Gestapo

Gestapo

Instrument of Tyranny

Edward Crankshaw

GREENHILL BOOKS, LONDON
PRESIDIO PRESS, CALIFORNIA

This edition of *Gestapo: Instrument of Tyranny*
first published 1990 by Greenhill Books, Lionel Leventhal Limited,
Park House, 1 Russell Gardens, London NW11 9NN
and 1991 by
Presidio Press, 31 Pamaron Way, Novato, Ca. 94949, U.S.A.

Lionel Leventhal
Celebrating 30 years of military publishing
1960–1990

British Library Cataloguing in Publication Data
Crankshaw, Edward, *1909–1984*
Gestapo: Instrument of Tyranny.
1. Germany. Geheime Staatspolizei
I. Title   363.2830943

ISBN 1-85367-077-4

Publishing History
Gestapo: Instrument of Tyranny was first published
in 1956 (Putnam & Co. Ltd.) and is reproduced now
exactly as the original edition, complete and unabridged.

Printed by Billing & Sons Limited, Worcester.

Contents

Illustrations

Acknowledgements

For their most helpful comment and advice, and for the willing assistance they have given me in checking and discovering facts, I take this opportunity of expressing my deep gratitude to my friends Mr. William Gutmann, Mr. Brian Melland, and Mr. Gerald Reitlinger.

Most of the direct quotations are taken from official reports of the Nuremberg Trials (see *Text References* and *Bibliography*). I also have to thank the following publishers for permission to quote directly from books carrying their imprint:

Messrs. Macmillan & Co. and St. Martin's Press, Inc., New York (*The Nemesis of Power* by John W. Wheeler-Bennett); Messrs. Vallentine Mitchell (*The Final Solution* by Gerald Reitlinger); Messrs. Jonathan Cape (*To the Bitter End* by Hans Bernd Gisevius); Messrs. Faber & Faber (*The Smoking Mountain* by Kay Boyle); Messrs. Hutchinson & Co. (*The Venlo Incident* by S. Payne Best); Messrs. Hurst & Blackett (*V2* by Major-General Walter Dornberger).

E. C.

Introduction

A REMARKABLE feature of the trial of the major war criminals at Nuremberg was the striving of various counsel for the defence to saddle each other's clients with the blame. This was especially evident when it came to the "organisations" which found themselves on trial: the S.A., the S.S., the Gestapo, the General Staff. In fact, there was little else counsel could do: they were faced with a miserable task. The facts were there and could not be denied. The crimes had been committed and could not be talked out of existence. It could not be denied, for example, that concentration-camps existed and that innumerable men and women from all over Europe had been tortured in them, or killed, or left to die of exhaustion and starvation; that there had been massacres of hostages and prisoners-of-war; that there had been a meticulously planned attempt to exterminate the Jews of Europe, children as well as adults, by gassing them to death. Cruelty and savagery unequalled in the history of modern Europe had been practised on a scale unequalled in the history of the world. It had been uncovered by the Allies, described by the survivors, and freely confirmed in detail by a host of witnesses.

Counsel's only hope, each for himself, was to make out that his own client was blameless in these matters by pinning the responsibility on to another. Some of them pursued this line so stubbornly that anyone with patience and a twisted sense of humour could go through the verbatim reports of the major trials and prove that although all these things had been done, and more besides, they had been done without the knowledge of anybody at all in Germany except for a few men who were dead, or missing, and a handful of witnesses who, for one reason and another, found comfort in confessing to almost unimaginable crimes.

Several million people (prosecuting counsel put it at twelve million; but that figure has since been shown to have been a little too high) had been put to death in atrocious circumstances; several million men, women, and children from the heart of Europe had been put to death in the heart of Europe; and nobody knew who had done it, or even that it had been done. This display of blessed ignorance made no difference to the upshot of the trials; but it did cause a good deal of unnecessary confusion. And to this day most people do not know what really happened.

This is an unsatisfactory state of affairs. The Germans, for reasons not plain to the outsider, regard themselves as being the most civilised race in the world. These things happened in their midst and were carried out by them. Germany is a part of Western Europe: she has made notable contributions to the culture of Western Europe. But these things happened only a few years ago, and not far away on the steppes of Central Asia, but in our midst: in the midst of the new European community. It is important for us all to discover how, and why, and who was really responsible—if only to decide whether they could happen again, and whether they could happen outside Germany, and, if not, why not.

It is necessary to understand the nature of these crimes, which shows important differences from the nature of the crimes committed, for example, by Russians under Stalin. And it is necessary to have some idea of how they happened. Otherwise the verdict oscillates senselessly between the two extremes of untruth: on the one hand, that all Germans were directly responsible; on the other, that they were due solely to Hitler and a hard core of Nazi brutes.

There are many ways into this subject. I have chosen the

history of the Gestapo because it offers an extreme example
of that purposeful confusion which covered, like a smoke-
screen, the most terrible activities of the Third Reich. Very
few people have a clear idea of what the Gestapo in fact was;
and it has come to serve in Germany as a kind of universal
scapegoat. Certainly the Gestapo stood behind the blackest
deeds committed by Germans all over Europe and inspired
and organised their execution. But it was essentially a small,
compact, and highly professional corps which participated
directly in only a part of the atrocities which horrified the
world. The activities of the Gestapo, for example, ended
more or less at the gates of the concentration-camps. This
fact will save us from the repetition of individual acts of
sadism which, by first sickening the mind, then numbing it,
could come between us and the object in view. At the same
time, by establishing what the Gestapo did and what it did
not do, we shall have a much clearer view of what was done
by other organisations whose membership accounted for a
very considerable proportion of the able-bodied population
of Hitler's Germany and which sought, not always un-
successfully, to saddle the Gestapo with their crimes.

Gestapo

CHAPTER 1

The Gestapo is Born

GESTAPO stands for *Geheime Staats Polizei*, or Secret State Police. The term was approved by Goering in April 1933, two months after he had taken over the Prussian Police and purged it, replacing many of its career officials by trusted Nazis. In its origins the Gestapo was simply Department IA of the old Prussian Political Police uprooted from its home in the Prussian Ministry of the Interior and transferred to a separate building, a commandeered art school in the Prinz Albrecht Strasse, which was to become notorious. This was done so that it could be more easily kept apart from the Prussian State apparatus as a whole, which still included many anti-Nazis and "luke warms".

Goering first thought of calling his new department the G.P.A. (*Geheime Polizei Amt*); but it occurred to him that this was too much like the G.P.U., as the Soviet Political Police was then called. He need not have bothered. The term Gestapo, which might have been made especially for Sir (then Mr.) Winston Churchill, was the invention of a clerk in the Berlin post-office, who simply needed an abbreviation for one more Government department.[1] He did not know what he was starting. Nor, probably, did Goering.

For although the Gestapo was born in Berlin in 1933 and at first limited to Prussia, its real history begins in Munich.

15

Those who think of the Gestapo as the creation of Heinrich Himmler are closer to the mark than the pedants, in spite of the fact that Himmler did not take it over from Goering until April 1934. For the Prussian Gestapo in the first year of its existence was, in effect, very little more than Goering's personal terror squad, the real business of smashing popular opposition to the Hitler régime being left to the S.A. and the S.S. It was only when Himmler came to Berlin that the Gestapo developed into the elaborate and terrible machine which became the scourge of Germany and was then perfected as an instrument to terrorise the populations of conquered countries and to exterminate certain categories of human beings, above all Jews, who were considered unfit to live. The beginning of this transformation coincided with the effective absorption of the Gestapo, a department of State administration, into the S.S., a purely Party organisation, and its union under Reinhard Heydrich with the S.S. Security Service, the *Sicherheits Dienst*, or S.D. The Gestapo, as it was to become known to the world, took its tone and meaning from the S.D.—so much so that throughout this narrative Gestapo and S.D. will be treated as being inextricably connected. This, indeed, they were, the protestations of the defence counsel at Nuremberg notwithstanding.

Here, then, is the first source of confusion. The Gestapo in its final form was a product of the S.S. The S.S. in the end was over half a million strong. But the Gestapo in its heyday, when its mastery extended from the Atlantic to the Volga, from the North Cape to the Mediterranean, was a strictly limited organisation, never employing more than 40,000 individuals, including women and clerks. The S.D. had only 3,000, and acted, in so far as its functions can be separated, as the long-range Intelligence Service of the Gestapo.[2]

These are facts which must be borne constantly in mind unless we are to lose ourselves in the confusion deliberately created by the Nazi leadership and so successfully exploited in the past.

Another relevant fact is the exceptional nature of the Gestapo. There had been a political police force in Prussia, as in other German states, during the days of the Weimar Republic, before Hitler came to power. Every government in the world relies in some degree on some kind of political police force to uncover conspiracy and protect the State from injury. The size and importance of such a force varies with the nature of the government: the wider the popular support for the government, the more insignificant the political police, and vice versa. In Victorian England, for example, the very idea of a political police force was remote from ordinary experience, and the majority of Englishmen would have said there was no such thing. Such a force did exist, nevertheless, its main duty being to keep an eye on the activities of exiles and refugees from less contented lands. In Russia, on the other hand, where most of the London exiles came from, the Government was neither popular nor democratic, and the political police, the *Ochrana*, as it was then called, was a highly developed arm, as, under a variety of names, it has remained to this day.

The Government of the United Kingdom is still more popular than most; but it has to counter dangers undreamt of a century ago: there are citizens who place loyalty to a foreign power above loyalty to their own land; there are spies and traitors seeking to discover those unhappy secrets of applied science which may win a war. Thus the apparatus of vigilance, the political police, has had to be enlarged and strengthened. It consists now, in effect, of the Special Branch of Scotland Yard and a branch of Intelligence known as M.I.5.

It is fashionable among apologists for the Nazis to pretend that in principle the Gestapo differed in no way from M.I.5

B

in Britain or the F.B.I. in America. Nothing could be more false. The political police of Britain and America and a number of other countries exercise a purely defensive function, designed to uphold a *status quo* sanctioned by the people as a whole. The German Gestapo, on the other hand, was an instrument not of defence but of attack. The Gestapo was created by Goering to impose the will of Hitler upon his political opponents and his rivals within the Party. A year later it was captured by Himmler to be used as the spear-head in his grandiose campaign to establish with his S.S. thugs what amounted to a State within the State, and later to subdue the occupied territories and turn them into German colonies. Throughout its career it was an instrument of aggression.

There is one last fact which is commonly overlooked but which has a very direct bearing on the nature of the Gestapo: the extreme youth of the men who first frightened the German people into abject submission, and then went on to trample the flower of European culture. Himmler himself was only thirty-three when Hitler became Chancellor. Heydrich was twenty-nine. And so it went on through the whole apparatus of the S.S. These were the men who succeeded in breaking the spirit of the proud Army tradition—embodied in grey-haired military leaders of proved courage and distinction. Schellenberg of the S.D. when he seized on behalf of Himmler the whole apparatus of Military Intelligence was only thirty-five. It is impossible to obtain a clear image of the mood of those days unless it is borne constantly in mind that many of our heroes, men with resounding names and ranks, occupying positions of great responsibility and holding the power of life and death over millions, were in fact young toughs with fair hair of the kind that in England after the first world war gravitated naturally into the Black and Tans. In Germany they were called by Hitler to rule, and allowed by the nation to do so.

CHAPTER 2

Himmler and the S.S.

THE original function of the S.S. was to provide a personal bodyguard for Hitler in the days of his struggle for power. S.S. stands for *Schutz Staffel*, or Guard Detachment, and the members of the S.S. in those early days belonged to Hitler alone and were devoted to him body and soul. They formed, organisationally, a part of the S.A., the brown-shirted Storm Troops, who represented the military arm of the Nazi Party, and who were used to intimidate opposition and beat up, or murder, those who would not be intimidated. But the S.S. in their black uniforms soon came to regard themselves as members of a race apart and to look down on the numerically far superior S.A.

When Hitler discovered Heinrich Himmler, the S.S., under Erhard Heiden, were only 280 strong.[1] That was in 1929. Already there had been stirrings of antagonism between Hitler and the leaders of the S.A. Hitler had set himself the task of capturing the Wehrmacht and the bankers and the industrialists to assist him in his rise. The S.A., led by Hitler's old friend and supporter, Ernst Roehm, was fundamentally a revolutionary army and, as such, had nothing but contempt for bankers and industrialists: at the same time they saw themselves as swallowing up the Wehrmacht and doing away with the stiff-necked General Staff. It was this conflict between the political leader and his brawling, strong-arm corner boys that led to the rise of Himmler and the S.S. Hitler needed a private army, but it had to be obedient and regard itself as his instrument. In Himmler he found a man whose chief qualities seemed to be blind loyalty, a certain organisational flair, and an impassioned faith in all the nonsense he chose to propagate about race and honour.

In quieter times Himmler might never have discovered his peculiar gifts. He was trained as an agriculturalist, had acted as a fertiliser salesman, and had finished up running a poultry farm in a Bavarian village. His brother has gone on doing that sort of thing ever since. He himself might very well have lived out his days in this innocent activity, quiet and efficient, but prevented by temperamental caution from becoming a tycoon, and remarkable for the number of bees in his bonnet—a harmless crank: the sort of man who combines business acumen with a belief in the secret of the pyramids. He was essentially a romantic. The undistinguished, puffy countenance concealed visions. The son of a schoolmaster, he was infected early with the romanticism of the German Youth Movement. He developed a passion for the good earth and the regeneration of Germany through an enlightened peasantry. Later he was to bring to the task of exterminating millions of human beings the spirit of the eternal *Wandervogel*.

Although he pinned his faith to Hitler in the first days of the movement and actually marched as Roehm's standard-bearer on the occasion of the farcical *Bierhalle Putsch*, he had no comprehension of the true inwardness of his Leader, and found himself attracted to the radical wing of the Party, which would have no truck with the Ruhr financiers. Thus one day he was taken up by Gregor Strasser, who, with Goebbels at his side, made a strong bid for the leadership of the Party after the failure of the *Putsch*. He became Strasser's adjutant.

This sounds grander than it was; for it should be remembered that the Nazi Party was very young and extremely disreputable. The men who were going to build the most terrible fighting force in the world, and then break it, were by the standards of more mature societies callow and raw. (We hear a great deal in these days about youth having its chance and the stifling influence of old men in office; but the two parts of the world in which youth has had its chance, Nazi Germany and Soviet Russia, have not made the best of impressions.)

In due course both Strasser and Goebbels were to be won over by Hitler's uncanny sense of reality; and the Fuehrer saw in Strasser's unprepossessing lieutenant the sort of man he needed for his bodyguard: utterly loyal—*treuer Heinrich*, he came to be called—quietly and unemotionally efficient, and so literal-minded that he could be relied upon to take at the foot of the letter anything in writing that came from an acknowledged authority.

All attempts to analyse the character of Himmler have failed, as I think all must fail—unless, perhaps, in casebook form with a far fuller documentation than exists—because they entail the understanding of a madman in terms of normal human experience. For if there is one thing clear about Himmler, it is that he was amiably and to some degree contentedly mad. Madness is a loose term. It is used here to characterise a man adrift from normal human experience. It is impossible to analyse Himmler's motives, because to understand a character one must be capable to some extent of entering into his thoughts and feelings and obtaining a recognisable idea of the world as it appears to him. This can be done with a number of Himmler's assistants, who were unbalanced to a degree and ogrish in their conduct. But it cannot be done with Himmler, because he was one of those terrifying human beings foreign to normal human behaviour.

He was not distinguished by cruelty, by lust, by excessive vanity, by overweening ambition, by systematic deceitfulness. His qualities were unremarkable, vices and virtues alike. But there was no centre: the qualities simply did not cohere.

There are men like Himmler in the prisons and criminal lunatic asylums all over the world—and, more fortunately placed by virtue of the possession of private incomes, leading retired and slightly dotty lives in seaside bungalows along our coasts. They are the sort of men, good husbands and fathers, kind to animals, gentle, hesitant, soft-spoken, absorbed in some mild hobby and probably very good at it, who murder their wives because they wish to marry another girl and flinch from the scandal of a divorce. As a rule such men are not particularly gifted, if only because the total number of particularly gifted men is small. Himmler, however, was an extremely gifted administrator.

He believed not only in the German race; he also believed in astrology and runes. With Hitler's Reich crashing down over him, and in the supreme moment of his life when he was prepared to betray Hitler and take on the leadership of the broken German people, he interrupted his conversations with Count Bernadotte, designed to lead Germany out of the war, in order to hold forth about the hidden secrets of Nordic runes.[2] He was convinced that if they could be deciphered they would prove to have a close affinity with the characters of the Japanese alphabet; and this was extremely important, because it would mean that the Japanese, in spite of their alien appearance, were in fact also Aryans and thus fit allies of the Germans. The only thing Hitler knew about race was that he hated the Jews and considered them the root of all evil. But for Himmler this was not propaganda. When he called a Slav an animal, he meant precisely that, with no ill-feeling; and it oppressed him to think that Germany was allied with a people who were, on the face of it, sub-human.

He went through life like this. In the middle of transacting arrangements for the extermination of whole peoples he pursued with no less care and far greater enthusiasm his own real interests. The activities of the Gestapo and the S.D., the building of gas-chambers, the massacre of prisoners-of-war, were simply routine police matters: unpleasant chores in the life of a man who was devoted to making the world fit for Germans to live in. The development of the S.S. Institute for Anthropological Research, however, was something after his own heart. He was determined to discover the secret of Aryan origins, and rich men subscribed millions of marks to this project in order to be numbered among Himmler's friends. For him the Russian war offered a glorious opportunity for comparative anatomy: while immense armies were manœuvring over the frozen plains and smashing each other to pieces, Himmler set himself the urgent task of building up a collection of skulls of Jewish–Bolshevik Commissars: such things were impossible to come by in Germany.

The story of this collection of skulls, with the Allies drawing closer to Strasbourg, where they were deposited, provided one of the few moments of farce in the grim drama of the trials of the war criminals. The instructions as to their collection and preservation, issued in all solemnity in the midst of a world toppling in ruins by a man who had not the faintest idea that he was doing anything out of the ordinary, illuminate very clearly the nature of Himmler's lunacy. It is worth quoting *in extenso* the report of Professor Hirt, director of the Anatomical Institute of Strasbourg, who was also a departmental chief in Himmler's *Ahnenerbe*:[3]

"Subject: Securing skulls of Jewish–Bolshevik Commissars for the purpose of scientific research at the Reich University at Strasbourg.

"We have a large collection of skulls of almost all races and peoples at our disposal. Of the Jewish race, however, only very few specimen skulls are available. ... The war in the East now presents us with the chance of overcoming this deficiency. By procuring the skulls of the Jewish–Bolshevik Commissars, who represent the prototype of the repulsive, but characteristic, sub-human, we have the chance now to obtain scientific material."

Professor Hirt then goes on to emphasise the necessity of catching the Jewish-Bolshevik Commissars alive, so that scientific measurements can be made by qualified persons before death:

"The best practical method of obtaining and collecting this skull material is to direct the Wehrmacht to turn over alive all captured Jewish–Bolshevik Commissars to the *Feldpolizei*. The *Feldpolizei*, in turn, should be given special directives to inform a certain office at regular intervals of the numbers of these captured Jews and where they are detained, and to give them every attention and care until a special delegate arrives. This special delegate, who will be in charge of securing the material (a junior physician of the Wehrmacht or the *Feldpolizei*, or a medical student, equipped with a motor-car and driver), will be required to take a previously agreed series of photographs, make anthropological measurements, and, in addition, determine as far as possible ancestry, date of birth, and other personal data."

When that much has been accomplished the unfortunates can be put to death and the serious business proceeded with:

"Following the subsequently induced death of the Jew, whose head should not be damaged, the physician will sever the head from the body and will forward it to its proper point of destination in a hermetically sealed tin can especially made for this purpose and filled with preservative fluid. Having arrived at the laboratory, the comparison tests and anatomical research on the skull, as well as the determination of the race membership and of pathological features of the skull form, the form and size of the brain, etc., can be undertaken by photographs, measurements, and other data supplied on the head and skull itself."

This was the world in which Himmler existed. He believed absolutely in the sub-humanness of Jewish–Bolshevik Commissars. When foreign diplomats occasionally suggested that his conduct verged on the brutal, he was completely and sadly uncomprehending. "But they are animals," he would say. And to him they were. He had no more qualms about cutting off the heads of Russian Jews and sending them in tin cans to Strasbourg than the trained pathologist has about killing animals for dissection. The Jews, like the animals, were to be well cared for until they were put to death. . . . Or perhaps that is an over-simplification. All the reports agree that Himmler suffered the most atrocious headaches, which on occasion nearly drove him frantic, that he was hesitant in arriving at decisions, that he did suffer and was sometimes appalled at the necessity of such wholesale slaughter.[4] But from all descriptions of this conscientious man it seems likely that the headaches came not from a battle with conscience so much as from a battle with his sense of responsibility. What was difficult was to decide what was necessary. Once that was decided, there were no more hesitations.

It was in this spirit that he presided over the appalling experiments on living human beings carried out by a remarkable assortment of doctors in the concentration-camps of the S.S.

These experiments had nothing to do with the Gestapo, as such. The Gestapo delivered the prisoners as a routine matter, and the concentration-camp commanders, on direct orders from Himmler, saw to the rest. Dachau was the principle centre for this particular horror; but experiments of one kind or another went on in most of the camps. At Neuengamme, for example, Dr. Heisskeyer carried out a series of experiments on Jewish children, injecting them with T.B., and watching them die—until the advance of the Allies spoilt the beauty of the experiments, and the children had to be killed prematurely to remove all traces of Dr. Heisskeyer's activities.

The heroes of Dachau were Dr. Sigmund Rascher of the Luftwaffe, Dr. Schillings the malaria specialist, and Dr. Schutz, who was interested in blood poisoning. Dr. Rascher was the chief of these, and he was Himmler's special favourite. A charming, well-spoken, and resourceful man, Rascher applied himself single-mindedly to experiments designed to save the lives of German Luftwaffe crews. Prisoners were used freely to discover what happened to pilots without oxygen at high altitudes and when immersed for varying periods in icy water. What happened was that they died. There was a special van, to hold twenty-five men, with an observation window in the side, from which air was progressively extracted until the prisoners in the van started dying of hæmorrhage of lung or brain: those who survived were usually killed. There was a tank full of ice-cold water in which other prisoners were placed and kept until they became unconscious. Blood was taken from the neck each time the body temperature fell by one degree, and analysed. One man was kept alive at 19 degrees Centigrade, but most died at 25 or 26 degrees. One aspect of these experiments was the attempted resuscitation of men apparently dead. Sun-lamps, hot-water bottles, electro-therapy were all tried in vain, until somebody had the brilliant idea that the application of animal warmth might do the trick—the animal warmth was to be provided by women. It was a new use for prostitutes, and a number of these unsuspecting females were earmarked for this purpose on Himmler's direct instructions to Pohl, his deputy for concentration-camps: his only proviso was that they had to be non-German prostitutes.

At the trial of the doctors at Nuremberg nobody managed to sort out the question of complicity in these experiments. Goering and high-ranking officers in the Air Ministry were all involved. Respectable members of the German medical profession as well as cranks and scallywags had guilty knowledge. But the driving force was Himmler—Himmler the scientist *manqué*, the collector of the skulls of Jewish–Bolshevik Commissars. And we find him breaking out petulantly against what he called " Christian medical circles" who tried to obstruct him in his starry-eyed rôle as protector of science and seeker after truth.[5]

There was also Himmler the crusader and visionary, the man who built a romantic castle in a German forest where the knights of the S.S., many of whom could hardly read or write, were required to repair at intervals to contemplate the glory of their order and establish spiritual contact with the heroes of mediæval Germany. We see the crusader in action in the notorious speech of 4th October 1943, to his S.S. Generals at Posen:[6]

"One basic principle must be the absolute rule for the S.S. men. We must be honest, decent, loyal, and comradely to members of our own blood and nobody else. What happens to a Russian and a Czech does not interest me in the least. What the nations can offer in the way of good blood of our type we will take, if necessary by kidnapping their children and raising them here with us. Whether nations live in prosperity or starve to death interests me only in so far as we need them as slaves for our culture: otherwise it is of no interest to me. Whether ten thousand Russian females fall down from exhaustion while digging an anti-tank ditch interests me only in so far as the anti-tank ditch for Germany is finished. We shall never be rough and heartless where it is not necessary, that is clear. We Germans, who are the only people in the world who have a decent attitude towards animals, will also assume a decent attitude towards these human animals. But it is a crime against our blood to worry about them and give them ideals, thus causing our sons and grandsons to have a more difficult time with them. When somebody comes up to me and says: 'I cannot dig the anti-tank ditch with women and children, it is inhuman, for it would kill them,' then I have to say: 'You are the murderer of your own blood, because if the anti-tank ditch is not dug German soldiers will die, and they are the sons of German mothers. They are our own blood. . . .' Our concern, our duty, is our people and our blood. We can be indifferent to everything else. I wish the S.S. to adopt this attitude towards the problem of all foreign, non-Germanic peoples, especially Russians. . . .''

The S.S. did.

And again, referring to the massacres of Jews:

"Most of *you* know what it means when a hundred corpses are lying side by side, or five hundred, or a thousand. To have stuck it out, and at the same time—apart from exceptions caused by human weakness—to have remained decent fellows, that is what has made us hard. This is a page of glory in our history, which has never been written and is never to be written. . . . We had the moral right, we had the duty to our people, to destroy this people which wanted to destroy us."

This was the tone set by Himmler for all the organisations under his command, including the Gestapo and the S.D. They obeyed it in the spirit and in the letter. Himmler was mad; but not all his many tens of thousands of subordinates were mad. Numbers of these to this day, still sane, hold responsible positions throughout the two Germanys.

There was also Himmler the animal lover. We glimpse him in the Posen speech. Here he is again, in conversation with his masseur, Felix Kersten, of whom he made a confidant and who was able, in this commanding position, to save the lives of some who would have been put to death. According to Kersten, Himmler used to condemn all blood-sports as "cold blooded murder of innocent and defenceless animals". And he would fulminate against Goering, the huntsman (another animal lover):

"Goering, that damned blood-hound, kills every animal he can shoot. Imagine, Herr Kersten, some poor deer is grazing peacefully, and up comes the hunter with his gun to shoot that poor animal. . . . Could that give you pleasure, Herr Kersten?" [7]

Himmler did not like blood at all; but he had his duty to do, and he did it unflinchingly. When he addressed his S.S. Generals at Posen referring to the terrible sights they had all seen, the spectacle of hundreds of men, women, and children lying side by side at the bottom of the trench they had been forced to dig with their own hands, and congratulated them on sticking it out, he was proudly speaking as one of them. Although his preoccupation with headquarters business made it unnecessary for him to be present at the massacres he was compelled to order, he was not one to ask others to do what he would not do himself; and in the very early days of the Russian campaign, in August 1941, at Minsk, visiting one of Heydrich's Action Groups (it was the one, incidentally, commanded by Artur Nebe, the friend of Hans Bernd Gisevius, whom we shall shortly encounter), he ordered Nebe to bring out a hundred prisoners for a sample execution in his presence. S.S. Lt.-General Erich von dem Bach-Zelewski, Higher S.S. and Police Leader for the Central Russian front, was also there. In an affidavit he described how he watched Himmler closely and saw him stagger at the first volley and almost fall to the ground in a faint. When the execution squad failed to kill two Jewish women outright Himmler could not control himself and cried out—so that afterwards Bach-Zelewski had to reproach his chief for upsetting the firing squad and ruining its nerve.[8] But, although upset, Himmler, like his generals, had stuck it out. This was Himmler the hero and stoic.

Himmler was also interested in power. Many people have queried Himmler's capacity, unable to believe that a man so colourless and dreary should have either the will or the strength for power. It is also pointed out that for many years he was Hitler's most devoted slave. But while some men are born to achieve power, others develop the taste for it as it is thrust upon them. It is improbable that Himmler, as a chicken farmer, dreamt of ruling Germany—as Hitler in his equal obscurity most certainly dreamt. It is improbable that when he took over the S.S. with its membership of three hundred professional thugs he saw in this modest institution the future janissaries of the New Order. It is improbable that when he created the Waffen S.S. to fight with the Reichswehr that he looked forward to the day when he would be virtual commander-in-chief under Hitler. But quite early in his political career he must have discovered that he was a born administrator with a marked capacity for intrigue.

He was, in fact, one of those intriguers, not energetic and demonstrative, who, with a fixed idea, are ready to let affairs take their course until the moment to strike presents itself. In his later years he let many things take their course, including an active conspiracy against Hitler conducted in part by his own subordinates. He profited by them invariably, until the very end, when, as Commander-in-Chief of the Home Armies, he sought to assume the leadership of the Reich and make peace with the Western Allies. Then Hitler in his Bunker in Berlin, discovering the treachery of *treuer Heinrich*, finally broke him, as his last act.[9] Then, too, Himmler rounded off his character, which had no centre, by regarding himself unquestioningly and in all innocence as the sort of man the Western Allies would be prepared to do a deal with.[10]

As for his physical appearance, it is familiar enough from photographs. It gave him great pain because it accorded so ill with the standard laid down for the knights of the S.S. But he had to put up with it; and, indeed, it served him well. It served others well, too. With very few exceptions surviving members of the S.S. have expressed pained surprise that Himmler should have done such terrible things. He was so benevolent, so diffident, so mild. They simply had no idea . . . though what passed through their minds when this old woman of a man spoke to them coldly of mass destruction, as at Posen, is not recorded. The best contemporary description so far comes from Major-General Walter Dornberger, who did not belong to the S.S. but was responsible for the development of the V.2 at Peenemuende. Himmler visited the station, and afterwards made himself a great trouble:

"He looked to me like an intelligent elementary schoolteacher, certainly not a man of violence. I could not for the life of me see anything outstanding or extraordinary

about this middle-sized, youthfully slender man in grey
S.S. uniform. Under a brow of average height two grey-
blue eyes looked out at me, behind glittering pince-nez,
with an air of peaceful interrogation. The trimmed
moustache below the straight, well-shaped nose traced a
dark line on his unhealthy, pale features. The lips were
colourless and very thin. Only the inconspicuous, reced-
ing chin surprised me. The skin of his neck was flaccid
and wrinkled. With a broadening of his constant, set
smile, faintly mocking and sometimes contemptuous
about the corners of the mouth, two rows of excellent
white teeth appeared between the thin lips. His slender,
pale, and almost girlishly soft hands, covered with blue
veins, lay motionless on the table throughout our conversation." [11]

CHAPTER 3

Heydrich and the S.D.

WILLY HOETTL, alias Walter Hagen, an intelligent but rather prolix Lieutenant-Colonel in the S.D., a prosecution witness at Nuremberg, and the author of a book on the German Secret Service, has contributed largely to the confused impression of Himmler by attributing all his remarkable achievements to Reinhard Heydrich.[1] He makes the common mistake of confusing power with dynamism.

Dynamism Heydrich had in plenty. It is scarcely open to doubt that he used Himmler's inoffensive person and hesitant ways as a camouflage for his own highly purposeful activities. It is still less open to doubt that Himmler frequently used Heydrich when Heydrich thought he was using Himmler. This is not to say that superficially at least Heydrich was not a stronger man than Himmler, or that he did not conceive highly dangerous ambitions sooner than Himmler. But it is permissible to doubt very strongly indeed the assumption so often canvassed by surviving members of the S.S. that Heydrich, had he lived, would have one day become the new German Fuehrer. He would certainly have tried it on. But Himmler would as certainly have seen to it that before he succeeded he would have broken his neck.

The only thing interesting about Heydrich was the extreme to which he carried certain traits widely admired in

Germany, when presented with some moderation, but not attractive to others. He was very young, very handsome, save that his eyes were too close-set; an outstanding example of that blond mixture of effeminacy and toughness which may be observed in any Teutonic night-club. He had immense drive, which was liable to carry him too far; total ruthlessness in the attainment of his own ends, which were wrapped up in personal ambition; no active enjoyment of cruelty except sometimes, perhaps, almost as an afterthought; and a devilish sense of humour. Vain as a peacock, but mockingly aware of his own vanity, clever, perhaps too clever by half, and contemptuous of the clumsiness of most of his colleagues and superiors, he nevertheless could be clumsy in his use of force and, unlike Himmler, was liable to overreach himself. He was dynamite, like a character in an American gangster story; and in the S.S. he was able to canalise his nihilism into a constructive purpose.

He had started life as a naval officer and, at the age of twenty-six, with a promising career before him, was cashiered by Admiral Raeder for getting the daughter of a dockyard superintendent into trouble and taking an unusually independent line about it. The girl was his official fiancée, but he had had enough of her and told her outraged father that the engagement was off: no self-respecting Naval officer, he pointed out, could conceivably marry a girl who was prepared to give herself away so easily.[2] Plenty of cads, however, have lived and died without becoming mass executioners; and this disreputable incident in Heydrich's life seems to be made too much of by German writers as a formative incident. It is rather a typical incident in a character already formed.

Certainly Heydrich was surprised, angry, and disgruntled when he found himself out of a job and with a broken career. Certainly this drove him earlier than otherwise into that haven of the resentful and disgruntled, the infant S.S. Certainly it was in the Hamburg branch headquarters that Himmler found him, his attention having been directed to the enlistment of a new member who had been an officer if not a gentleman and who knew how to read and write—who had, moreover, been employed in Naval Intelligence. Certainly, sensing which way the tide was running, and observing that Himmler's preoccupation with racial purity, at least as regards physical appearance, was filling the S.S. with a remarkable collection of fair-haired morons, Heydrich saw his opportunity. But he had the ability as well. And he was one of those very few born leaders who have the boldness and the confidence to surround themselves not with sycophants but with the cleverest men they can find.

Himmler took him to Munich and confided to him a pet project. The S.S. was all very well as a *corps d'élite* of guards; but it needed to be more than that. If the S.S. was to be the fountain-head of German manhood it had to impose itself as a minority power on the sprawling, brawling shape of revolutionary Germany. It needed a highly organised intelligence system, and Reinhard Heydrich was the obvious man to create it.[3] Heydrich thought so too.

He took his new assignment in a very broad sense. The drilling and recruitment of the S.S. could be left to those who liked that sort of thing. He would provide its brains. He decided quite soon that it was easier to turn brilliant young men after his own heart into useful S.S. officers by offering them careers which they could not hope to make elsewhere, than to turn the existing membership of the S.S. into brilliant young men with the brains and character to carry out the tasks envisaged for them. So he proceeded to build up a *corps d'élite* within the S.S., just as Himmler was already building up the S.S. as a *corps d'élite* within the S.A.

The basis of this body was known as the S.S. *Sicherheitsdienst*, or Security Service, called hereafter by its initials the S.D. And to the end of its history the S.D. remained a purely S.S. organisation, playing no official part in the apparatus of State, although, when Himmler took over the Prussian Gestapo (not as leader of the S.S., but as a police-officer under Goering), the S.D. became in theory the long-arm, or intelligence service, of the Gestapo, and later became inextricably merged with it.

The two men, Himmler and Heydrich, made indeed a terrible combination. With the advent of Hitler to power and his immediate domination of Prussia they represented the strength of the Nazi movement in Bavaria, and with their rapidly developing organisation played a major part in carrying out the *coup d'état* after the March elections which secured Munich for Hitler. During those two months neither Himmler nor Heydrich had official Government standing: their sole authority was the power of the S.S. Nor was Himmler, much less Heydrich his very young lieutenant, a member of the inner Nazi circle. He had no pretensions to high office. And, indeed, when the Bavarian Government was overthrown, Himmler contented himself with asking for the post of Chief of Police in Munich, which he received.

We shall probably never know whether it was Himmler or Heydrich who hit on the idea of getting control of the police, first of Bavaria, then of all Germany. Himmler himself was so preoccupied with the organisation and recruitment of the S.S. and his dreams for a knightly order that it was probably Heydrich, restless and thrusting. But Himmler had thoughts of his own. His administrative skill and his romantic visions dwelt in rigorously separated compartments, and he was never blinded by passion in the conduct of his intrigues. Heydrich, although he prided himself on

his superior finesse and flexibility and despised the idiocies of
his master, was nevertheless very much at the mercy of his
own destructive impulses. We shall see how he was to drive
with all his power at the final centralisation of his authority
under Himmler; and we shall see how Himmler profited by
this to the extent of allowing Heydrich to build up what was
virtually a state within a State—within which, nevertheless
(and here, I think, is the real significance of the odd and
anomalous relationship of the Gestapo and the S.D.),
Himmler kept certain features fluid. We shall also see how
when Heydrich was killed in 1942 by Czech patriots
Himmler hesitated some months before appointing a successor; and then he chose a man of very different stamp from
Heydrich: the Austrian lawyer, Ernst Kaltenbrunner. This
is generally taken to indicate that Himmler had come to fear
Heydrich and was happier to replace him with a lesser man,
lacking in vaulting ambition.

It seems more likely that Heydrich had served his purpose
by building up under Himmler's eye the immense apparatus
which was now running smoothly. For Heydrich was not
the only dangerous man whom Himmler allowed and encouraged to play a dangerous game. At the very end of the
war, when Himmler was at last deciding to commit himself
to the bid for supreme power and a deal with the Allies, he
"allowed himself to be persuaded" by one of the late Heydrich's most gifted discoveries, Schellenberg, who started
life in the foreign-intelligence section of the S.D. and later
came to control the unified intelligence service of the Reich, to
treat with Count Folke Bernadotte. One of Himmler's qualities which struck all beholders was his extreme caution and
slowness in action. It seems likely, however, that he understood the desirability of swiftness and boldness as much as
anybody else, but preferred to cover himself until success
had been attained by allowing his subordinates, who could

always be thrown over in a crisis, to indulge in the swiftness and the boldness.

Certainly nobody who had not realised for himself the over-riding importance of police activity in the new Germany could have set about the methodical conquest of police power with such steadiness of aim and sureness of foot. It could not all be done by Heydrich. One of the men Himmler had to conquer was Goering himself, who, those early days, was scarcely aware of the existence of Heydrich. The younger man may well have counselled and prompted; but when it came to action it was Himmler who had to meet Hitler and Goering face to face and make good his case—or rather his two cases: for Hitler he had one story, for Goering another. And he could not do this without knowing exactly what he was doing, and why. Anybody in a subordinate position who has ever tried to brief a superior officer to fight a battle with his equals on a matter which he does not understand will realise the truth of this.

CHAPTER 4

Gestapo and Revolution

THE battle for the Gestapo began even before Himmler took over the Bavarian Police in April 1933. At first it was a long-range battle. By the time Hitler became Chancellor, Himmler and Heydrich between them had raised the numbers of the S.S. to 50,000, and the organisation was very strongly officered. Himmler himself was known as the Reichsfuehrer S.S. (RfSS). Beneath him there tailed away a complete quasi-military hierarchy, from Generals to Privates, known by the terms invented for the S.A., of which the S.S. was still on paper a part.* It had been Heydrich's idea to recruit in addition to the open membership a shadow corps of S.S. officers who were to keep their affiliations secret until the Nazis came to power.[1] Thus, in key positions all over Germany, including Government offices in which membership of any Party was forbidden, there were high-ranking S.S. officers waiting for the moment to reveal themselves and put on the black uniforms they had never worn. The regular police forces of the Reich had their quota of these, a striking example being Artur Nebe of the Prussian Criminal Police or Kripo, a sort of C.I.D., who will become a familiar apparition in these pages. It was the in-

* Throughout this narrative the special ranks of the S.S., meaningless to the reader without German, have been translated into their military equivalents. Thus *Hauptsturmfuehrer* becomes S.S. Captain. A complete glossary is appended.

filtration technique which has now become notorious in another context. The fifth column did not begin in Spain: it began in Germany under the Weimar Republic. The Nazis began their career of treachery not against foreign states but against their own.

When on 30th January 1933, the ancient and decrepit Hindenburg crowned his post-war career of ineptitude and deceit by inviting Hitler to become Chancellor of Germany, he committed to the care of the Nazis the whole State apparatus of a system they despised. For the moment Hitler had to accept what was called a coalition, which meant that important offices were filled by men he proposed to get rid of at the first opportunity. For instance, von Papen, not a Nazi, who by his own *coup d'état* of the year before had shaken the inadequate foundations of the Federal Republic, became Vice-Chancellor and Prime Minister of Prussia. But Hitler was able to make certain key appointments, and the most critical of these was the elevation of Goering to be Prussian Minister of the Interior, with control of the Prussian police. Goering, of course, did not report to von Papen, who was his technical superior: at that time, with Goebbels, he was closer to Hitler than any other man, and more than any other man he had the responsibility of carrying out the Nazi revolution, which could not begin until Hitler had achieved power by constitutional means.

With the war between us and the early thirties it may seem odd to think of the blusterer who was going to smash Britain with his Air Force as a revolutionary; but, indeed, Goering was precisely that. He was, in spite of soft living and expensive habits, a man of immense energy and drive. His vicious temper and his appetite for pleasure, his hatred of his enemies and his generosity to his friends, were all equally unbridled. This ex-fighter pilot of the first world war, gross, debauched, yet physically very brave, a buccaneer by nature, had developed a mystique of loyalty: he demanded it, he gave it. He became a revolutionary because he wanted power and riches, to play the despotic patron as well as to destroy—unlike Goebbels, who was a revolutionary because he hated others having power and riches. When he had achieved both, and allowed himself to believe that the war was won, he ceased to be a revolutionary and became a conservative. It was only then that he took to wearing snow-white togas and jewelled head-dresses.

In 1933 he was a savage driver. He enjoyed his own savagery so much, and could be such a good companion on occasion, that it seemed almost a shame when people with less zest for living objected to his activities as the chief policeman of Prussia. But there was a great deal to object to. And the savagery was deep-seated. He showed it to the whole world for the first time during the Reichstag Fire Trial, when he could not contain himself, and roared apoplectic threats across the court at Dimitrov, then an admired and pitied figure, who was later to become a dictator himself and to end his days in Moscow. And Goering retained his savagery to the end. In the closing stages of the war he was talking to Ciano in Berlin: Greece was starving.

"We cannot worry unduly about the hunger of the Greeks. It is a misfortune which will strike many other peoples beside them. In the camps for Russian prisoners they have begun to eat each other. This year between twenty and thirty million people will die of hunger in Russia. Perhaps it is well that it should be so, for certain nations must be decimated. But even if it were not, nothing can be done about it. It is obvious that if humanity is condemned to die of hunger, the last to die will be our two peoples." [2]

He retained his savagery. But he also retained something of an individual charm which was the undoing of many—of people as far apart as Sir Nevile Henderson, His Majesty's Ambassador to Berlin, and Rudolf Diels, the first head of the Gestapo under Goering. Even in Ciano's report of that terrible conversation there is something of the Goering which made able strangers lose their judgement. Hitler, Himmler, and others had been saying the same thing, but flatly, defiantly, and without a shadow of irony or philosophic doubt. In Goering's tones there is just such a shadow. He was a complex villain if ever there was one. He also kept his bravery to the end and made a showing at Nuremberg which shamed his colleagues. He also kept his stubborn cunning, defeating the hangman.

All these attributes have tended to obscure the simple fact that in the early days of the Nazi revolution Hitler relied on Goering's savagery to beat down the opposition ruthlessly. And Goering did what was required of him. The rôle of Goering himself, as controller of the Prussian police, is as clear as daylight. The rôle of the Gestapo, of which he was nominal head, and which he created, is far less clear. The main evidence concerning its first activities derives from two sources, from two men who detested each other and contradict each other at every turn. Rudolf Diels, who actually started the Gestapo under Goering and ran it for a year, and Hans Bernd Gisevius, who vainly aspired to the job and turned his defeat to advantage.

The S.A., the Storm-troopers, the louts in brown shirts and jack-boots who had roared and bullied their way to power, expected blood when their Fuehrer was translated, and they were determined to have it. They had the freedom of the streets and beat up or kicked to death in their improvised "bunkers" anyone they took a dislike to. Their chief enemies were the Communists, who, at the last election, had voted nearly 6,000,000 strong; but anybody with either a liberal or a Marxist attitude was their predestined victim; and soon they had seized so many that they improvised special holding centres where they could torture their prisoners to their hearts' content.

The man who first thought of this idea was Edmund Heines, the S.A. chieftain of Dresden, who put up a barbed-wire stockade for his captives; [3] but soon there were others. And in March 1933 the idea of the concentration-camp was officially blessed, and Oranienburg was set up by Goering himself just outside Berlin and staffed by the S.A.[4]

The S.S. kept a little aloof from the crudest of the street bullying. They had their own self-consciously superior code. Apart from the higher leadership, they were racially pure and looked like a set of blond Commandos; they had their rigidly idiotic marriage rules, laid down by Himmler, who himself died in doubt about his own ancestry; they had their motto: My Honour is Loyalty. They also had their own select torture-chamber in the Columbia House.[5]

The regular police, as such, took little part in these activities; but, then, the regular police had taken little part in anything very much for some years past. Following the lead of the democratic politicians, they had virtually abdicated, while retaining their nominal positions; and the various private armies brawled and killed at will, while they stood by: they stood by most steadfastly when the Nazis were winning. "Parliamentarianism is not sick because it is threatened by dictators; it is threatened by dictators because Parliament has abdicated," said Chancellor Wirth in the Reichstag three years before Hitler came to power. And this was a true verdict. There were many in the Government offices who were appalled at the prospect of Nazi rule, and had everything to lose by it; but they had done nothing to prevent its coming, and so were disarmed when it came. The same might be said of the police: "The police are not abject because they are threatened by Himmler; they are threatened by Himmler because they are abject."

Goering, when on 31st January he strode in high spirits into his new office in the Prussian Ministry of the Interior, was bent on a purge of the police, and not so much because the police were anti-Nazi as because they were no good. As Chief of the Prussian Police, responsible to him as Minister of the Interior, he appointed the young S.S. General Kurt Daluege, then twenty-nine years old, blond and crass, recommended by Himmler as Chief of the S.S., and cast by him to be the spear-head of his projected advance on Berlin. But Goering had no idea of letting the S.S. come between him and his own personal aims. He needed a small, compact apparatus of his own. He needed his own man, not too scrupulous, who knew his way about the files of the pre-Hitler police, files which contained confidential information not only about the political enemies of the Nazis, but also about the leading Nazis themselves, Goering's colleagues and rivals; he needed, moreover, a man who, with the authority of the State Police, could put pressure where pressure might be required in his, Goering's, own material interests. He needed, in a word, an instrument of blackmail.

Thus it was that one of the few regular officials he spared was Rudolf Diels, then thirty-three, an up-and-coming careerist (not a secret Nazi: Diels was not the sort of man to commit himself to any cause until it had clearly won), who had been specialising in anti-Communism in the Political Department. He had met Diels before in circumstances which are still obscure, and now decided that he was the very man to act as his personal combination of spy, blackmailer, and bulldog. The arrangement worked so well that after two months, and when Hitler had won his election, Goering decided to detach Diels's office from its proper home as a branch of the Prussian Ministry of the Interior and set it up in a headquarters of its own, where it would be free from interference by Himmler's S.S. henchmen.[6] Thus Department IA of the Prussian Political police became the Gestapo, with Rudolf Diels as its first head, under Goering.

It was an odd partnership: on the one side the Renaissance figure of the supreme Nazi bully, on the other the shady apparition with no roots, who had graduated from one of the extreme right-wing Students' Corps to the Civil Service of the crippled Weimar Republic, which he despised. Brilliant, inordinately ambitious, hag-ridden, Rudolf Diels shows himself as a queer combination of a twilight adventurer, man of affairs (cynical in the German tradition), and intellectual. He is shrewd and yet humourless; highly educated, and yet illiterate when it came to true understanding; a man clever and balanced enough to impress Goering, but sufficiently lacking in judgement to take on the incomparably more able Heydrich in single combat. He is weak enough to need bolstering up with the delusion that his duty lay in serving the Nazis, yet strong enough to fight the S.A. and the S.S. in his own interests with boldness and cunning. He saw in Goering's favour not only a supreme opportunity for advancement, but also the chance to influence the course of German history. In the end he was broken by a stronger and more single-minded power, to which he had to surrender the whole apparatus of the Gestapo. By that time he had given up fighting and took what offered. Under Goering's protection (for Goering was loyal to his friends) he survived in nominally high positions until, in the end, Himmler caught up with him and he found himself in the basement of the requisitioned art school in the Prinz Albrecht Strasse, a prisoner of the organisation which, with hopes so high, he himself had founded in the first flush of the Nazi Revolution.[7]

When it was all over he wrote a remarkable book which he

called characteristically *Lucif.. Ante Portas*, a sustained and closely argued apology for his career in the Gestapo. In it he represents himself as the man who stood between countless innocents and the vicious brutality of the undisciplined brown-shirt mob and the evil fanaticism of the black S.S. In this defence there can be found that golden thread of truth which knits together the really superior lie. Torture in those early days was the perquisite of the S.A. and the S.S., who had restored to Europe on a large and open scale the practice of degrading the spirit by breaking the flesh which for centuries had survived only in a hole-in-corner manner. It was not until later that the house in the Prinz Albrecht Strasse became the chief torture-chamber of the Reich; and, although the infant Gestapo made its arrests and handed its victims over to the care of the S.A. concentration-camp commanders, it also intervened on occasion to save individuals seized by the S.A. and the S.S. It warned others of imminent danger in time for them to escape. At Christmas, the first Christmas of the new régime, Diels himself was influential in obtaining Goering's amnesty which emptied the camps of many prisoners. In such engagements he quarrelled dangerously with both S.A. and S.S. leaders and frequently irritated Goering in the process—for although Goering resented the power of both organisations and was determined to keep his grip on his own Gestapo, he needed them to batter down the enemies of the régime. This made it difficult for Diels.

What the author of *Lucifer Ante Portas* omits to indicate, however, is that his long and ultimately vain battle with the S.S. and the S.A. was in the main a part of his own struggle for power. He was fighting not for order and justice as such, but for order to be imposed by Rudolf Diels and not by Heinrich Himmler. It is clear, however, that he was not a natural brute and took no delight in wanton violence. He was not a totally ruthless man like Heydrich, a totally conscienceless stooge like Daluege, a methodical madman like Himmler. If Diels had been able to maintain himself at the head of the Gestapo and defeat the S.S., events in Germany would have taken a milder course. But it is equally clear that he was committed completely to the Nazi revolution and, to retain his own position, was prepared to go along with it while fighting for personal ends the men who were most actively helping to make it. The reader of *Lucifer Ante Portas*, to say nothing of certain evidence at Nuremberg, might gain the impression that the Gestapo in those early days was a sanctuary of justice and a solace for the afflicted. Diels, as the career official, the regular policeman, is represented as standing for order and sanity in a howling wilderness of barbarity. The picture was a good deal less idyllic than that.

Diels was a regular police official. His new master, Goering, had immediately started making clear his attitude towards the regular police, the colleagues of Diels. It was due to the purge of the regular force that Diels got his chance.

Diels was also an opponent of the S.A. and the S.S. His whole defence rests on the plea that only by remaining where he was could he curb the excesses of the S.A. and the S.S. But Goering had not been in office for more than a few days before he issued a directive to the reorganised police which defined them as accomplices of the S.A. and the S.S.:

"The police have at all costs to avoid anything suggestive of hostility to the S.A., S.S. and Stahlhelm, since these organisations contain the most important constructive national elements . . . it is the business of the police to abet any form of national propaganda."

Objective justice, on Hitler's specific orders, was defunct. Men, like the young lawyer Heinz Litten, who insisted on defending enemies of the revolution, were taken away and tortured and killed—or driven to kill themselves.[8] Arbitrary violence was to take its place. So Goering continued:

"Police-officers who make use of fire-arms in the execution of their duties will, without regard to the consequences of such use, benefit by my protection; those who out of a misplaced regard for such consequences fail in their duty will be punished in accordance with the regulations. . . . Every official must bear in mind that failure to act will be regarded more seriously than an error due to taking action."

On 22nd February these instructions to the regular police were rendered superfluous. By a special decree Goering added 50,000 Auxiliary Police to the regular forces, by the simple expedient of issuing white arm-bands to as many S.A. and S.S. men, arming them, and giving them full police powers.[9]

In March, in a whole series of speeches to mass audiences in the course of the election campaign, he developed his attitude. It was now that he ordered the construction of the first official concentration-camp, Oranienburg, at Sachsenhausen outside Berlin, to be run and staffed by the S.A.

"Fellow Germans," he declared at Frankfurt-am-Main, "my measures will not be crippled by any bureaucracy. Here I don't have to worry about justice; my mission is only to destroy and to exterminate; nothing more."

He then proceeded to describe how he intended to carry out this modest mission:

"This struggle will be a struggle against chaos, and I shall not conduct it with the power of any police; a bourgeois state might have done that. Certainly I shall use the power of the State and the Police to the utmost, my dear Communists, so do not draw any false conclusions. But the real struggle to the death, in which my fist will lie heavily on your necks, I shall conduct with those down there—and they are the brown-shirts."

To a mass meeting a few days later in Essen he declared:

"Even if we make many mistakes, at least we shall be acting: I may shoot a little wildly, one way or the other. But at least I shoot."

And on another occasion:

"Every bullet which leaves the barrel of a police pistol now is my bullet. If one calls this murder, then I have murdered: I ordered all this. I back it up. I assume the responsibility, and I am not afraid to do so."

And lest it should be thought that this was simply bombast, designed to strike terror into the hearts of an audience of sheep and create a general feeling of hopelessness in the hearts of the opposition, here is Goering again, speaking officially as Chief of Police to his own police-officers in Berlin. The date is 20th February, seven days before the Reichstag Fire, four days before the police raid on Karl Liebknecht House, the Communist Party H.Q., two days before the enrolment of the S.A. and the S.S. as Auxiliary Police:

"I can do nothing against the Red mob with a police force which is afraid of being punished for doing what is only its duty. The responsibility must be placed squarely where it belongs. It does not lie with the junior official in the street. I want to hammer it home into your heads that the responsibility lies with me alone. You must be quite clear about that. When you shoot, I shoot. When a man lies dead, it is I who have shot him, even if I happen to be sitting up there in my office in the Ministry. For it is my responsibility alone."

D

Nothing, one would think, could be more unambiguous than that. Goering, as Controller of Police, categorically instructs his police to shoot first and ask questions afterwards, threatens them with punishment if they falter in this duty, and takes upon himself full responsibility for his actions. The thugs of the S.A. and the S.S. are enrolled as policemen, and the S.S. and S.A. as a whole are above the law and enjoy Goering's full protection. Rudolf Diels in his first two months under Goering heard all this, knew all about it, and by 4th April, when he took over the newly founded Gestapo, knew precisely what sort of a man his master was. Diels himself has quoted these passages from Goering's oratory in his own book.

Also, before he took over the Gestapo, he knew what sort of a man Hitler was. He gives us a vivid description of the scene on the balcony of the great hall of the Reichstag with Hitler staring down in silence at the great sea of flame, and then suddenly beginning to rant:

> "His face was scarlet with emotion, and with the heat, which, up there in the dome, was intense. He started yelling as though he would burst and with a more total abandonment of self-control than I had ever seen in him before:
>
> " 'Now there must be no mercy. Anyone who stands in our way will be trampled underfoot. The German people won't understand mercy. Every Communist official will be shot out of hand. The Communist Deputies must hang this very night. . . .' " [10]

CHAPTER 5

Vendetta and Intrigue

I F the atmosphere throughout Germany as a whole was
dominated by the sudden overflow of pent-up violence,
with what remained of the regular forces of law and
order struggling to keep their footing and being swept along
by the brown flood, inside police headquarters in Berlin there
was a mood of sustained and deadly vendetta and limitless
intrigue.

One basic fact was that Goering controlled the Prussian
Police, and was determined to keep it, and saw in the Gestapo
his private instrument. The other basic fact was that outside
Berlin, in Munich, Heinrich Himmler, the Chief of the
S.S., had been made Chief of Police in Bavaria, and, egged
on by his new right hand, Reinhard Heydrich, was determined to become the Police Chief of all Germany.

The almost total destruction of the Gestapo archives makes
it impossible to follow in detail the progress of the intrigues
which followed from these facts. We need not regret this.
Nothing could be more tedious in detail than a consequent
narrative of the arid, repetitive moves in any struggle for
power. In essence they are limited and restricted in the
extreme. They include the double-cross; the playing off of
one faction against another; the playing of both ends against
the middle; the bluff; the double-bluff. They include blackmail and they include flattery. They include, in a word, all

the tricks of self-advancement, old and dreary as the desert hills, but still, in the hands of the master, infallible in their effect. Himmler versus Goering; Heydrich versus Diels; Gisevius versus Diels and Heydrich (a forlorn hope, if ever there was one); Daluege, cleverer, in spite of looking like an affronted duck and being to all appearances as stupid, floating on the tide and taking advantage of every current; Nebe playing Daluege's game, but, in the end, biting off more than he could chew, and failing to realise that in the last resort the individual must have an ally and that, although a master can play everybody off against everybody else some of the time, he cannot play them all off against each other all the time.

Who were these people, and how did they fit in together? Goering and Diels, Himmler and Heydrich, we have met. Gisevius flickers in and out of this narrative, as he must flicker in and out of all narratives concerned with the development of Hitler's tyranny and the pathetic, broken-backed resistance to it, not because he was in the least important but because he thought he was important and sometimes managed to impose himself on others. He was able to do this because he was a born go-between and, by German standards, an accomplished intriguer.

He appears on the scene as a very young man brought into the Prussian Ministry of the Interior by one of Goering's nominees, Under-Secretary Grauert. That was in July 1933, three months after Diels had installed the new Gestapo in the Prinz Albrecht Strasse. He was a young lawyer on the make, who had decided that the Nazified Civil Service offered the best chances. With a complaisant and idle Minister in times of comparative stability he would have gone far. But he arrived on the scene at a time of revolution, when the negative and colourless were being swept away by the unscrupulous and the dynamic. He did not grasp his own limitations: bumptious, tactless, unsnubbable, yet sly, not at all a brute, but a place-man who would do anything required of him to hold his place, he was lucky never to get one. He is alive today, and he owes his life to Heydrich. But for Heydrich he might have intrigued Diels out of existence and risen high in the Gestapo. He would then have been doomed to ruination, instead of being fêted as a star witness for the prosecution. For he might not have found it desirable to make common cause with the men who were ineffectually plotting Hitler's death.

Daluege was Himmler's man, placed by him in Berlin to represent the spear-head of the S.S. penetration of the police. In time he came to command the *Ordnungspolizei*, or uniformed police, and, as such, was responsible for many of the most dreadful crimes loosely attributed to the Gestapo. We shall meet him later on. His cleverness seems to have been confined to a highly developed instinct for self-preservation, which, however, proved in the end inadequate, and he was hanged in Prague in 1946. In those early days in Berlin he pinned his faith to Himmler and kept fairly quiet. Throughout his dreary little career (he was only forty when he was executed) he seems never to have taken a decision of his own but always to have acted as the literal-minded and joyless administrator of the death and torture sanctioned by his superiors.

Nebe was an altogether more colourful character; but he was able to change his colours and sink into the background of the moment like a chameleon. He was one of the most able members of the regular Prussian Police, and functioned as head of the *Kriminal Polizei*, or Kripo, in effect the Prussian C.I.D. He was also in secret a member of the Nazi Party and of the S.S., which he had joined in 1929 in defiance of a law forbidding membership of political parties to members of the Civil Service.[1] He was, however, a man so accustomed to playing his own hand, and that so close to his chest, that his real affiliations will probably never be known. He led a lonely life, achieving and maintaining a high position in the police hierarchy, but never exceeding his own powers, a secret member of the S.S. when it looked as though the S.S. was going to sweep the board, a secret member of the Opposition when it looked as though Germany was going to lose the war.[2] He is supposed to have been overtaken and hanged by the avenging host of his police colleagues after the failure of the Stauffenberg plot; but we have no proof of this: he ran away, was chased—and never heard of again. For all we know, like Mueller, Chief of the Gestapo; Eichmann, exterminator of the Jews, and a host of other conscientious murderers, he may be alive to this day.

Gisevius, who, for reasons best known to himself, professes a reverence for Nebe little short of idolatry, and as fanatical as his hated of Diels, presents his idol as an idealist —who joined the Party in secret for reasons of idealism, went on being a policeman under Goering and Himmler for reasons of idealism, turned against the Party again for reasons of idealism, continued to hunt with the hounds and run with the hare, still for reasons of idealism, and finally ended as a martyr. He does not, however, refer at all to the period when Nebe commanded one of the notorious Action Groups in Russia and gave a personal demonstration to Himmler of how Jews were executed.[3] So we shall probably never know whether this adventure was also undertaken in a spirit of idealism—or in a fit of absent-mindedness.

These were the chief figures among the bunch of officials who were intriguing against each other with murderous intent in and around the headquarters of the Prussian Police, under Goering. Everybody feared everybody else. There are occasions when it is permissible to believe both Diels and Gisevius: for example, when each confirms the other in describing the mood of those days:

". . . . We were living in a den of murderers," writes Gisevius (who, it should be remembered, was doing his level best to make good in that den). "We did not even dare step ten or twenty feet across the hall to wash our hands without telephoning a colleague beforehand and informing him of our intention to embark on so perilous an expedition. Not for a moment was anybody's life secure. Nebe, of all persons, Nebe the Nazi, the old fighter who had the best of connections, used to impress this on me forcibly, morning, noon, and night. His own opinion of his illustrious department was quite clear. As a matter of principle he entered and left by the rear staircase, with his hand always resting on the cocked automatic in his pocket. And again and again he angrily reprimanded me for coming incautiously upstairs near the banister—which could be seen more easily from above—instead of stealing up against the wall, where a shot from above could not easily reach me.

"It was so usual for members of the Gestapo to arrest one another that we scarcely took notice of such incidents, unless we happened to come across a more detailed example of such an arrest—by way of the hospital or the morgue." [4]

That is a leaf from the album of an aspiring member of the early Gestapo, describing life in the Prinz Albrecht Strasse—Nebe had been seconded to the Gestapo from the Kripo. But life also had its colour in the old Prussian Police headquarters in the Ministry of the Interior across the road. And Gisevius gives a vivid account of the excitement when Diels was brought back to the Prinz Albrecht Strasse to resume his old functions after Heydrich's first major assault had all but succeeded:

"At the end of September, Diels was removed from office with the lightning swiftness common to all Nazi actions. The Gestapo chief was assigned to the post of assistant police commissioner of Berlin; but he sensed that his career was in a bad way and thought it better to fly to Czechoslovakia on a false passport. Nebe and I, who had persistently intrigued for his removal, breathed more freely." [5]

But not for long. Diels has himself described at length and with some pathos his feelings in exile and the highly patriotic motives which induced him to return.[6] We have no reason to doubt that he felt homesick in Prague. He also wanted to get on in the world, and Berlin was the place for that. And so, says Gisevius, "From his retreat in Bohemia he threatened embarrassing revelations, and asked a high price for keeping his mouth shut. By the end of October he had moved in again." [7] This rings true, and it is also the only reasonable explanation of Diels's power over Goering. Diels himself describes how after Goering had "pleaded" with him to return he, Diels, demanded extensive guarantees and a free hand.[8] For the time being he had both. And it was at this moment that Goering, who had now succeeded von Papen as Prime Minister of Prussia, quite unconstitutionally removed the Gestapo from the Ministry of the Interior and continued to run it, through Diels, as his private police force.

"I can still see Nebe collapsing into his chair when he returned from the Ministry with the bad news," writes Gisevius, who, however, was made of sterner stuff. "My immediate reaction was to decide that I must not sleep at home that night. So I hid in a hotel; and that was fortunate for me, for the hangmen were already out looking for me." [9]

Next day he decided to throw himself on the protection of Kurt Daluege. Instead of going to his own office in the Prinz Albrecht Strasse, he went off to the Ministry of the Interior and slunk in through a back entrance. Nebe, who knew Daluege very well, joined him there, and together they went up to Daluege to decide what to do. They could not think of anything. One of Daluege's subordinates, who had gone with them, also in fear of his life from Diels, had the bright idea that Diels should be called over to the Ministry for a conference and then, when he appeared, Nebe and Gisevius should "grab him and throw him out of Daluege's third-floor window". But even as they discussed the pros and cons of this expedient the door opened, and Daluege's secretary came in to tell them that a Gestapo agent was waiting outside and wished to arrest Gisevius—"in the office of the Chief of Police, of all places!"

But the Chief of Police, Daluege, did not seem to share the indignation of Gisevius at this sacrilege. "In fact, the spark of courage that remained in him seemed to go out." He was finding it difficult to make up his mind whether Diels or Heydrich was going to win the next round—and in any case neither Heydrich nor Diels had any use for Gisevius. "Nevertheless, he was generous enough to show me how to escape through an emergency exit."

What to do next? With presence of mind Gisevius remembered his original protector, Grauert, who had been put into an under-secretaryship at the Ministry of the Interior by Goering in the flush of his first purge. "Grauert was not a man to get excited easily," reports Gisevius. "Yet even he was somewhat put out." He told the egregious young man that everything would be all right, he would see to that; and meanwhile he had better go home and wait for things to blow over. But this Gisevius flatly refused to do. He would not budge from the sanctuary of Grauert's office—until, at last, Grauert agreed to ring up Goering, who "pretended to be outraged by what had happened and ordered a strict investigation."

Three days later Gisevius was back again in his own office, still a member of the Gestapo. And there was Diels to welcome him:

> "My dear fellow, what a shocking misunderstanding! I knew nothing about it at all. It was all a piece of insolence on the part of the S.A. You're my very best adviser!" [10]

Diels's own account of the events that led up to his precipitate flight from Germany, referred to by Gisevius, is part and parcel of the same mood. One night round about midnight he was rung up by his wife, who was in a highly agitated condition. Their apartment had been broken into by a gang of roughs who had locked her up in her bedroom while they went methodically through their belongings and carried off what they wanted. Diels hurried home and was able to establish that the gang of roughs must have been a well-known S.S. Group under a certain S.S. Capt. Packebusch which had recently been active in various parts of Berlin as a self-appointed anti-Communist mobile squad. Packebusch was used by Daluege to do his dirty work.

Not only was this aggravating to Diels in principle, since he himself was the great expert on Communism, but also, worse than this, Nebe had been telling the S.S. that he, Diels, of all people, was a Communist in disguise.[11] Gisevius insists that his beloved Nebe, a simple soul, really believed this. But while there is every excuse for believing almost anything of Diels, there are certain things that those who knew him really could not have believed: and one of these was that Diels would ever associate himself with a losing cause. He certainly had a curious relationship with the German Communist leaders, Thaelmann and Torgler.[12] This was probably in essence no more than the sort of attraction which so often binds together deadly adversaries in a private duellist's universe. But there may have been more behind it than that.

In the interests of his career, Diels had deserted his chief among the Social Democrats, Sievering, for von Schleicher. He had deserted von Schleicher for Goering. There had been a time when nobody could tell whether the Nazis or the Communists would win; and it is conceivable that during this period of uncertainty Diels, with his deep knowledge of the Communist Party in Germany and his personal acquaintance with its leaders, may have deliberately left himself several lines open. We do not know. All we know is that a man with Diels's established record cannot justly complain if, when in doubt, we believe the worst of him. Certainly on that winter's night Captain Packebusch of the S.S. had broken into the flat of the Chief of the Gestapo in the hope of discovering incriminating documents linking him with Communist leaders. He failed, and Diels acted with resolution.

As soon as he had decided whom he was dealing with he telephoned an old friend, Commandant of the Tiergarten Police-station, a man "who had often helped me in the past, and was not afraid of his chief, Daluege". The old friend responded, and, within an hour, the house in the Potsdamer Strasse, where Packebusch "carried on his unholy activities at Daluege's behest", was surrounded by members of the uniformed police, armed with hand grenades and automatics. Diels, according to his own account, himself stepped forward to knock on the door. An S.S. sentry opened, and, taking Diels and the little group at his heels for friends, showed them the way to Packebusch's room, Diels still leading.

"I chose to expose myself in this affair," he writes, "because, in the last resort, it was my own personal interest that was at stake. The most dangerous part of the enterprise now lay before me: the arrest by my own hand of the worst of the gangsters."

It was a dramatic moment. There, in the small hours, sat the S.S. Captain—

"the very prototype and image of the later concentration-camp commandants, harshness and callousness written deep into his face. He sat there, brooding over the papers on his desk like a scholar working into the night. . . . They were my papers he was working on, and defacing, as I soon discovered, with inept annotations. . . .

"Packebusch had no time to recover from his shock. He stared at me as though I were a ghost. As I said, 'I've come to take you away', the uniformed police who had entered with me seized him without particular gentleness. They removed the pistol from the belt he had hung up on the wall with his black uniform jacket. His accomplices, in turn, were seized in their own rooms."

But by the time Diels had got Packebusch to his own office on the Prinz Albrecht Strasse it was a different story. They started roaring and shouting defiance at each other. Diels threatened Packebusch with prison, and Packebusch threatened Diels with arrest for treason.

"As I jumped up to refute this insolence he pulled an automatic from his trousers' pocket and pointed it at me, yelling unprintable obscenities. But before he could steady his aim and press the trigger the great Alsatian dog which had been observing the progress of the scene from his corner of the big room threw himself at the jack-booted thug." [Diels, as usual, was in civilian clothes.] "Two policemen wrenched the weapon from his hands." [13]

The upshot of that evening's entertainment was that with Himmler protesting to Goering and calling for the blood of the Chief of the Gestapo, it looked as though the S.S. had won. But there were obscurities in the case, almost certainly involving scandals among the high and mighty of the Nazi Party. Diels was demoted, fled to Czechoslovakia, returned in triumph to a stronger position, himself was offered rank in the S.S., and managed to hold out against Heydrich for several months to come.

While the police leaders fought each other for power, the work of the police went on. And always the Gestapo was being strengthened. These incidents in the lives of Gisevius and Diels are recorded here not for their own sakes but to illustrate the atmosphere inside Gestapo headquarters in its early days. To the outsider the building in the Prinz Albrecht Strasse was the headquarters of a smoothly functioning terror machine. To the victims it was a pit of organised torture and injustice in which their bodies, and sometimes their spirits, were broken by remote inquisitors who knew how to be affable and bland when occasion called for it and how to beat and kick a man until he whimpered for mercy when occasion called for that. But the remote inquisitors, as we have seen, had problems of their own.

The sorting out of these problems reflected the development of the Gestapo from a small private instrument in Goering's own war against all comers, from Communists to the S.A., into the dread and comparatively stream-lined apparatus, which, partnered by the S.S. *Sicherheitsdienst*, was ready to apply its deep experience to the subjugation of occupied Europe.

It is clear, however, from the illustrations already given, that there can be no sorting out of those problems. We are dealing with the struggle for power between rival gangs, and there is nothing more tedious and repetitive. There are no records left to speak of, and if records exist in full they would not be worth losing time over. It is enough to establish the nature of the soil which nurtured the Gestapo, and from which it sprang. And it is only by appreciating the utter demoralisation of the German police force, a regular body which should have had a proud tradition, but which had not, that we can understand how that arch-gangster and master of iniquity, Reinhard Heydrich, the type of adventurer without a shadow, was able to seize the whole apparatus after barely a year of quiet application to the task, with such effortless ease.

The members of the regular German police were Civil Servants, reflecting the moral condition of their country as a whole no less clearly than Civil Servants everywhere. Diels was given his chance because of the general demoralisation. He failed; but after the war he came back, and for some time held office in the West German administration.

CHAPTER 6

Confusion as a Fine Art

IT is time to take a wider view, to look beyond the building in the Prinz Albrecht Strasse, and to see the burgeoning Gestapo in relation to the administrative pattern as a whole.

If the reader finds himself muddled by the strange overlappings and divisions of authority and executive power, he may be assured that he is in good company: the Germans themselves were also muddled. Even at Nuremberg, with its remarkable gathering of forensic talent, the court never succeeded in unravelling the tangle and laying bare the outlines of the hierarchy—for the very good reason that no rigid outline ever existed. In the light of accumulated knowledge we can get a clearer picture than was possible at Nuremberg; but it will only be to find that behind the apparently iron front of Teutonic organisation there was a sort of willed chaos.

It will be for each reader to decide for himself to what extent the confusion was deliberate and calculated, to what extent it was spontaneous and involuntary. Be that as it may, the Germans have brought to a high pitch the art of evading responsibility by losing all sense of it in total confusion; and it comes to much the same thing in the end whether the fostering of such confusion is due to calculated cunning or a more generalised intellectual dishonesty. The general impression created is of a system knocked together in an *ad hoc* manner by the members of a ruling caste intent on re-insuring themselves, never content to commit themselves finally to a single course, but for ever contriving to hedge and lay off.

Confusion first arose from the dualism of the German police as such, and was magnified by the equivocal rôle of Himmler.

Strictly speaking, until the Nazis completed their central-ising action, there was no German police. Germany was a Federal Republic, and the various States, or *Laender*, as well as a number of important municipalities, ran their own police forces. There was indeed a Reichs Ministry of the Interior (R.M.d.I.), but this had little effective power and was a shadow compared with the Prussian Ministry of the Interior. Prussia, in theory, was one *Land* among others; but in fact it controlled two-thirds of Germany and dominated the whole. The capital of Prussia was also the capital of the Reich. Only one other *Land*, Bavaria, was ever strong enough to assert its own independence to any effect.

When Hitler became Chancellor, he knew very well that with Goering in control of the Prussian State Administration and the Prussian Police he would soon be able to do what he liked with Germany. Von Papen, when he agreed to serve as Vice-Chancellor, was also aware of the importance of Prussia and reserved to himself the office of Minister Presi-dent, with Goering at the Ministry of the Interior as tech-nically his subordinate: he would be able, he thought, by this means, to curb Goering's activities, and thus Hitler's. What he failed to see, however, was that Goering, with the appara-tus of Prussian State power under his hand, would be serving the leader of the Nazis, who also happened to be Chancellor of the Reich, not the Minister President of Prussia, his con-stitutional superior. So von Papen was by-passed by his own police, and through that same force Hitler achieved more or less absolute control over Prussia as his first step to dictatorship over Germany as a whole.

Germany, by the standards of other Western countries, had long been over-policed. In Prussia the plain-clothes branches had consisted of the Criminal Police (Kripo), a sort of C.I.D. (headed by Artur Nebe, the secret Nazi), and the Political Police, or Stapo, a sort of Special Branch (taken over by Diels and turned into the Gestapo). The uniformed police consisted of the Order Police, or Orpo, who lived in barracks in the large cities and were used as mobile squads for use in case of rioting and strikes; the Protective Police, or Schupo, the equivalent of the ordinary urban constabulary; the Gendarmerie, who acted as a constabulary for rural areas; and certain specialised forces—the Fire Police, who ran the fire brigades, and the Railway and Water Police. All these bodies, some of which were concerned with duties carried out in other countries by voluntary associations or local councils, were run for the Prussian Minister of the Interior by a supreme head, the Chief of Police in the Prussian Ministry of the Interior, and, in his hands, constituted a formidable body.

We have already encountered S.S. Lt.-General Kurt Daluege, and we shall encounter him again. We have spoken of him as Himmler's personal agent in Berlin. But here is another source of confusion. He was technically responsible to Himmler only as the leader of the Berlin S.S. His official position was Chief of the Prussian Police, under Goering; and Himmler, as Chief of the Bavarian Police, had no jurisdiction over him in this capacity. His first task in Berlin was to carry on Goering's purge of doubtful elements of the police, replacing them with old Party men and members of the S.A. and the S.S. (which was then still a part of the S.A.). Until Goering put the Gestapo under Himmler in April

E

1934, Daluege was technically the superior officer of Rudolf Diels, a fact which makes the scene in his office when Gisevius and Nebe discussed the feasibility of throwing Diels out of the window, a project suggested by Daluege's own lieutenant, even more extravagant than may at first sight have appeared.

Daluege's second task, however, was to assist Himmler and Heydrich to realise their aspiration of getting control of the Prussian Police. And in this task he worked against Goering. The unseating of Diels was part of the general plan; and the incident of Captain Packebusch was an attempt in this direction. It was not until April of the following year that Diels was finally got rid of on the pretext that he had been plotting against Goering, and Himmler was formally installed in the Prinz Albrecht Strasse as Deputy Chief of the Prussian Gestapo, Goering still retaining for reasons of prestige, as well as one other reason which we shall come to later, the nominal office of Chief of the Prussian Gestapo. By that time the opposition to the Nazi advance had been crushed and trampled to death, in the streets, in the rigged law-courts, in the bunkers of the S.A. and the torture barracks of the S.S., in the concentration-camps and in the cellars of the Prinz Albrecht Strasse under Rudolf Diels. The new Deputy Chief of the Gestapo was able to concentrate on smashing the radical wing of the Party itself, led by Ernst Roehm at the head of the S.A.

This brings us to a further source of confusion: the structure of the S.S. and its relationship to the State administration. This confusion, as we have seen, existed from the first day of the Nazi revolution, 30th January 1935. The Gestapo itself developed and ramified steadily in an unpredictable way for the next three years. It did not, however, receive an official stamp and sanction—so that, one might say, judicial and administrative confusion became a basic plank of State policy—until 1936 when Himmler, already Reichs-fuehrer of the S.S. and Chief of Political Police throughout Germany, was formally inducted as Chief of German Police. Only then was the oppressive apparatus of the State and of the Party brought under one hand—thus providing a perpetual source of alibis for all who served under Himmler in any capacity whatsoever, and making the letters of his style the most terrible initials in the history of Europe: RfSS u.Ch.d.d.Pol.im. R.M.d.I.

In 1933 he still had a long journey before him.

CHAPTER 7

The Totalitarian State

DURING that first year of the Nazi régime Hitler, who had started carefully, with only a solitary Nazi in the cabinet (this was the colourless Frick, at the Reichs Ministry of the Interior), had been consolidating his grip on the country with resounding success. By the time Himmler and Heydrich were ready to come from Munich to Berlin the stage was set for totalitarian action in the grand manner.

The first enemy had been the Communist Party, with its six million voters, many of whom by the time the year was out had joined the Nazis. In his diary on 31st January, the day after Hitler became Chancellor, Goebbels had written:

> "In a conference with the Fuehrer we arranged measures for combating the Red terror. For the present we shall abstain from direct action. First the Bolshevik attempt at a revolution must burst into flame. At the given moment we shall strike." [1]

And so it was—except that what burst into flame was the Reichstag, and it was not fired by the Communists.

On 24th February the Berlin Police raided the Karl Liebknecht House, the Communist headquarters. A communiqué was issued immediately afterwards which said that

complete plans for the Bolshevik revolution had been discovered. These documents were never published.[2]

On 27th February the Reichstag burst into flames and
Hitler struck. Of all the incidents of the Nazi revolution this
is the most familiar and the least rewarding of study. There
is no need to recapitulate the details, and it is fairly certain
that the Gestapo as such, under Diels, was not directly involved. The fire was supervised by Goering and Goebbels
working through the S.A. It is established that Karl Ernst,
the Chief of the Berlin S.A., taking a small group of his followers, got into the empty Reichstag on the evening of the
27th by means of an underground passage which ran from
the Palace of the President of the Reichstag (i.e. Goering) to
the Reichstag building itself. There they sprayed a special
preparation used in the past by Berlin hooligans (it bursts into
flames after some exposure to the air) over carpets, curtains,
and upholstery.

When this task was finished, and as they left the building
by the way they had come, the wretched young Dutch Communist, degenerate and half insane, who had been chosen by
the S.A. as their tool because of his known propensity for
setting fire to things, got into the building through a window
and started his own incendiarism in an amateurish way. To
this day nobody knows what methods the S.A. used to persuade van der Lubbe to play his part at the given moment.
But play it he did. It would have been better for Hitler and
Goering if he had failed. The Reichstag would have gone up
in flames just the same. The Communists could have been
accused and liquidated without the farcical and damaging
superfluity of the trial which turned Dimitrov and Torgler
into martyrs.

It was the sort of clumsiness that was later to distinguish
the work of Heydrich—notably in the assassination of Dr.
Dollfuss in the Ballhausplatz in Vienna. But it was not the

work of Heydrich, who was in Munich. Nor was it the work
of Diels, though he had a great deal to do with the arrests that
followed. It was the work of the higher Nazi leadership,
using their trusted S.A. And, indeed, the exclusion of the
Gestapo from this action is a fine example of the sort of madness that existed in those days.[3]

Diels must have known all about it afterwards. In his
book he protests too much, and his argument against the
proper view that Goering and Goebbels were responsible is
almost inconceivably lame.[4] It is possible in his protestations
to discover a certain pique at his exclusion from the delibera-
tions preceding this great drama: for one thing Diels can
never resist, and that is magnifying his own importance, even
if, by doing so, he has to show himself a bigger rascal than
he cares to seem to be. Gisevius, of course, has his story—
prolix and circumstantial down to the last detail—too circumstantial to be true. But in one particular he carries con-
viction—on broad lines if not in detail. And that is in his
description of the liquidation by Diels and the Gestapo of certain S.A. participants in the Reichstag plot who had afterwards talked too much.[5] That is what the Gestapo were for.

And it was the Gestapo which profited most from the fire
itself. Next day, on 28th February, came the decree for
"The Protection of the People and the State", which Hitler
induced President Hindenburg to sign. Described as "a
defensive measure against Communist acts of violence", it
made an end of personal liberty as it had been guaranteed by
the Weimar Constitution:

"Thus restrictions on personal liberty, on the right of
free expression of opinion, including freedom of the Press;
on the rights of assembly and association; violations of the
privacy of postal, telegraphic and telephonic communications; warrants for house searches; orders for confiscation

as well as restrictions on property, are permissible beyond
the legal limits otherwise prescribed." [6]

The Police, in a word, were now given a free hand. But
still Hitler was not dictator, and the Nazi Party was still a
minority Party in a coalition government. The Reichstag
Fire and the President's decree opened the last week of the
election campaign which, on 5th March, was to give Hitler
his majority. But in spite of the terrorism; the torchlight
processions of marching brown-shirts; the frenzied speeches
(it was on 3rd March that Goering made his speech at Frankfurt in which he declared: "Here I don't have to worry about
Justice; my mission is only to destroy and to exterminate;
nothing more"); individual acts of terror against Communists, Left Wing journalists, Trade Unionists, and opposition
leaders of every kind; the shameless inactivity of the Police,
who stood by and watched the S.A. beat their enemies to
death and break into offices and shops—in spite of all this
the Nazis won less than half the votes, while the Communists
still got nearly five million to the Nazis 17 million. But it
was enough for Hitler, and the subsequent proscription of
the Communist Party gave him an absolute majority in the
Reichstag.

And so the new phase began. The Communists were pro-
scribed. And by a judicious mixture of blatant force and
flattery of the aged President and the Nationalists, Hitler
managed to pass by constitutional means (a majority of two-
thirds), on 21st March, 1933, a law which in effect did away
with the Constitution. This was the basic Enabling Act
(Law for Removing the Distress of People and Reich) which
gave the Government power for four years to enact laws without the co-operation of the Reichstag, to deviate from the Constitution. It gave the Chancellor personally the power to draft
such laws, to come into effect the day after publication. [7]

The Revolution had now started in earnest. It was called the *Gleichschaltung*, the process of bringing the totality of German society under direct Nazi control. First Hitler had to do for the various *Laender* what Goering had done for Prussia. On 9th March, aided by Himmler and Heydrich, Ritter von Epp, on instructions from Berlin, carried out a *Putsch* against the Bavarian Government—and Himmler became Chief of Bavarian Police. A few days later Frick, at the Reichs Ministry of the Interior, appointed Reich Police Commissioners in Baden, Wuertemburg, and Saxony, who promptly turned out the existing governments. On 31st March Hitler, through Frick, decreed the dissolution of the Diets of all other *Laender*, and a week later appointed a *Reichstatthalter* to every State with the power to appoint and remove governments, promulgate State laws, appoint and dismiss State officials.

Then it was the turn of the Trade Unions. Through March and April the S.A. ran wild and looted the Trade Union branch offices. On the second day of May the offices were formally occupied by the S.A. and the S.S., officials were arrested and sent to concentration-camps, and the Unions were merged into the New Labour Front under Robert Ley.

Finally came the dissolution of the opposition parties. On 10th May Goering occupied the buildings and newspaper offices of the great Social Democratic Party and ordered the confiscation of its funds. On 19th June what remained of the Party was put under a ban. On 26th May the assets and property of the Communist Party were confiscated. On 14th June all parties were officially banned and the National Socialist German Workers Party was declared "the only political Party in Germany". It became an offence to seek to maintain existing parties or to start new ones—an offence punishable with up to three years penal servitude or imprisonment, "provided the action is not subject to a greater penalty under other regulations".

In all this tumult the new Gestapo played only a small part. The youth of Germany, alive and ardent after years of frustration and apathy, stood behind the man who at last seemed able to do something active and bold to rehabilitate their shabby lives, and marched to the rhythm of "*Sieg Heil*", intoxicated by a new sense of power which found its natural expression in revolutionary violence. The liberals, the sober thinkers, the balanced sceptics had failed, and Germany was still sunk in resentful chaos. The liberals now tried to block the new drive led by the magician Hitler which held the first real promise for many weary years. They had to go. They had nothing to offer but the infinite negative. If they would not go of their own accord they had to be trampled underfoot. And so they were. And so also were the Communists, who, instructed by the tortuous crassness of Stalin in Moscow, had made it clear that they would do nothing to support the liberals and the socialists in face of the new menace—because they believed that their own way to power led through the swift rise and fall of Hitler.

The conspiratorial leadership of the Nazi Party and the thugs who took to violence for the sake of violence were reinforced and upheld by the genuine revolutionary enthusiasm which Hitler had evoked and by the distrust of the Communists aroused by their own dreary methods. They caught up in their wake millions who should have known better, and few stopped to ask whether an advance towards the promised land led by Goering and Goebbels and organised by Himmler and Heydrich could in cold blood be regarded as desirable. The fathomless German cynicism which separates absolutely political action from private morals was never more manifest than during the spring and summer of 1933. It prepared the way for all that was to come.

By autumn the new police were controlling the levers of a State organisation which had been completely transformed. While Rudolf Diels, at the head of the infant Gestapo in Berlin, was conducting the fight for his own career in a welter of intrigue and violence, while the Gestapo itself was being used partly as a weapon in this fight, partly as a private weapon by Goering, partly to establish a dark, secret terror over Prussia—which ran parallel with, but much deeper than, the spectacular terror of the S.A.—Himmler and Heydrich waited and planned in Munich.

With Daluege in Berlin they already had a hold on Prussia through their S.S. cohorts, now very much a power in the land, and infiltrating every Government office. And when in October 1933 the last restraints to the Nazi revolution were finally broken down and Hitler became in effect dictator of the Reich, it seemed the most natural thing in the world to centralise the various police forces in their political aspects on the Himmler machine.

In the next three months this was done, and the German people fearfully watched the rise of a new star in their midst —until, in early 1934, Heinrich Himmler had become, step by step, Chief of Political Police throughout the whole of Germany, except in Prussia. Himmler's Political Police was modelled on Goering's Gestapo—but with a difference: it was monolithic. It did not have to fight the S.S.—because it was the S.S. It could devote itself with single-mindedness to the task of smashing the S.A. and winning for itself the physical power upon which Hitler was to rest. It could devote itself to this task with all the more freedom since in the first year of the revolution the general political opposition had been broken—largely by the S.A.

But first Himmler had to conquer Prussia. He could not hope to smash Goering: the most he could do was to use him. Goering, too, wanted to smash the S.A. Thus there

existed in the making an excellent arrangement for all. And
in April 1934 Himmler took over the running of the
Prussian Gestapo and came with Heydrich to Berlin—
Himmler in the Prinz Albrecht Strasse, Heydrich with his
S.D. in the Wilhelmstrasse, the two buildings separated
from each other by a pleasant garden.

CHAPTER 8

The End of the S.A.

IT was the Army which gave Himmler his supreme opportunity. It was the Army, therefore, the proud, stiff-
necked Generals, who regarded Hitler as a distasteful
necessity—for it was Hitler alone who could give them a
Germany in which they could prosper—who must accept
direct responsibility for the rule of the Gestapo in its final
and irresistible form.

Nobody knows precisely what took place at the interviews
between Himmler, Goering, and Hitler which preceded the
announcement, made on 10th April 1934, that Himmler was
to be Deputy-Chief of the Gestapo under Goering. Goering
clearly did not give in without a struggle. The Gestapo was
his personal creation, and Rudolf Diels his private agent.
Without any authority at all beyond that of his own pleasure,
he had detached the Gestapo from the Prussian Ministry of
the Interior when he became Prime Minister of Prussia and
retained it as his own personal preserve. Even when Himmler
took over effective control, it was as Goering's Deputy. But
there were two things which influenced Hitler, and one of
them also had a strong appeal to Goering.

The first was that Himmler could show how throughout
Germany security had been brought to a very high pitch of
efficiency as a result of the hand-in-glove working between
the State Police and the Security Service of the S.S., under

Heydrich. Sooner or later all the police forces of the Reich would have to be unified and centralised, like everything else; and he, Himmler, was clearly the man for the job. The second, and the decisive point for Goering, concerned the future of the S.A.

Hitler's mind at this time was full of the coming showdown with Roehm, the highly ambitious S.A. Chief of Staff. Roehm was one of his oldest friends, but already the differences that had flared up between them in 1930 were beginning to show again. To reassure Roehm and soothe his injured susceptibilities Hitler had given him Cabinet rank a few months before. But this had not helped a great deal. The S.A., who had carried Hitler to power, were in a mood of disillusionment and apprehension. The revolution had not brought them to the promised land. After all the shouting and the tumult they faced a future which appeared by no means rosy in a land in which big business and Army caste, far from being swept away, were prospering more than ever. Their old, trusted leaders of the outlaw days seemed either to have given way to the corruption of power and the blandishments of the old ruling classes or else, like Hitler himself, to be so immersed in cares of State that they were separated from them by a gulf which, to all intents and purposes, was infinite.

Roehm strove to interpret their mood to Hitler, who understood perfectly well what was going on, but dared not quarrel with the financiers, who had backed him, and the Reichswehr, whose continued support he was going to need. In these months at the beginning of 1934 he had the choice of remaining with his old comrades, attempting by violence to carry through the National Socialist revolution to its logical end, with a very strong risk of defeat and downfall—or of abandoning the men who had carried him to power, making a pact with the men who had the cheque-books and the arms, and thus retaining his personal position. He chose the latter course, supported by Goering, who, with the acquisition of high rank, was becoming daily more authoritarian (he had been made a General by President Hindenburg some months before, which had pleased him mightily and brought out all his latent *Junker* snobbery). Goebbels, alone among his closest comrades, opposed him; but Goebbels could be relied upon to change his mind when he saw which way the cat was jumping.

The first manifestation of his choice was when, in February, Roehm presented a memorandum to the Cabinet demanding that the S.A. should form the basis of a new and expanded German Army, and that a new Minister of State should be appointed to control the Armed Forces together with all para-military formations—that Minister, it was clearly implied, was to be Ernst Roehm himself.[1] The Army reacted indignantly to this idea, and Hitler refrained from supporting Roehm. At the same time he sought to exploit necessity to his own advantage by offering the sacrifice of the S.A. as a concession to the British, who were beginning to be alarmed. Then he confided to Mr. Eden that he had plans for cutting down the S.A. from its present strength of three million to some 750,000.[2] At one blow he proposed to appease and reassure the Generals and gain the goodwill of the British Government, which was showing signs of uneasiness at the strength of Germany's para-military formations, as well it might. But it was not as easy as that. Roehm, besides being Hitler's oldest friend, the only one of his followers with whom he was on terms of natural intimacy, was, with his three million devoted brown-shirts, very much a power in the land.

This was the situation when Himmler was appointed Deputy-Chief of the Berlin Gestapo: a move which brought into action at Goering's side the growing might of the S.S.

and the whole apparatus of the German police outside Prussia. It was the counterweight that Hitler needed.

There is no evidence to indicate that Hitler himself was then contemplating a massacre of his old comrades: he was intent only on clipping their wings. With the Army, the Police, and the S.S. on his side, this had become a possibility. Thus, eleven days after Himmler's appointment, Hitler embarked at Kiel on the cruiser *Deutschland* to take part in Naval manœuvres; and with him went the German High Command. On that April cruise from Kiel to Koenigsberg among the bleak waters of the Baltic the Generals sold themselves to Hitler, and Hitler sold his old comrades to the Generals.[3] In return for the support of the Reichswehr Hitler agreed to keep the S.A. down. The men who were going to do the job were Goering and Himmler, and behind Himmler was Heydrich.

It is improbable that on the occasion of what was to be known as the *Deutschland* Pact either Hitler, or General von Fritsch, or Admiral Raeder, or anybody else were clear in their minds that the S.A. could be kept down only by the murder of its leaders. But Goering and Himmler, with Heydrich behind them, were more lucid. Goering detested Roehm for personal reasons: Goering himself had been the first Chief of the S.A. and deeply resented the growing importance of his successor. Himmler and Heydrich saw in him the only obstacle to the infinite expansion of the S.S. As far as Hitler was concerned, there was a tense situation which had to be resolved by means which were not yet clear.

Throughout May and the greater part of June that situation smouldered. But as far as Goering and Himmler were concerned, the issue was settled. They simply had to perfect their plan and then jockey Hitler into a position from which he would be forced to give his consent to its execution. It was the first major operation of the new Gestapo, allied with Heydrich's S.D. And it entailed, as future operations were to entail, the fabrication of a bogus conspiracy and its subsequent "discovery". Events, meanwhile, played into their hands. They had only to prepare the ground and wait.

Hitler, reluctantly, had been forced in April to face Roehm with a point-blank negative when he made a further demand that the Army should be based on the S.A. Roehm, resentful, and also bewildered by the course the revolution was taking, but still not contemplating the removal of Hitler personally, found himself confiding in General von Schleicher, the gallant war-horse of pre-Nazi intrigue, who, sniffing disruption in the air, had come out of his discreet retirement. Goering and Himmler watched this reunion and magnified tremendously the rumours which sprang from it. In the words of Wheeler-Bennett:

"Through the evil fertility of their minds the stories current in Berlin and elsewhere in Germany were built up into a nightmare of horrible appearance. It was no longer a meeting together of disgruntled persons, it was a plot, a conspiracy to murder, to be met and fought with its own weapons. Plans were laid for a drastic purge of the Party, which should include within its scope all enemies of the régime, both past and present, to the Right and to the Left. Lists of those to be 'liquidated' were prepared and a certain bargaining went on whereby the friends of one were to be removed from the list of the other in return for reciprocal treatment. The date was fixed for mid-June, and all that was lacking was the Fuehrer's final consent for action." [4]

Still Hitler persisted in his strange reluctance to murder his oldest friend, and 15th June passed with Roehm still alive. But there was in being a strong movement of fate, which could not be arrested. Everything conspired to favour the conspirators (Goering and Himmler were the conspirators, not Roehm) and to overcome Hitler's absurd scruples. Thus, on 15th June itself, Hitler met Mussolini, still dazzling, still patronising, in Venice, and received some valuable advice as from an old dictator to a young one: Roehm, Heines, and others, the Duce had heard on good authority (the authority was the German Ambassador, von Hassell, who was later to be hanged after the failure of the Stauffenberg attempt on Hitler's life), were men of loose morals and extremist tendencies who were getting the Party into disrepute: it would be a wise thing to remove them before they did more harm.[5] Hitler still hesitated.

And then, only two days later, while the Nazi chieftains were assembled in the provincial city of Gera to hear Hitler's report on the Mussolini meeting, came the dramatic intervention of von Papen. It might have been engineered by Himmler, but it was not: it was the last, brave attempt of a vain, unstable, too-clever-by-half patriot, who had seen himself outwitted at every turn in the very battle of wits which he had backed himself to win, to break the back of the Nazi revolution. At the University of Marburg he made a great and gallant speech. It was great because it had been written by Edgar Jung, a blazing spirit of the Catholic Action, who, with his friends, had captured von Papen to express their own ideas. It was gallant because even von Papen with his remarkable blend of crassness and naïveté must have realised that he was exposing himself to danger of the most deadly kind. It was the last free and defiant utterance to be heard in Germany until after the death of Hitler, and it was fittingly cast in terms of extreme dignity and distinction. It attacked Goebbels, Roehm's only powerful supporter, without mentioning him by name; and it called upon the German people

F

to resist a new wave of the Nazi revolution, which was then about to engulf them.

To the Nazi leaders it meant that they had to choose between the President and Reichswehr, who stood behind von Papen, on the one hand, and the radical wing of their own movement on the other. It was the decisive moment. Hitler at last had to act. The coalition was disintegrating under the Fuehrer's eyes; for von Papen, von Neurath, and others refused to put up with the calumnies now spouted against the Right by Goebbels, and sent in their resignations. The Army and the President stood by them, and Hitler had to give way. Goering and Himmler were called into action, and the conspiracy they had been fabricating was improved and extended. So were the lists of those to be done away with. Von Papen had done his bit in assuring the triumph of Himmler, with Heydrich behind him.

The plot, Goering's and Himmler's plot, long perfected, now ceased to be the private scheme of two conspirators: it became, like the Reichstag Fire plot, part of the policy of State. It was taken over by Hitler, and the Army itself prepared the way for its execution. On 25th June the Reichswehr all over the country was placed in a state of alert by its Commander-in-Chief, von Fritsch; leave was cancelled and troops were confined to barracks. Germany was in effect handed over to Himmler, while the Army kept indoors. The S.S. was secretly mobilised and ordered to stand-by for immediate action on 28th June. On that very day Roehm was formally expelled from the German Officers' League: he could now be arrested and charged with high treason without affecting the honour of the Reichswehr. It is likely that this is what the Generals expected would happen; but the conspirators, who now included Hitler, had other views. Roehm was to be murdered; with him, his chief supporters; with them, anybody else Hitler, Goering, and Himmler between them, to say nothing of Heydrich, wanted out of the way.

The operation started soon after dark on Friday, 29th June. Hitler flew to Munich and arrived before dawn, leaving Goering and Himmler to look after Berlin. Hitler himself confronted the local S.A. leaders, who were under arrest, raved at them, and tore off their insignia with his own hands. Roehm and Heines were dragged out of bed in the Hanselbauer Hotel at Wiessee, a resort quite close to Munich. In his broadcast two days later, which sickened the world, Goebbels described the shooting of these two men, of whom, until a few days before, he had been the impassioned champion. The rest of the S.A. in Munich were rounded up and shot by an execution squad supplied by Hitler's S.S. bodyguard—the S.S. *Leibstandarte Adolf Hitler* commanded by Himmler's crony, Sepp Dietrich.

In Berlin their colleagues were taken to the Lichterfelde Barracks and shot there. It was in Berlin, too, that General von Schleicher and his wife were shot down and left lying in their own blood on their drawing-room floor. Von Papen was arrested, and would have been shot on Goering's orders but for Hindenburg's special protection. Two of his adjutants were shot dead at their desks, while the man who had written the famous Marburg speech for von Papen, Edgar Jung, was killed on the run. Karl Ernst, the Berlin S.A. leader, was out of town.

The S.A. was supposed to be actively conspiring against Hitler, but Roehm and Heines were on holiday near Munich, and Ernst was at Bremen about to embark on a pleasure cruise. The Gestapo were sent after him and brought him back to Berlin, where he was shot almost at once in the Lichterfelde Barracks, still believing that he was the victim of a *Putsch* by Goering against Hitler and Roehm. Gregor Strasser, Himmler's old chief, was declared to have committed suicide. But in fact he was shot in the Gestapo building on the Prinz Albrecht Strasse. Gisevius, who had been hanging about the place all day, trying to piece together what was going on, said:

"Strasser had been taken to the Gestapo prison at about noon. By that time some hundred arrested S.A. leaders were crowded together in one big room. These men had no idea why they had been arrested, nor did they know about the shootings that were going on in Munich and at Lichterfelde in Berlin. They were therefore inclined to look at the situation in its most humorous light, a mood which is common when people are arrested *en masse*. They cheered Strasser when he was brought in as a new comrade in misery.

"Some hours passed and there was a great deal of coming and going. Then an S.S. man came to the door and called out Strasser. The man who had formerly been next in importance to Adolf Hitler was to be moved to an individual cell. No one thought anything of it as Strasser walked slowly out of the room. But scarcely a minute later they heard the crack of a pistol.

"The S.S. man had shot the unsuspecting Strasser from behind and hit his main artery. A great stream of blood had spurted against the wall of the tiny cell. Apparently Strasser did not die at once. A prisoner in the adjoining cell heard him thrashing about on the cot for nearly an hour. No one paid any attention to him. At last the prisoner heard loud footsteps in the corridor and orders being shouted. The guards clicked their heels, and the prisoner recognised Heydrich's voice saying: 'Isn't he dead yet? Let the swine bleed to death.'

"The bloodstains on the wall of the cell remained for weeks. It was the pride of the S.S. squadron, a kind of

museum piece. These cut-throats showed it to all the
terrified inmates and boasted that it was the blood of a
famous man, Gregor Strasser. It was only after he had
received numerous complaints that Heydrich ordered the
bloodstains to be cleaned." [6]

The building on the Prinz Albrecht Strasse was finally
shaking down into its true character. Himmler was not there
most of the time: he was supervising the executions in the
Lichterfelde Barracks, familiarising himself with the sort
of work he required his subordinates to do and lending them
moral support.[7] On the Sunday evening, while the shooting
was still going on, Hitler gave one of his special tea-parties
in the garden of the Chancellery. It was to become a familiar
gesture after a particularly gruelling time.[8] (He was to give
another, one of his last, ten years later, while the conspirators
of the 20th July were being shot.) It was a sign of his remarkable resilience. For only the evening before he had arrived from Munich at the Tempelhof Airport in no condition
at all for tea-parties. Gisevius was at the airport with his
police cronies, Daluege and Nebe, to welcome him:

"The plane from Munich was announced. In a moment we saw it looming swiftly larger against the background of a blood-red sky, a piece of theatricality that no
one had staged. The plane roared down to a landing and
rolled towards us. Commands rang out. A guard of
honour presented arms. Goering, Himmler, Koerner,
Frick, Daluege, and some twenty police officers went up
to the plane. Then the door opened and Adolf Hitler was
the first to step out. . . .

"A brown shirt, black bow tie, dark-brown leather
jacket, high black army boots—all dark tones. He wore
no hat; his face was pale, unshaven, sleepless, at once
gaunt and puffed. Under the forelock pasted against his

forehead his eyes stared dully. Nevertheless, he did not impress me as wretched, nor did he awaken sympathy, as his appearance might well have done. It was clear that the murders of his friends had cost him no effort at all. He had felt nothing; he had merely acted out of his rage.

"First Hitler silently shook hands with everyone within reach. Nebe and I, who had taken the precaution of standing some distance away, heard amid the silence the repeated monotonous sound of clicking heels. . . .

"On his way to the fleet of cars, which stood several hundred yards away, Hitler stopped to converse with Goering and Himmler. Apparently he could not wait a few minutes until he reached the Chancellery. He listened attentively as the two made their report, though he must have been in constant telephone communication with them all day.

"From one of his pockets Himmler drew a long, tattered list. Hitler read it through, while Goering and Himmler whispered incessantly into his ear. We could see Hitler's finger moving slowly down the sheet of paper. Now and then it paused for a moment at one of the names. At such times the two conspirators whispered even more excitedly. Suddenly Hitler tossed his head. There was so much violent emotion, so much anger in the gesture, that everybody noticed it. Nebe and I cast significant glances at one another. Undoubtedly, we thought, they were now informing him of Strasser's 'suicide'.

"Finally they moved on, Hitler in the lead, followed by Goering and Himmler. Hitler was still walking with the same sluggish tread. By contrast, the two blood-drenched scoundrels at his side seemed all the more lively. Both Goering and Himmler, for all the bulkiness of the one and the drabness of the other, seemed cut out of the same cloth today. Both manifested the same self-importance, loquacity, officiousness, and the same sense of guilt. Without a sound, the rest of the procession followed at a discreet distance. Everybody behaved with abashed deference, as if he had been permitted to touch the hem of world history or to carry the blood-streaked train that dragged behind the unholy triumvirate." [9]

The S.A. was finished. Roehm was succeeded by colourless von Lutze, and the brown-shirts were never to play a major rôle again. The Army had triumphed. That is to say, it had kept proudly and virtuously aloof while Goering and Himmler had employed the methods of Chicago gangsters to break their most dangerous rivals. The Generals were quite oblivious of the fact that by allowing Himmler, with his black-shirts and his Gestapo, to break the power of the S.A. they had put them in a position to dominate utterly not only the despised civilians but also the Army itself. For the Generals, the 30th June was the start of their melancholy progression to the dock at Nuremberg.

CHAPTER 9

Gestapo Ueber Alles

THERE was nothing now that could hold back Himmler and Heydrich except the will of the Fuehrer: and Hitler was well satisfied with them both. He had got Germany where he wanted her. He was comparatively uninterested in domestic politics. His concern was to turn the nation into a first-class fighting power. "For us the revolution is no permanent condition," he declared in his speech defending the massacre of 30th June. And indeed it was not. Already, a year earlier, he had said: "Many more revolutions have been successful at the outset than have, after their initial success, been checked and brought to a standstill at the right moment." The right moment, a little belatedly, had been caught. The revolutionary flame was dead. Hitler was free to build up the might of Germany in collaboration with the Generals, the manufacturers, the financiers.

There was to be no political life in the country. All parties were banned, and he, Hitler, proposed to govern by decree. The administration was provided by the purged offices of local government. The discipline and the drive would be provided by a police terror. Himmler and Heydrich had shown that they knew how to provide that, and they could be safely left to carry on. Goering, with his own position secured by the murder of Roehm and the final abasement of Goebbels, could from now on afford to loosen his grip on the police.

But Himmler and Heydrich went very quietly. They settled down to consolidate what they had and to extend the limits of their power. The Gestapo and the S.D. provided the brain; the general S.S., the physical threat; the S.S. Death's-head formations (the concentration-camp guards), the ultimate terror. It was the task of the Gestapo and the S.D. to penetrate into every aspect of public and private life secretly, and publicly to create a legend of terror designed to make them appear even more omniscient and ubiquitous than in fact they were. Their power soon outran their official mandate. Nearly two years were to pass before the Gestapo was legalised as such and Himmler became officially what he already was in fact, the Chief of the unified German Police. It was not until 1939, on the eve of the war, that the instrument of terror achieved its final shape.

The Gestapo was finally brought on to a legal footing on 10th February 1936, by virtue of a Prussian statute which recognised the peculiar position it had carved out for itself and regularised its ways. The statute which made it legal at the same time raised it above the law. Clause 7 stated that there was to be no appeal from the decision of the Gestapo, and the judiciary was forbidden to re-examine these decisions. This meant that once an individual was in the hands of the Gestapo he was debarred from any appeal to the law as traditionally understood. It meant, further, that a man could be acquitted by the courts, or released from prison on the expiry of a court sentence, and immediately rearrested by the Gestapo and taken into Protective Custody—i.e. sent to a concentration-camp. The spirit of the matter is best conveyed in the words of Hitler's notorious proclamation of 22nd October 1938: ". . . every means adopted for carrying out the will of the Leader is considered legal, even though it may conflict with existing statutes and precedents."

On 17th June 1936 Himmler was formally appointed

Chief of German Police; and from that moment began the long, calculated campaign to detach the Gestapo from the State apparatus and transfer it effectively to the S.S. and to put the S.S. into a position to dominate completely the police apparatus as a whole.

On 26th June 1936 the police was formally divided into two parts: the uniformed and the plain clothes; or the Order Police (Orpo) and the Security Police (Sipo), which included the Gestapo, the Kripo, and, in effect, the S.D. Daluege became head of the Orpo; Heydrich, of the Sipo. The two branches were run by Himmler as Chief of German Police; but he was working towards the day when he would run them as *Reichsfuehrer* S.S.

On 20th September Inspectors of Orpo (IdO) and Sipo (IdS) were appointed to each *Wehrkreis*, or Military District, to co-operate with the Gauleiter and the *Wehrkreis* Commander. At the same time it was decreed that the S.S. Leader in each main territorial sector of the S.S. (*Oberabschnitt*) should also be Chief of Police for his area. The State administration was being swamped by the S.S. On the same day the Prussian Gestapo became the headquarters of the Political Police throughout Germany. On 1st October the term Gestapo was extended to cover the unified Political Police of the Reich.

Eight months later, on 15th May 1937, Himmler, as *Reichsfuehrer* of the S.S. (RfSS), achieved a major objective. It was decreed that all rulings issued by his office were valid as Ministerial decisions. On 11th November the peculiar affinities of the Gestapo and the S.S. Security Service (S.D.) were recognised by law:

"The S.D. of the RfSS, as a Party and Reichs Government organisation, has to carry out important tasks: in particular it is required to assist the Security Police [i.e.

Gestapo and Kripo]. The S.D. is consequently active on behalf of the Reich; and this demands close and intelligent co-operation between the S.D. and the officials of the General and Interior Administration."

This decree was a logical outcome of a decree of 23rd June 1938, which laid it down that all Security Police (Gestapo and Kripo) personnel must be enrolled in the S.S. This meant, in effect, that the Gestapo, a State organisation, was brought under control of the S.D., a Party organisation.

The final stage was reached in 1939 when Heydrich achieved his personal ambition. The Main Office of the Security Police in the Reichs Ministry of the Interior, the Gestapo and the Kripo that is, was taken away from the State organisation and from the surveillance of the Minister of the Interior and merged into the Main Security Office of the S.S., which was henceforth known as the *Reichssicherheits-hauptamt*, or R.S.H.A., directly under Heydrich. The Gestapo became Section IV of this institution; the Kripo was Section V. The S.D. (home intelligence) was Section III; the S.D. (foreign intelligence) was Section VI. Sections I and II were concerned with Personnel and Administration.

There was also Section N (*Nachrichten*), the all important technical communications section; and, later, when the S.S. was making its bid to duplicate the armed forces, Section VII, which was concerned with Scientific Exploitation, and set up its own rocket research station in rivalry to Peenemuende.

In 1943 the circle was closed when Himmler himself became Reichs Minister of the Interior. By that time Heydrich was dead.

This tabulation of dates and appointments is not irrelevant. It is of extreme importance for an appreciation of the interlocking responsibilities of the Gestapo, the Orpo, the

Kripo, the S.D., and the S.S. in general. Great efforts have been made by interested parties to obscure the true picture. At one time and another members of all the organisations listed here have sought to disclaim all connection with each other. But the chain of command and the interlock are both unambiguous.

The Orpo and the Sipo were connected through Himmler as Chief of Police. The leadership of the police and the rank-and-file membership of the Gestapo and Kripo were restricted to the S.S. The Gestapo and the Kripo formed part of the security service of the S.S., first under Heydrich, then under Kaltenbrunner. The S.S. under Himmler also provided the concentration-camp guards (Death's-head formations), the concentration-camp administration (W.V.H.A.), and, later, the special S.S. divisions, the Waffen S.S., which fought at the front. The S.S. in the end became a state within the State, duplicating almost every aspect of the State administration. It captured the Intelligence services of the Armed Forces; it duplicated every administrative office; it duplicated even the most elaborate and costly research projects; it fought the armed services for supremacy all along the line, and in the end was winning. The Gestapo was its spearhead. In the end, as Amt IV of the R.S.H.A. under its shadowy chief, Lt.-General Heinrich Mueller, who reported directly to Heydrich, it dominated the whole of occupied Europe, and it contained the following sections and sub-sections, which illustrate its range:

R.S.H.A. IV Ia. Marxism; enemy broadcasting; enemy propaganda; partisans; Russian prisoners-of-war.

„ „ Ib. Reaction; monarchism; pacifism; liberalism; rumours; undermining morale; defeatism.

R.S.H.A. IV 2. Sabotage; radio jamming; parachut-
                ists; commandos.

"   "   3a. Counter-intelligence; careless talk.

"   "   3b. Economics; foreign exchange.

"   "   3c. Frontier control.

"   "   4a. Catholicism; Protestantism; Free-
                masonry.

"   "   4b. Jews.

"   "   5a. Anti-social behaviour; shirking.

"   "   5b. Party affairs; Press.

"   "   6a. Card index; personal dossiers; in-
                formation.

"   "   6b. Protective custody; concentration-
                camps.

All these came under Section IVA of the R.S.H.A. After
the outbreak of war Section IVB was added to cover the
occupied countries: IVB 1 for Western Territories; IVB 2
for Eastern; IVB 3 for South-eastern; IVB 4 for passes and
identification. A special sub-section, IVB A (*Arbeit*) was
created to look after the employment of foreign workers;
and another, IVB G (*Grenze*) to control Customs and frontier
protection and inspection. R.S.H.A. Amt IVA 6a at the
top of a letter-heading looks insignificant enough; but it
stood for the immense system of card indices and dossiers
which penetrated into the personal lives of every German
citizen. R.S.H.A. Amt IVA 4b, again, was responsible for
the rounding up, transportation, shooting, and gassing to
death of at least three million Jews.

There was no murdering of Jews, except incidentally, in
the early days of the new Gestapo. Himmler and Heydrich
were still manœuvring for the absolute power which would
make Auschwitz possible. The Jews could be picked off

when the time came. Meanwhile there were heavier antagon-
ists. The German people as a whole had to be regimented;
the Army had to be put in its place (Himmler and Heydrich
had no illusions about the enduring quality of the Army's
gratitude to them for breaking the back of the S.A., especially when it dawned on the Generals that Himmler was
going to prove a far more dangerous and purposeful threat
to the sovereignty of the Armed Forces than Roehm ever
was); the power of the Churches had to be undermined.

For the purposes of general supervision and repression the
Gestapo modelled itself closely on the Soviet Secret Police.
Himmler had at his command an extremely able police-
officer, Heinrich Mueller, who became known as Gestapo
Mueller, a close and devoted student of Soviet methods.
Mueller was impressed by the efficiency of the internal spy
system which had been perfected by the Soviet Government,
the effect of which, ideally, was to isolate the individual by
making it impossible for anybody to trust anybody else. He
set to work to reproduce this system in Germany by more
economical means.

He built up a cell system which enrolled quantities of
ordinary citizens as honorary part-time members of the
Gestapo. Thus there was the *Blockwart*, the concierge, who
had to report on the activities of every tenant in his apartment block. Every Air-Raid Warden was also a corresponding member of the Gestapo. Every labour group had a
Gestapo representative. And, on top of this, voluntary informers were encouraged by every possible means. As the
Russians had discovered, there is nothing like the voluntary
informer for creating a general atmosphere of unease and
apprehension: he operates by personal spite, or by the desire
to ingratiate himself with the authorities; he costs nothing;
his information is usually valueless in any specific sense; but
since every human being at some time commits some indis-

cretion, he enables the secret police to swoop where it is least expected (and often least needed) and give the desired impression of possessing an all-seeing eye.

As far as the regular membership was concerned, there was no difficulty in recruiting. Any regular police official was liable to find himself drafted into the Gestapo as a matter of routine posting; and although a handful of individuals at one time and another avoided such postings, by open refusal, or by subterfuge, the average police official seems to have taken it as part of the day's work and to have made no complaint, being prepared to carry out in the German manner the most atrocious orders without any sense of personal responsibility, or even involvement. There were also volunteers, of course, men like Heinrich Baab of Frankfurt, whom we meet later, who drifted into the regular Gestapo because the work suited them. Baab himself had been a Block supervisor in the S.A. He had volunteered as a Gestapo informer for 50 marks a month, proved his worth, and was then taken into the Frankfurt police for duties first with the Gestapo, then with the S.D. He was a loutish brute with a good working-class background, a man with a chip on his shoulder who found fulfilment in the uninhibited exercise of subordinate authority. There were many like him.

But not all members of the Gestapo were trained Gestapo agents. There was a large corps of administrative officials who had no police training at all, but were simply Civil Servants: in 1944 there were some 3,000 of these, or less than 10 per cent of the regular force. There were a host of junior clerks and typists, many of them, and particularly in wartime, women, often the wives and relatives of regular officials. The so-called Executive Officials, the true Gestapo agents, formed just under half of the total force of 40,000 in 1944, and they were divided into various grades. First the Senior Grade Civil Servants, the *Regierungsrat* and the *Kriminalrat*, who were highly educated men. Then the slightly lower grade, beginning with the *Kriminal Inspektor*; then the medium grade, beginning with the *Kriminal Assistant*. All these, most of them Civil Servants by nature with an ingrained police outlook, were sent to special training courses at the Fuehrer School, where they were inculcated with the outlook and techniques of Gestapo Mueller. They were German officials called upon to carry out specialised work in accordance with the orders of Hitler, and most of them were convinced that all they were doing was their duty, which frequently called for harshness and an iron will.

Mueller, who came to control and who built up this apparatus for Heydrich, will repeatedly appear by name in these pages. But we shall never meet him. He was the arch-type of non-political functionary, in love with personal power and dedicated to the service of authority, the State. Although he was a high-ranking officer of the S.S. and had worked under Himmler from the moment he took office as Bavarian Chief of Police, it was not until 1939 that he joined the Party, and even then he took no stock in it. He worked anonymously, and he has left hardly a trace behind. We find his signature on orders authorising the most atrocious deeds. We glimpse him once or twice in action, and are surprised to discover that this man without a shadow, this office bureaucrat, could walk about and use a gun. But we know nothing about him, neither where he came from nor where he went. Even his subordinate, Eichmann, the murderer of the Jews, who never on any account put his signature to a document, left behind friends and acquaintances who have given us vivid glimpses of the man. Mueller left nobody. We see him lunching at the Adlon Hotel with Heydrich, Nebe, Schellenberg, later with Kaltenbrunner. They are all dead. Even Willy Hoettl, who has things to say about most people, can tell us nothing about Mueller.

One of the few recorded interviews with him is given us by General Walter Dornberger, the chief of rocket research at Peenemuende. In his memoirs Dornberger shows a marked talent for describing the most varied personalities and making them live. But Mueller defeats him.

"He was the unobtrusive type of police official who leaves no personal impression on the memory. Later, all I could remember was a pair of piercing grey-blue eyes, fixed on me with an unwavering scrutiny. My first impression was one of cold curiosity and extreme reserve." [1]

And yet it was a critical meeting. Himmler had been interfering with the management of the Peenemuende station (this was in 1944), and Dornberger had gone to Berlin to demand the release of two of his men who had been arrested for no apparent reason at all. Mueller's behaviour indicated how deeply he had been impressed by his Soviet model. He heard Dornberger out, and then, without warning, instead of arguing, came back with a counter-attack:

" 'You are a very interesting case, General. Do you know what a fat file of evidence we have against you here?'

"I shook my head in surprise. He raised his hand a few inches above the table. I couldn't help asking him: 'Why don't you arrest me then?'

" 'Because it would be pointless as yet. You are still regarded as our greatest rocket expert, and we can't very well ask you to give expert evidence against yourself.' "

There was some desultory discussion of General Dornberger's alleged negligence and sabotage, and that was that. The only time Mueller showed emotion at this interview was when Dornberger referred to the arrests as being carried out by the S.D. This upset the Chief of the Gestapo: "As a

G

General on the active list you should surely know the difference between the S.D. and the Gestapo." Dornberger retorted that nobody knew the difference. Mueller gulped, but said nothing.

He disappeared as silently as he arrived. We hear of him last in Hitler's Bunker two days before the end.[2] Professional as always, he had turned up in that madhouse on Hitler's instructions to interrogate, as head of the Gestapo, the ex-riding-master Fegelein, the brother-in-law of Eva Braun, and one of Himmler's personal links with the Fuehrer's inner circle. Fegelein had to be investigated because the news had just come to Hitler that Himmler had turned against him and was conspiring to usurp the leadership. It is characteristic of all we know of Mueller that he should not have been held compromised by the treason of his master.

Mueller did his job, while Berlin rocked, shuddered, and disintegrated under the Russian artillery and Hitler prepared himself for the end. Then, with Fegelein shot for a conspiracy with which he had nothing to do—Hitler's last execution—the chief of the Gestapo vanishes, whether to die in the streets of Berlin, to escape under an assumed identity to Austria or Spain or the Argentine, or to join the Russians he admired so much, we do not know. Willy Hoettl believes that he did just that. For some time he had been using captured Russian agents to communicate false intelligence to the Soviet armies, using their own codes and their own wireless sets; and it would have been entirely possible for him to enter into detailed communication with the enemy by this means without anyone being the wiser.[3] Be that as it may, like a perfect Civil Servant, he went, leaving not a trace, his files totally destroyed.

CHAPTER 10

The Dustbin of the Reich

IF every member of the R.S.H.A. had been as efficient and careful as Gestapo Mueller it would have been very hard indeed to piece together the story of that remarkable institution. But many members were not. Documents with the signatures of Himmler, Heydrich, Kaltenbrunner, and even Mueller himself were found by the Allies all over Europe. These should have been destroyed when read by their recipients; but they were not. Further, prisoners from the concentration-camps, many of whom had been interrogated by the Gestapo, lived in considerable numbers to tell their tale. These, too, should have been done away with before their release by the Allies; but, although Kaltenbrunner and others gave orders for their liquidation, they survived.[1] Finally, on a much smaller, yet decisive, scale, certain colleagues, associates, and subordinates of Mueller fell into Allied hands and satisfied some inner need either by denouncing their superiors and associates or else by confessing to all but unbelievable actions committed by themselves. These, had they been made of the stuff of Mueller, would have destroyed themselves or else gone into hiding; but they did not.[2] So, all in all, the discretion of Gestapo Mueller was practised in vain.

It should not be thought that all his associates were captured. Some committed suicide, like Himmler himself; many

99

others—a remarkably high proportion, indeed—simply disappeared, like Mueller, and have never been heard of again.
Nor did all those who were captured allow themselves the
luxury of confession. For example, Kaltenbrunner, Heydrich's rather dreary successor, sourly refused to admit his
complicity in anything at all, even when confronted with his
own signature and his own photograph in what might be
called compromising contexts.[3] Others sought to put all the
blame on to their colleagues. Some succeeded in this; but
some did not—like the gentlemanly and well-dressed Dr.
Lindow of sub-section Ia of the Gestapo, who busied himself with Russian prisoners-of-war, and, two years after his
release from formal internment as a second-degree Nazi, was
shocked and outraged to find himself suddenly under arrest
for mass murder.[4] But there were others who felt the need
to confess, and described their activities, and those of their
associates, with conscientious care and in clinical detail.

These were various. There was the imposing figure of
S.S. Lt.-General Erich von dem Bach-Zelewski, Higher S.S.
and Police Leader of the Central Russian front, and, as such,
immediately responsible to Himmler for everything that
happened behind the fighting armies in his immense command.[5] There was one of the star performers among Heydrich's bright young men, an intellectual thug, the brilliant
young economist Otto Ohlendorf, who became an S.S.
Major-General and head of the domestic S.D., the German
version of those Oxford dons who did so well in the British
Intelligence during the war; unlike his English, or Scottish,
or Welsh counterparts, he got out of his depth and found
himself commanding one of Heydrich's notorious Action
Groups (*Einsatzgruppe* D), and later admitted responsibility
for the murder of over 90,000 Jews in Southern Russia, men,
women, and children.[6] There was S.S. Captain Dieter Wisliceny, a trusted aide of S.S. Colonel Eichmann (Chief of the

Gestapo's Jewish Office (R.S.H.A. Amt IVA 4b)) in his task of delivering the Jews of Europe to the gas chambers.

It was Wisliceny who related at Nuremberg how Eichmann had told him that he would kill himself if Germany lost the war, and "would leap into his grave laughing, because the feeling that he had five million human beings on his conscience would be for him a source of extraordinary satisfaction".[7] (Eichmann could not help boasting, even in terms of horror, as Mr. Reitlinger in his monumental and terrible study of the attempted extermination of European Jewry has shown: he personally did not have a hand in more than three million murders.[8] Most would be well satisfied with this; but Eichmann, like so many of his compatriots, had to exaggerate, even to himself.)

There was S.S. Lt.-Colonel Rudolf Franz Hoess, not a member of the Gestapo or the S.D., and so inferior. As Commandant of Auschwitz, however, he was a particular crony of Eichmann's and his chief customer; later, he became Deputy Inspector of Concentration-camps under S.S. Lt.-General Gluecks. Gluecks vanished, but Hoess was caught and hanged.[9] There was Helmut Naujocks of the S.D., a plain-clothes expert, who only killed for a useful purpose, but who was able to throw some light on the conspiratorial aspects of the Gestapo: his modest contribution to history was the faking of the frontier incident which started the world war.[10]

There were others: so many, that, in spite of the silences of Gestapo Mueller, the picture builds up; it is time to look at it.

At Nuremberg they did not talk about the activities of the Gestapo: they talked about its crimes. They listed these crimes in a manner which makes for convenient reference, and, at the same time, offers a useful and comprehensive survey of the ground we have to cover. The best list was provided by Colonel Story of the United States Prosecution. When he speaks of "the conspiracy" he means the Nazi conspiracy, first against Germany, then against the world:

"The Gestapo and the S.D. played an important part in almost every criminal act of the conspiracy. The category of these crimes, apart from thousands of specific instances of torture and cruelty in policing Germany for the benefit of the conspirators, reads like a page from the devil's notebook:

"They fabricated the border incidents which Hitler used as an excuse for attacking Poland.

"They murdered hundreds of thousands of defenceless men, women, and children by the infamous Einsatz groups.

"They removed Jews, political leaders, and scientists from prisoner-of-war camps and murdered them.

"They took recaptured prisoners-of-war to concentration camps and murdered them.

"They established and classified the concentration camps and sent thousands of people into them for extermination and slave labour.

"They cleared Europe of the Jews and were responsible for sending hundreds of thousands to their deaths in annihilation camps.

"They rounded up hundreds of thousands of citizens of occupied countries and shipped them to Germany for forced labour and sent slave labourers to labour reformatory camps.

"They executed captured commandos and paratroopers, and protected civilians who lynched Allied fliers.

"They took civilians of occupied countries to Germany for secret trial and punishment.

"They arrested, tried, and punished citizens of occupied countries under special criminal procedures, which did not accord fair trials, and by summary methods.

"They murdered or sent to concentration camps the relatives of persons who had allegedly committed crimes.

"They ordered the murder of prisoners in Sipo and S.D. prisons to prevent their release by Allied armies.

"They participated in the seizure and spoliation of public and private property.

"They were primary agents for the persecution of the Jews and churches." [11]

This was the pattern of terror. Himmler used to go about asking visiting foreigners why it was that the Gestapo had got such a bad name for itself.[12] Heydrich, on the other hand, knew why, and gloried in this reputation:

"Secret State Police, Criminal Police, and S.D. are still adorned with the furtive and whispered secrecy of a political detective story. In a mixture of fear and shuddering —and yet, at home, with a certain feeling of security because of their presence—brutality, inhumanity bordering on the sadistic, and ruthlessness, are attributed abroad to the men of this profession." [13]

Heydrich was speaking to his officers and men on German Police Day in February 1941. He was happy that things should be so. He could make a joke about it. In the same speech, he said:

"It is natural that people do not want to be involved with us too much. There is no problem down to the smallest egotistical longing which the Gestapo cannot solve. Regarded in this way we are, if a joke is permitted, looked upon as a cross between a general maid and the dustbin of the Reich."

The joke was permitted. The problems were solved by killing and torture: the Gestapo knew no other way. There was scarcely an exception to this. Once Himmler was in the saddle there were few major actions undertaken by the Gestapo which did not involve the torturing or killing of somebody. The massacre of 30th June set the tone. When Himmler was allowed by the Generals to murder their rivals in cold blood, when during this massacre Himmler saw fit to kill off for good measure some of the Army's closest friends, without producing any reaction from the Generals—then the game was up. It was too much to expect that the ordinary citizens of a powerful country should show resistance to an evil condoned by their most venerated caste. If Himmler, under Hitler, showed no scruple in murdering his fellow Germans—Communists, Socialists, Liberals of all kinds— it was a fair deduction that he would show no scruple in murdering his fellow Party members. And if he was prepared to murder his fellow Party members, then plainly he would be even more prepared to murder such foreigners as might come his way. This happened. And the Generals who had condoned the murders of Roehm, Strasser, and their old friend von Schleicher, were to find themselves condoning before very long—and, indeed, as we shall see, actively assisting in— the murder of hundreds of thousands of human beings, men, women, and children, under their own noses and within the areas of their commands.[14]

They could not help it, they said. The whole affair was outside their control. It could be so: it is not for us to say. The issue is too large for the outsider. Only the Germans can decide. So far, as a nation, they have evaded decision.

But why should we pick on the Generals? Why assume in

them a special responsibility towards the German people? The answer is that they claimed such responsibility. The officer caste regarded itself, and was so regarded by large sections of the population, as the repository of German honour. It was also powerful. Hitler could do nothing without its assent and connivance. It tolerated Hitler, whom it despised, because Hitler promised it a return to its vanished glory. For this it was prepared to put up with Himmler and Heydrich too, and the methods of this precious pair. It was the only organised body which could have stopped Himmler in time. It did not do so because Himmler was helping Hitler to consolidate his power, and the Generals needed Hitler to restore their arms. In order that they might once more hold up their heads before the world and recover their lost confidence, the German Generals were prepared to condone, and did condone—and later largely assist in—the murder of innumerable innocent civilians, men, women, and children. And in the end, of course, they found they could not hold up their heads after all.

It was not as if these men had no warning. In June 1934, after the nation as a whole, in the high hysteria of revolutionary violence, or in the defeatism of cynicism, opportunism, or despair, had been gathered into Himmler's net, the Generals were still outside. They had the aged President at their head; General von Fritsch, the most able man after von Seekt, was their Chief-of-Staff. They had a man of the quality of General Beck, later to resign in disgust, to play Cassandra. They made their deal with Himmler and handed over the S.A. to the S.S. for slaughter almost certainly without knowing what they were doing. But by the first day of July they knew exactly what they had done. And if in that moment they were too dazed and sickened to take resolute action, they still had another chance. Two more chances. Three.

When Hindenburg died and Hitler supplanted him, the Generals took a new oath of allegiance to him personally. There was no force in Germany to make them do this. They did it of their own free will. It was to tie their hands, or to serve as an excuse for refusing to act in the interests of decency, for ten more squalid years—until most of them could no longer recognise decency when they saw it. That was the first chance.

Their second chance came in what was to prove their first and last major engagement with the Gestapo. Heydrich all but over-reached himself, as he was to over-reach himself in Austria with the murder of Chancellor Dollfuss. But the Generals let him win. It was a bloodless victory. No General died in the action which led to the final demoralisation of the High Command.

This was one of the Gestapo actions not mentioned by the Prosecution at Nuremberg. It was achieved by the now familiar means of a frame-up. In January 1938 the Minister of Defence, Field-Marshal von Blomberg, an ageing widower, marrying for the second time, chose a typist in the War Ministry, Fraülein Erna Gruehn. Goering assisted in this operation by sending off to South America a younger aspirant for the hand of Fraülein Gruehn. Hitler gave his blessing. But soon afterwards Berlin was alive with the most astonishing rumours, and the rumours were true. Fraülein Gruehn was found to have a police record: there was a routine dossier in existence showing her to have been a professional prostitute, and clipped to the dossier were photographs of the most compromising kind.[15]

The Gestapo had nothing to do with this discovery. It was accidental; and the Police President of Berlin, Count Hell-dorf (although a Nazi, Helldorf retained to the end certain feelings of decency, and paid for these ultimately with his life) immediately decided that on no account must Himmler know anything about the affair. He knew what would happen. Innocently he took the dossier for advice to von Blomberg's own son-in-law, who had risen from obscurity by the unfortunate Field-Marshal's grace, and was now head of the *Wehrmachtamt* in the Ministry of War. The son-in-law was Wilhelm Keitel (who never had any feelings of decency, and was to pay for this ultimately with his life). Keitel would have liked to save his old father-in-law, just as later he would have liked to have saved the hundreds of thousands who were shot by the Wehrmacht or handed over to the Gestapo in every country in Europe. He was fond of the old man. But there was nothing he could do without risking his career. And that was not to be considered. So he took the dossier to Goering. And Goering, full of pleasurable anticipation, took it to Hitler, who had one of his fits.[16] Meanwhile the news got round. And Himmler began to move.

In the coming and going of the next few days, with demands for Blomberg's immediate resignation, divorce, expulsion from the officers corps—with Hitler vacillating as usual—there was one purposeful figure: Himmler, with Heydrich behind him. For the next move was to appoint a successor to von Blomberg as Minister of Defence. The next in line of succession was von Fritsch. But Goering himself coveted the office; and although Himmler did not in the least want to see Goering in that particular chair he was prepared to put up with it if he could get rid of von Fritsch. He thought he could do so, and in such a way that von Fritsch's disgrace, coming on top of the von Blomberg scandal, would shatter the confidence and unity, as well as the popular reputation, of the General Staff for ever.

What Hitler minded most was homo-sexuality among his national leaders—not, as far as is known, because he had any particular objection to it as such, but because he was trying to build up a system admired for its puritanical morality. So von Fritsch was to be cast as a homo-sexual. It was easy enough. Heydrich managed to dig up an underworld character, a professional blackmailer who specialised in well-to-do homo-sexuals. He featured in an existing dossier about a junior cavalry officer called Frisch. He was threatened by Heydrich and told he would be killed if he refused to identify General von Fritsch as the man Frisch from whom he had extorted sums in the past. The confrontation took place in the presence of Hitler. Von Fritsch, who had coldly and categorically denied the charge against him, was so outraged when the disreputable figure emerged from a side door and made his identification that he became incoherent and could find no words. Hitler immediately assumed his guilt.

It was not one of the more polished Gestapo actions. Very soon the truth was widely known, and at the Court of Enquiry the blackmailer broke down and told the whole story. But the damage had been done. Only resolute and violent action on the part of von Fritsch could save the situation. All those who had been waiting impatiently for the pretext for such action, which would sweep the filth of Nazidom away, thought the moment had come. But von Fritsch preferred the way of proud resignation—or sulking. "At the moment of confluence of his own Fate with that of Germany, he was found wanting", in the words of Wheeler-Bennett, who goes on to use an image so crude and raw that for a moment the reader is shocked—until he realises that, in the end, the Chief of the great General Staff deserved no more sounding epitaph: "The Man of Steel, the Hero of the Army, bewildered and shocked by what had happened, at that moment of destiny resembled a cross between a puzzled virgin and a petrified rabbit." [17]

Hitler himself took over the Army. Von Blomberg's son-in-law, Keitel, as head of the newly constituted O.K.W., became Hitler's military mouth-piece. Himmler, with Hitler now concerned almost exclusively with military matters, became effective master of Germany.

The third chance of the Generals came with the outbreak of war. They could have stopped it; they wanted to stop it; but they did nothing.[18] The Gestapo, as such, for once had nothing to do with this, it is a pleasure to record.

The Gestapo set the scene for the outbreak, however. And since this was the first major excursion of the Gestapo into the international field; since it shows how that organisation, after its modest start, had now become privy to the highest secrets of State; since, finally, although it involved the actual killing of only a dozen individuals, it inaugurated a movement of destruction spectacular even by the standards of Himmler —because of all this it is worth recording in detail.

The Gestapo were called upon, in their capacity of "dustbin of the Reich", to fake the frontier incidents which were to be Hitler's excuse for attacking Poland. The whole operation was known as "Undertaking Himmler". It involved more than one incident, organised between them by Heydrich and Mueller. But the one we know most about was run by Alfred Helmut Naujocks of the S.D., already referred to, who was to fake an attack by Polish troops on Gleiwitz radio station, just inside the German border. It had to be done without Poles. Naujocks said in his sworn affidavit, presented at Nuremberg:

"On or about 10th August 1939, the Chief of the Sipo and S.D., Heydrich, personally ordered me to simulate an attack on the radio station near Gleiwitz, near the Polish border, and to make it appear that the attacking force consisted of Poles. Heydrich said, 'actual proof of these attacks of the Poles is needed for the foreign Press, as well as for German propaganda purposes.' I was directed to go to Gleiwitz with five or six S.D. men and wait there until I received a code word from Heydrich indicating that the attack should take place."

He was to seize the radio station when he got the code word, and hold it long enough to let a Polish-speaking German, detailed for the purpose, make an inflammatory speech into the microphone. The speech, according to Heydrich, was to exhort Poland to a show-down with Germany and urge the Poles to take immediate action. Heydrich also told Naujocks that he expected Germany would attack Poland "in a few days".

So Naujocks went to Gleiwitz and hung about. He was bored and thought nothing would happen, and after a fortnight asked if he could return to Berlin, but Heydrich told him to stay where he was. Then:

"Between the 25th and 31st of August I went to see Heinrich Mueller, head of the Gestapo, who was then near by at Oppeln. In my presence Mueller discussed with a man named Mellhorn plans for another border incident, in which it should be made to appear that Polish soldiers were attacking German troops. . . . Germans in the approximate strength of a company were to be used. Mueller stated that he had twelve or thirteen condemned criminals who were to be dressed in Polish uniforms and left dead on the ground at the scene of the incident to show that they had been killed while attacking. For this purpose they were to be given fatal injections by a doctor employed by Heydrich. They were then also to be given gunshot wounds. After the assault, members of the Press and other persons were to be taken to the spot of the incident. A police report was subsequently to be prepared."

It was Mueller who told Naujocks that he could have one of these "criminals" for his own use to add verisimilitude to his own incident. The "criminals" had a code name, which showed that Mueller had as good a sense of humour as any English police-officer. The code-name was "Canned Goods".

Naujocks continues:

"The incident at Gleiwitz in which I participated was carried out on the evening preceding the attack on Poland. As I recall, war broke out on the 1st September 1939. At noon on the 31st August I received by telephone from Heydrich the code word for the attack which was to take place at eight o'clock that evening. Heydrich said, 'In order to carry out this attack, report to Mueller for "Canned Goods".' I did this and gave Mueller instructions to deliver the man near the radio station. I received this man and had him laid in the entrance to the station. He was alive, but he was completely unconscious. I tried to open his eyes. I could not recognise by his eyes that he was alive, only by his breathing. I did not see the shot wounds, but a lot of blood was smeared across his face. He was in civilian clothes.

"We seized the radio station as ordered, broadcast a speech of three to four minutes over an emergency transmitter, fired some pistol shots, and left." [19]

If it is asked what the Gestapo did with itself in the long, dull intervals between the high-lights of its career, when it was not massacring the S.A. leaders, or breaking the power of the Generals, or touching off the Second World War, the general answer is that it was perfecting its machine and thinking up ideas for the day when it would have more people to kill than could conceivably be spared inside Germany. It had plenty of time to run its machinery in and discover the weak spots. It managed to get in good practice of the most realistic kind when first Austria, then, by stages, Czechoslovakia, were overrun. And inside Germany itself it was able in peace and quiet to develop its technique of persecution and oppression.

There was no organised resistance by the time Himmler had taken over. The last time the braver and soberer German masses made their voices heard was during the March elections in 1933, when, after over a month of S.A. rule, there were still 22 million Germans out of 39 million with the courage to vote against Hitler. With the banning of political parties three months later, and the smashing of the Trade Unions, there was no more sectional opposition. But there was incessant grumbling and a great deal of sporadic underground activity, which, but for the vigilance of Heydrich, would soon have made itself felt. All over Germany groups of anti-Nazi workers were meeting in secret, and it was the job of Heydrich's S.D., with its fabulous network of honorary informers, to smell out this activity. Then, as a rule, it was the job of Himmler's Gestapo to investigate more closely, often by insinuating one of its own agents into a group of dissidents, before taking action. There were many actions of this kind between 1934 and 1939 of which the outside world heard nothing, and the prisons and concentration-camps were filled with the victims.

One that the world did hear about, rather belatedly, was the case of the Stettin group, which involved the arrest of 280 factory workers in 1936, their being held in prison for eleven months "on remand", and being sentenced to terms ranging from one to six years for a variety of offences: the reading of prohibited newspapers (one to two years); the passing on of prohibited newspapers (two to three years); using a private dwelling as a meeting-place (three years); enrolling new members (three to four years); working on an illegal newspaper (four to six years).[20] This was one aspect of life in Germany in the days when people looked over their shoulders before mentioning politics in case there might be someone standing by who could be an agent (unpaid) of the Gestapo or the S.D.

The general idea was to produce an atmosphere of uncertainty and suspicion, a sort of all-enveloping fog, through which naked terror might suddenly loom to destroy the individual. The Nazi authorities made no bones about the fact that the job of the Gestapo was not so much to capture and punish individuals who had acted against the interests of the Fuehrer State as to arrest on suspicion before action could be taken.

"The number of criminal proceedings continually pending in the People's Court for treasonable acts against *Land* or Reich is the result of this work," wrote the *Volkischer Beobachter* early in 1936, in an article glorifying the Gestapo and the S.D. "As, since the National Socialist revolution, all open struggle and all open opposition to the State and to the leadership of the State is forbidden, a secret State Police as a preventive instrument in the struggle against all dangers threatening the State is indissolubly bound up with the National Socialist Fuehrer State. The opponents of National Socialism were not eliminated by the prohibition of their organisations and newspapers, but have withdrawn to other forms of opposition to the State."

The newspaper then went on to explain the rôle of the S.D.

"The preventive measures of the Secret State Police consist first of all in the close surveillance of all enemies of the State in the Reich territory. As the Secret State Police cannot, in addition to its important executive tasks,

H

perform this surveillance of the enemies of the State to the extent necessary, there enters to supplement it, the Security Service of the Reichsfuehrer of the S.S., set up by the Fuehrer's deputy as the political intelligence service of the Movement, putting thereby into the service of the security of the State a large part of the forces of the Movement mobilised by him."

The article then develops the ideal behind "protective custody" as a means of silencing opposition. Protective custody meant concentration-camps. The Gestapo, of course, had the exclusive right to send people to concentration-camps, and there was no appeal outside the Gestapo. The Decree of 10th February 1936, already cited, had put it above the law.

If it is wondered how the S.D. and the Gestapo knew the enemies of the State from its friends, the answer is that there was no difficulty about this. There were the informers. There were also innumerable devices. The S.D., for example, developed an elaborate organisation for the secret marking of ballot papers, which told them who had voted "No", or deliberately spoilt his paper, in the referendum. The result would then be passed on to the Gestapo for action.[21] And so it went on.

The S.S. weekly newspaper, *Das Schwarze Korps*, was developed by Heydrich into an extremely powerful instrument of blackmail and persecution. Unrestrained by any considerations of libel, it hit out right and left with the general aim of humiliating and frightening into inaction conspicuous figures who could not be simply arrested and sequestered by the Gestapo without fuss. *Schwarze Korps* could draw freely for its material from the secret dossiers of the S.D., and it did so, so that as often as not it was able to mix truth with its lies. It acted as a spear-head in Heydrich's attack on Christianity, which was one of the major pre-occupations of the Gestapo in those peaceful days before the war. For the Christian Church was the exception to the rule which permitted no organised bodies outside the Nazi Party. Himmler, though nominally a Catholic, resented its power, and Heydrich seems to have had a pathological hatred of the Churches, which was perhaps his strongest sustained emotion. He sought to ruin them by discrediting them through a long and sustained campaign of slander, backed up by Gestapo action.

The cartoonists of *Schwarze Korps* were let loose on the priests and the nuns, and the paper was full of unfounded charges against individuals—from embezzlement and currency offences to homo-sexuality and rape. At the same time the Gestapo made frequent raids on monasteries and convents and rarely came back with empty hands. To the very end there were numbers of German priests who fought back bravely—to the end, that is to say, of their freedom. Himmler and Heydrich were correct in recognising in the Church a serious and dangerous opponent, and they gave a lot of thought to it as a long-term problem. They were far-sighted, and they were prepared to wait a long time for the final undoing of a worthy opponent. And it was in this mood that Heydrich conceived his plan for disrupting the Church from within.

He proposed to introduce into the Churches selected youths who would be enrolled in the S.S., instructed in their future rôle, and then sent as ordinary seminarists into the theological colleges, passing out after ordination into the priesthood with the aim, in Heydrich's good time, of organising a spectacular revolt from within. This plan came to nothing because Hitler, for once, drew the line at it; he refused to exempt Heydrich's candidates for the priesthood, drawn from the Hitler Youth, from their compulsory military service. This we have on the authority of S.S. Lt.-Colonel Willy Hoettl, one time assistant of Heydrich in Amt VI of the R.S.H.A.[22]

The campaign against Christianity, indeed, never made much progress. The Gestapo had to rely too much on charges which were obviously trumped up, and the German people, having squandered their right to think and act for themselves all along the line, clung stubbornly to the last link with an exterior reality. They refused to believe Heydrich's charges, which by their insolent extravagance developed a resistance not unlike the resistance to his own attitudes developed by Senator McCarthy in America. Also, of course, there were the Jews, who were easier game. But the persecution, and then the attempted extermination, of the Jews is a story in itself.

CHAPTER 11

Streamlined Violence

At the trial of Heinrich Baab, a Frankfurt Gestapo
official of low rank, in 1950, there appeared as the
hundred and fifty-second witness an intelligent and
dapper figure who gave his name as Kurt Lindow, Doctor of
Philosophy. He seemed an excellent type of German, who
had already paid for allowing himself, perhaps weakly, to
support the Nazi régime to the extent of engaging himself
in one of its more disreputable institutions. He had, indeed,
at one time been an S.S. Colonel, in charge of subsection
IVA 1a of the R.S.H.A.—i.e. that section of the Gestapo
concerned with Russian prisoners-of-war. Because of this,
after giving evidence for the prosecution at Nuremberg, he
had been given three and a half years imprisonment at a
Darmstadt trial in 1948, as a member of the second category
of Nazis. Since he had been interned since 1945, he was
deemed to have served his sentence and set free.

The trial of Heinrich Baab was an affair of extreme
squalor. Baab was a minor official of gross aspect and plebian
background whose job had been to get rid of the Frankfurt
Jews. He had beaten and tortured, dragged shrieking children away from their mothers, despatched his quotas of
human cargo in sealed box-cars to the frontier, until finally
he was able to declare that there were no more Jews in Frankfurt. He had done all this without knowing that he was doing

it, and so was able to face the court of his fellow-countrymen with assurance, a clear conscience, and massive self-respect. For example, he was asked by the Prosecution whether it was true that when mothers herded in the market-place had asked him in desperation what was to become of their children, he had answered: "Don't worry about those Jewish bastards. You'll soon be on your way up the chimney and your troubles will be over." He replied: "I was an idealist in my profession. If I used such expressions as 'Jewish bastard' or 'Jewish sow', it simply meant that this official language had become so much a part of my flesh and blood that I saw nothing unusual in it. I never used anything but spiritual weapons in dealing with offenders."

This creature, this Baab, with his spiritual weapons, was in the end found guilty on fifty-five counts of murder, on twenty-one counts of attempted murder, on thirty counts of assault and battery, and a variety of lesser offences. There was nothing remarkable about him, except that his trial was recorded with extreme virtuosity by Miss Kay Boyle.[1] There were thousands like him all over Germany, subordinate Gestapo officials of plebian origin and plebian mentality who were given absolute authority over their fellow citizens.

What seemed remarkable, although it was not, was the sight of Dr. Kurt Lindow in that gallery. It seemed almost indecent to suggest that this excellent and dapper citizen could conceivably have any connection with Herr Baab. He was a cut above that sort of thing—or he would have been but for the fact that the Gestapo made all its members kin.

To quote Miss Boyle:

"Lindow was clearly a man of intelligence and education. Both before and during the war, he travelled widely in a diplomatic capacity, representing Nazi interests at international conferences. His oval face was tanned, his dark hair was perfectly groomed, and his gray felt hat, his black shoes, his well-creased trousers, and his white shirt were impeccable.''

He gave his evidence politely but in the usual evasive manner. The whole thing, one would have said, was a little below him. And, indeed, he implied as much himself. "The implication was that he had operated on a very high level and that he knew scarcely anything of what went on below." He was quite willing, however, to tell the few things he knew. For example, he knew what "protective custody" was. It was a measure to "protect from persecution individuals who had been under suspicion or under arrest"—that was his definition of Belsen, Ravensbrueck, and Buchenwald. But he did not really know about the Jews: certainly he had noticed that there were no more people in the streets wearing the Star of David, and he had supposed that the Jews had all been resettled in Eastern ghettos.

It seemed a shame to worry the cultivated Dr. Lindow with these sordid matters, and he evidently thought so too, but was prepared to do his duty willingly. When he had finished giving his evidence the judge told him that he might go.

"And then three things happened simultaneously. The faces of the spectators turned wearily towards the door, awaiting the entry of the next witness; Lindow rose from his chair, and, immaculate gray felt hat in hand, began his bow to the Court before taking leave; and Kosterlitz [the Prosecutor in the Baab case under trial] jumped to his feet and called out, in a voice that roused the courtroom from its sleep, 'Herr Wachtmeister, place Dr. Lindow under arrest! I accuse him of defying all international and human law by murdering Soviet prisoners-of-war who were under his care.'

"The police officer so addressed made his way to Lindow and requested him to follow him from the room. Lindow completed his bow to the Court with dignity, and, as two men in plain clothes fell into step flanking him, he walked towards the door. Some members of the Press hastened from the courtroom and walked beside him and his escort along the hall and up the stairs. And there, as he climbed, his composure left him. The colour drained from his face, and with each step he took and each breath he drew, he sobbed like an aged man. When a member of the Press speculated on his being extradited to Russia for trial, this one hundred and fifty-second witness covered his face with his hands, leaned against the soiled plaster wall for strength, and groaned."

Why did Dr. Lindow groan and suddenly look like an old man?

He had been nothing but a Gestapo officer doing his duty in charge of sub-section IVA 1a of the R.S.H.A. But this duty, among other things, and at one time and another, made him responsible for issuing the execution warrants for Soviet officers screened by the Gestapo in the prisoner-of-war camps and deemed fit only to be exterminated. . . . To him, also, in his office in the R.S.H.A., had come the periodical reports of the massacres of Jews and Communists in Russia by the *Einsatzgruppen*—who used, literally, to compete with one another for the highest number of killings day by day, in order to please Himmler. All this was now going to come out, and Lindow knew, as he leaned groaning against the wall, that if ever he were extradited to Russia he would be shot or hanged. He need not have worried. He was not even tried. But the officers of the Gestapo, and other German official bodies concerned with killing people on a large scale, almost invariably turned out to be strangely sensitive when it came to being killed themselves—unlike their opposite numbers in the Soviet N.K.V.D., who, though they kill far less frequently, are inclined to take it as all part of the day's work when their own turn comes. It is this mixture of brutality with cowardice and righteous indignation which makes these people more unpleasant to write about than any other body of men in the world: few things are more repellent than the brute who bursts into tears.

But there were so many like him. Dr. Lindow is chosen from among thousands, partly because we have an unusually clear picture of him, partly because he is representative of a large class of S.D. and Gestapo officials, the gentleman thugs, whose background was sympathetic and cultivated, who in their first youth had become economists like Otto Ohlendorf, lawyers like Ernst Kaltenbrunner and Karl Adolf Eichmann, but who worked side by side with the Baabs and the dregs of the underworld, and exhibited always a perfect readiness to commit with their own hands the most frightful atrocities. It is this aspect of the Gestapo and the S.D. that is most puzzling of all. The commandants of concentration-camps were usually chosen for their brutality, their staffs always.[2] Thus it was axiomatic that the Kramers, the Kochs, the Mewes would find their way to Belsen, Buchenwald, and Ravensbrueck. Their particular activities, whether it was horse-whipping naked women prisoners, watching police dogs tear human beings to pieces, selecting prisoners with elaborate tattoo patterns to be killed and skinned because they wanted the patterns for their lamp-shades, killing prisoners with perfect teeth so that their unblemished skulls might be used for paper-weights—their particular activities are of no more interest than the particular activities of any psychopath anywhere: every country has women like Dorothea Binz, the head wardress of Ravensbrueck, who specialised in setting dogs on people.[3] In countries other than Germany, however, they are kept under restraint, and their fantasies, if translated into action, are deemed to have only a clinical interest. From what we have already seen of Himmler and Heydrich and senior S.S. villains it is understandable that they should have staffed their concentration camps, which were officially regarded as extermination camps ("extermination through work" as opposed to "extermination by gassing", as in the annihilation camps),[4] with the scum of Germany.

What is not understandable is how the bright young men of Heydrich, many of them recruited in the first instance as intelligence officers from the intellectual professions, should have been prepared to work with this scum. How did Dr. Lindow do it? What made him think, as he evidently did think, that, after doing so, he was a worthy citizen of a worthy race? And the even larger question: why, when it was all over, did so many Germans clamour, not by any means always in vain, for the release of some of the worst offenders? What made them do it?

There is a general belief that what was in fact the normal routine of the Gestapo was confined to exceptional cases. Thus, in various memoirs of survivors, and in statements by unimpeachable eye-witnesses, we are told of all but inconceivable behaviour on the part of this or that Gestapo or S.D. official, and, for want of easily accessible evidence to the contrary, are inclined to assume that these were excesses on the part of individual sadists. For example, we know that Mrs. Peter Churchill, "Odette", had her toe nails pulled out, one by one, to make her speak.[5] We know that Wing-Commander Yeo Thomas had to submit to the deliberate crushing of his testicles, as well as to being all but battered to death and half drowned in baths of ice-cold water, with the girl typists and secretaries of the Gestapo prison looking on.[6] But these were not exceptions, though every member of the S.S. and a large number of other Germans would like us to believe they were. They were part of a recognised drill, a drill which every Gestapo official must have known by heart.

It is a thousand pities that this statement cannot be conclusively proved by documentary evidence. The truth of it can only be deduced; and the materials upon which the deduction is based, the circumstantial evidence, is of the cumulative kind, which would require a large volume for its proper presentation. The material is there. It exists, scattered through the mass of documents presented at innumerable trials, from the trials of the major war criminals at Nuremberg downwards. In case after case, in affidavit after affidavit, from witness after witness, we get the same story.

In every Gestapo prison in every city of occupied Europe —which extended from Brest on the Atlantic to the Volga, from the North Cape to the Mediterranean—we find the same tortures being repeated. If it was only a matter of beating up and kicking—beating to the point when the kidneys are all but torn away from their protective fat; kicking until the face is a shapeless gap-toothed jelly—it could still be put down to individual sadism. When all is said, this technique was developed in the earliest days of Nazidom by the young hopefuls of the Party, and evidently expressed some deep-seated need in certain sections of the German young. If the Gestapo had confined itself to crudities of that kind it could still be put down to individual acts of violence: one would simply record that Nazi Germany contained a remarkable number of sadists in positions of responsibility. But it was not as simple as that.

While it might reasonably be argued that beating and kicking a helpless prisoner to death is the sort of thing that might well occur simultaneously to thousands of German Government officials scattered throughout the length and breadth of Europe, it is too much to ask us to believe that these same officials would simultaneously hit on some of the more elaborate methods of torture which we find practised with monotonous regularity in towns as far apart as Lyons and Stavanger, Amsterdam and Odessa.[7] Thus we find the testicle-crushing technique in almost universal use, and involving the employment of a little machine which even a nation of inventors could hardly be expected to duplicate very often. Again, there was a fairly elaborate exploitation of the principles of electricity, which involved passing an electric current through electrodes fastened to the penis and the rectum. If this was thought of simultaneously in a dozen Gestapo offices throughout the length and breadth of Europe, then the Germans are more ingenious and inventive than we have hitherto believed. But, of course, they were not.

The torturing, as such, took place invariably at the interrogations of prisoners and suspects in the Gestapo offices. After interrogation the victims were, equally invariably, either sent to a concentration-camp or killed. The ostensible idea of the interrogations was to make the victim talk—not, as with the Soviet interrogations, to make him confess to his own crimes, but to make him say what he knew about others. More often than not—in fact, nearly always—the interrogations were conducted with extreme clumsiness and lack of finesse. It is not to be expected that the Heinrich Baabs would be very good at cross-examination; but it is remarkable that the "gentlemen" Gestapo officials were not much better. Even when they had a fairly clear idea of what they wanted to know, as when they had captured a known Resistance leader, they seem to have brought a minimum of subtlety to the interrogation, relying on the effect of one or two questions repeated to infinity against an accompaniment of battery and torture. On the rare occasions when battery was not used for reasons of high policy they still shouted and threatened to produce an atmosphere of terror, and seemed at a loss for the next move if the victim did not succumb.

Captain Best, one of the chief figures in the Venlo incident, who from the moment of his kidnapping with Major Stevens from Dutch territory by a dubious individual who turned out to be none other than Schellenberg himself, was treated very much as a privileged prisoner, was one of the few who were interviewed by Gestapo Mueller in person and lived to tell the tale. Mueller, too, shouted, like any Baab (Captain Best, who knew the Germans as well as he knew himself, gives the German word for this shouting technique: *anschnauzen* or snorting) and Captain Best's description of Mueller in action is the only one extant:

"Mueller was a dapper, exceptionally good-looking little man, dressed in imitation of Adolf Hitler, in a grey uniform jacket, black riding breeches and top boots. He started his 'snort' immediately he entered and, as he walked towards me, increased the pitch and the volume of his voice with great virtuosity. He managed to get right up close to me before his vocal chords tore into shreds. 'You are in the hands of the Gestapo. Don't imagine that we shall show you the slightest consideration. The Fuehrer has already shown the world that he is invincible and soon he will come and liberate the people of England from the Jews and Plutocrats such as you. It is war and Germany is fighting for her existence. You are in the greatest danger and if you want to live another day must be very careful'. Then he sat down on a chair in front of me and drew it up as close as possible, apparently with the intention of performing some mesmerising trick. He had rather funny eyes which he could flicker from side to side with the greatest rapidity and I suppose that this was supposed to strike terror into the heart of the beholder."

Best also met Heydrich, who shouted too:

"Almost as soon as I entered a young and very resplendent officer whom I recognised as Heydrich (his enlarged photograph hung in every room) jumped up and started shouting at me in a most threatening manner:

" 'So far you have been treated as an officer and a gentleman, but don't think that this will go on if you don't behave better than you have done. You have two hours left in which to confess everything. If you don't, I shall hand you over to the Gestapo, who are used to dealing with such gangsters and criminals—you won't enjoy their methods a bit.'

"I turned to Mueller, who was standing at my side and asked: 'Who is this excitable young officer?' At this Heydrich really went off the deep end and literally foamed at the mouth; at all events, he sprayed me liberally with his saliva. Mueller quickly pushed me out of the room and into my own. Later on he came in again and told me I must not take the matter too seriously: 'Soup is never eaten as hot as it is cooked.' " [8]

It is only fair to Mueller to record these impressions of Best, as well as his conclusion: "In my experience I always found Mueller a very decent little man." But this verdict of a British officer who exhibited a remarkable talent for getting on with the Germans is the last good we shall hear. As a rule the interrogation of the Gestapo was a prelude to the concentration-camp and slow, laborious death, or to immediate killing.

The battery usually began with arrest and continued intermittently until the more formal tortures were started. The general object of knocking prisoners about even before interrogation started seems to have been to break their nerve by shock tactics and so daze and humiliate them that they would never have a chance to recover: they were knocked off balance, in a word, and only the bravest or most insensitive ever found their feet again: it is hard to be calm and collected and lucid when your face is streaming with blood, your eyes are closed up, your lips swollen and your front teeth adrift; and when with every word you try to say you are knocked down again and kicked as you try to get up it is very hard indeed to retain a balanced view. So this was the almost universal preliminary treatment, though whether a drill laid down in Gestapo regulations or a custom spontaneously generated among the like-minded it is impossible to say. The torture began with the interrogation proper.

The basic torture was flogging, and this was the only form of torture ever admitted to by the Germans. Numerous members of the Gestapo, among them the all-too-familiar Heinrich Baab, told of the existence of an R.S.H.A. order authorising in exceptional cases a treatment called "Rigorous Examination", which was to consist of not more than twenty-five blows with a stick. Corporal punishment of up to twenty-five blows "on the loins and buttocks" was also authorised in the official "Concentration Camp Statutes", and records were to be kept. The Yugoslavs, however, found a blank form used by the Gestapo and the S.D. in Slovenia which was intended to be filled in to cover "especially rigorous interrogations". This contained a space to be filled in by the authorising official: "The especially rigorous interrogation should consist of . . . Minutes of the interrogation should be kept. A doctor may (or may not) be asked to be present." [9]

We do not know exactly what the central office of the R.S.H.A. had in mind in the way of "especially rigorous" torture. But it clearly had something. And we do know what in fact happened.

One of the most comprehensive first-hand descriptions of the Gestapo's methods of torture was given by the Frenchman, M. Labussière, a schoolmaster, and a captain of the reserve. His testimony was presented by the French Prosecuting Counsel at Nuremberg, and it concluded with a general statement of the methods used:

"(1) The lash.

"(2) The bath: the victim was plunged head-first into a tub full of cold water until he was asphyxiated. Then they applied artificial respiration. If he would not talk they repeated the process several times consecutively. With his clothes soaking, he spent the night in a cold cell.

"(3) Electric current: The terminals were placed on the hands, then on the feet, in the ears, and then one in the anus and another on the end of the penis.

"(4) Crushing the testicles in a press specially made for the purpose. Twisting the testicles was frequent.

"(5) Hanging: the patient's hands were handcuffed together behind his back. A hook was slipped through his handcuffs and the victim was lifted by a pulley. At first they jerked him up and down. Later, they left him suspended for varying, fairly long periods. The arms were often dislocated. In the camp I saw Lieutenant Lefevre, who, having been suspended like this for more than four hours, had lost the use of both arms.

"(6) Burning with a soldering-lamp or with matches.

"On 2nd July my comrade Lalbue, a teacher from Cher, came to the camp. He had been subjected to most of these tortures at Bourges. One arm had been put out of joint and he was unable to move the fingers of his right hand as a result of the hanging. He had been subjected to flogging and electricity. Sharp-pointed matches had been driven under the nails of his hands and feet. His wrists and ankles had been wrapped with rolls of wadding and the matches had been set on fire. While they were burning, a German had plunged a pointed knife into the soles of his feet several times and another lashed him with a whip. Phosphorous burns had eaten away several fingers as far as the second joint. Abscesses which had developed had burst, and this saved him from blood poisoning." [10]

It is unnecessary to pile horror upon horror. The instances of this kind of torture are innumerable. They may be found in quantity in the documents submitted by the French and Soviet prosecutors at the Nuremberg trials, and in the reports of hundreds of lesser trials. There were variations in detail from place to place. In Russia, for example, the Gestapo were especially fond of immersing their victims in barrels of icy water until they drowned or were frozen to death. Different Gestapo chiefs would have their own variants of the technique of hanging up by the wrists. What might be called the Kiev-Pechorsky variation was to twist the suspended victim round and round until the rope was tightly knotted, and then let go, so that the rope unwound in a dizzy rush. Most inquisitors preferred the rubber truncheon to the whip, and used it to break bones. Some preferred the more sophisticated machines to the boot and the bludgeon. There were iron bands which were placed round the head and contracted; and there was a special apparatus for mangling the wrists and ankles, consisting of rings set with alternate balls and spikes which could be tightened by a screw. There is no known case of the use of the rack; but in every other way the torture chambers of the Gestapo were better equipped than the dungeons of the Mediæval tyrants and inquisitors. A favourite activity was to torture a woman within hearing of a male prisoner under interrogation and to pretend that the woman was his wife. [11]

I

It is desirable to repeat that these were not the innocent excesses of the psychopaths who ran the concentration-camps, each of whom was a law unto himself. They were the prescribed routine of innumerable Gestapo prisons in all the occupied countries of Europe. The Chief of German Security in Denmark, S.S. Colonel Bovensiepen, admitted that the order to use torture "in certain cases" certainly originated from the higher authorities in Berlin. And the general instruction was that torture could be used to compel persons to give information that might serve to disclose subversive organisations directed against the German Reich, but not for the purpose of making the delinquent admit to his own deeds. Even Bovensiepen, however, insisted that the means prescribed were limited to a certain number of strokes with the rod. He did not explain the extraordinary unanimity of the more elaborate methods of torture employed thoughout the whole of occupied Europe.

As far as it is possible to establish, however, the general instruction that torture was only to be used to make the victim speak about his colleagues seems to have been fairly rigidly adhered to—though not in Germany itself. The chief victims of torture were members of Resistance groups and partisans, and they were questioned about their companions and tortured if they refused to speak. There are few known instances of a man or a woman being tortured to make him confess to his own misdeeds. On the other hand, most of the examples known to us involved questioning at random.

Anybody picked up by the Gestapo would immediately be assumed to have some knowledge of subversive activity, even if nothing positive was known against him. And he would be questioned, stupidly and aimlessly, often about subjects of which he was totally ignorant. In other words, he was tortured on the off chance that he might know something. And, once started, and firmly based on their instructions from Berlin, the local inquisitors, the Gestapo Commissars and Secretaries, as they were called officially, would find it very hard to stop. If a man had nothing to say under mild torture, the pressure would be increased, and frequently he was dying, or dead, before his interrogators could bring themselves to conclude that he had nothing to tell them at all. The torture might go on for days—and end only with the victim being shot as good for nothing.

So the Gestapo had it both ways. Sometimes, if for a technical reason—as when an arrest had been made on neutral territory—the Gestapo wished to avoid shooting a man outright they would smash his body and leave him lying in the middle of a public road to give the impression that he had been run over. When a man was not killed, torture was simply a prelude to the concentration-camp, where as often as not he died.[12]

CHAPTER 12

The Gestapo Goes to War

THE organisation of tyranny in the occupied countries was elaborately conceived and prepared in fine detail before the outbreak of war. The German police, like every other Nazi institution, was put on a war footing in 1938, and the attachment to each *Wehrkreis* inside Germany of a Higher S.S. and Police Leader was a part of this development; for the *Wehrkreis*, or military district, was to serve as the base for extra territorial expansion.

Technically the Higher S.S. and Police Leaders were Himmler's own representatives with the military commanders and the civil governors of their areas; but they varied very much from place to place in quality, character, and attack. As a rule they held the rank of S.S. General or Major-General. They were the hard core of the Nazi "old fighters", and they ranged in background from the promoted sergeant-major to the dug-out retired officer who had decided to go in with the Nazis for reasons of idealism or expediency. On the whole they were tough and apt to be stupid and extremely heavy in the hand. They represented the victory of the S.S. over the civil administration, and they owed their positions to the desire of the Nazi leadership to reward the faithful for their services in the wilderness. By the professional policemen like Mueller, Nebe, Best, and others, who ran the Security Police—the Gestapo and the Kripo—

they must have been regarded as a lot of blundering old men who had no comprehension of police matters—with certain notable exceptions, such as S.S. Lt.-General Franz Jaeckeln and others of his colleagues in Poland and Russia, who by their energy and ruthlessness set an example even to the Security Police and the S.D.[1]

To the bright young men of the S.D. they must have appeared as denizens of another world. But character and opportunity counted for a good deal and although there were undoubtedly a number of Higher S.S. and Police Leaders who were not active or interfering and hardly knew what was going on, and although there were others who were simply corrupt in a rather elephantine manner and chiefly concerned with loot, the most energetic among them were fully worthy of the organisation they were privileged to adorn and succeeded in having a finger in very many pies.

Their opportunities varied with the nature of the problems presented by their particular commands. In Denmark, for example, S.S. Colonel Bovensiepen was not much more than a repressive chief constable, often at loggerheads with the emissaries of the Gestapo and S.D. In Russia, on the other hand, where the front was far from static and there was much partisan warfare, men like von dem Bach-Zelewski, Jaeckeln, Herff, and Pruetzmann took their jobs very seriously, acted in liaison between Himmler and the Army, and entered with determination and enthusiasm into their task of terrorising the back areas, and massacring Jews, Commissars, and other undesirables.

In Poland outside the annexed areas, in the General Government that is, where an extremely energetic civilian Governor was charged with the task of starving the masses into submission, killing off their natural leaders, and liquidating the Jews, there was clearly immense scope for displays of energy. Thus S.S. Major-General Katzmann, based on

Lvov, actively supervised the killing of 400,000 Jews in
East Galicia, while S.S. Lt.-General Odilo Globocnik, the
butcher of Lublin—"dear old Globus", Himmler's crony—
officially organised and carried out "Action Reinhard", the
story of which will later be told.

In Yugoslavia, where there was constant chaos and much
internecine strife of great bitterness, a man like S.S. Lt.-
General Thomas of Belgrade (and Globocnik again, when,
after cleaning up Poland, he was sent to Trieste) was a professional and well-equipped hangman functioning among a
mob of amateurs.

In France, on the other hand, S.S. Lt.-General Kurt
Oberg found himself inevitably involved in politics of an
extremely delicate kind and, in the intervals of shooting
hostages, deporting Jews, and torturing the Resistance
leaders (all of which activities General Oberg is said to have
disapproved of), found himself involved in complicated
tangles with Vichy, the German military Governor, the German Ambassador, and the fire-eaters on the staff of the Sipo.

The exact position of the Higher S.S. and Police Leader
has never been defined. This vagueness contributed to the
fog with which the whole German police organisation was
enveloped. At the same time it is reasonable to assume that
Himmler created the office as part of a deliberate plan to
prevent Heydrich from completely dominating the whole
apparatus of repression—a plan which also denied the
Gestapo control of the concentration-camps, although Heydrich had taken active steps to obtain such control,[2] by putting them under a parallel organisation, under S.S. Lt.-
General Pohl, known as the Economic Administration
Main Office (W.V.H.A.). The Higher S.S. and Police
Leaders were superior in rank to the Gestapo representatives
in their area, the chief of which were attached to their own
staffs. For at the headquarters of each Higher S.S. and

Police Leader there were to be found the direct representatives of Heydrich (Security Police, or Sipo) and Daluege (Uniformed Police, or Orpo). Inside Germany, these were known as Inspectors of Sipo and Orpo (IdS and IdO); outside they were known as Plenipotentiaries, or *Befehlshaber* (BdS and BdO). The BdS was, in effect, the head of a miniature Prinz Albrecht Strasse, which was set up on the Berlin model in certain cities of occupied Europe. Thus, in Paris, there was the Higher S.S. and Police Leader for Northern France and Belgium, Oberg; and on his staff, as BdS, S.S. Colonel Helmuth Knochen, directly responsible for all the Gestapo and S.D. of his huge area. Scattered through the country the BdS had his deputies, known as Commanders of Sipo, or KdS, each with his own headquarters. Below the KdS were the *Leitstellen* and *Stellen*—main and subsidiary command posts of the Sipo.

The headquarters of a BdS consisted, typically, of five sections:

1. Administration.
2. Surveillance of local Police.
3. Economic affairs.
4. Gestapo.
5. Kripo.

"Administration" and "Economic affairs" sounds harmless enough; but the one would on occasion find itself concerned with the supply and maintenance of gassing vans; [3] the other with the supply of forced labour and the disposal of gold from the teeth of executed prisoners. [4]

The drive, it will be seen, save in certain cases, or when the Higher S.S. and Police Leader was an exceptionally strong and vigorous character, came from the BdS, who was usually a Colonel or a Lt.-Colonel, but might also be a Brigadier. Some of the better known BdS were S.S.

Lt.-Colonel Hahn of Warsaw; S.S. Lt.-Colonel Fuchs of
Belgrade; S.S. Colonel Knochen of Paris; S.S. Major Lange
of Latvia; S.S. Brigadier Naumann of Amsterdam; S.S. Lt.-
Colonel Witiska of Slovakia. These men, and dozens of
others, were Heydrichs in little. They were energetic, hard-
working, and professional. They worked sometimes hand
in glove, sometimes at loggerheads, with their Higher S.S.
and Police Leader. As a rule the latter was content to suggest, rather than to order, except in particular cases (above
all in Poland). The normal chain of command was Himmler
–Heydrich (later Kaltenbrunner)–Mueller–BdS. Often, but
not always, orders were repeated for information to the
Higher S.S. and Police Leader. The BdS was always supposed to consult with his nominal superior; but frequently
he only did this if the intervention of a high-ranking S.S.
officer was needed with, for example, the Higher Command
of the Army.

If this is confusing, the Germans have only themselves to
blame. The whole set-up was confusing in the extreme, and
was almost certainly intended to be so. Confusion, furthermore, extended all down the line.

For the BdS, or Chief of Security Police, himself had a
dual command, and over certain aspects of it he sometimes
had no more jurisdiction than the Higher S.S. and Police
Leader might have over him. In the first place, he had his
own headquarters staff, with its separate sections for Gestapo,
Kripo, etc.; in the second place, he had his "out stations"—
the KdS and the inferior Sipo posts covering his whole area.
But the members of his headquarters staff were by no means
exclusively staff officers, giving orders to, as it were, the
policemen in the field.

In a manner highly characteristic of German organisation
they mingled paper work with active investigation and interrogation. Just as Hitler astounded all his subordinates by

interesting himself in affairs of minute detail, remote from him in place and time, even to the fate of individuals, so, all the way down the line in the apparatus of tyranny, high-ranking officials were apt to turn from their in-trays, which contained documents for their signature which would move armies or condemn whole populations to death, and interest themselves directly in some particular segment of the vast mosaic of destruction. Gestapo Mueller himself would frequently take time off to conduct a special interrogation,[5] and the same was true of the area and local Sipo chiefs throughout occupied Europe.

Thus each BdS ran his own office, supervised the subordinate offices throughout his area, and took an active hand in interrogations. His own office, his miniature R.S.H.A., was run by section-heads, all of whom were liable at any moment to turn themselves into practical policemen in the Nazi manner. So that there was no clear-cut chain of command, and in the great Gestapo network which covered Europe it could never be predicted with any certainty which individual official would be found dealing directly and in detail with which particular offence.

The matter was complicated still further by the special position occupied by certain sub-sections of the office of the BdS. While the Gestapo was Section IVA, within the Gestapo was the usual range of sub-sections; and one of these, IVA 4b, which was the Jewish office, led a private existence of its own almost completely outside the normal hierarchy. The BdS had virtually no control or, indeed, sometimes no detailed knowledge of the activities of the junior official who, on paper, was a wholly subordinate officer, usually with the rank of S.S. Captain. In all matters relating to the deportation and resettlement of Jews the departmental head of IVA 4b received his instructions directly from Berlin, from IVA 4b of the R.S.H.A., which was housed in a separate building and run by S.S. Colonel Eichmann. The chain of command here was rigid: Hitler–Himmler–Heydrich (later Kaltenbrunner)–Mueller–Eichmann–then straight out, by-passing the Higher S.S. and Police Leader, by-passing the BdS or other regional Sipo Chief, to Eichmann's local representative, who had virtually unlimited power.

Section IVA 4b in Paris, for instance, was run by an obscure and pedantic little creature called S.S. Captain Dannecker, who was absolutely responsible for deporting the French Jews to the concentration-camps and the gas-chambers. He had a harder task than most of his colleagues in other lands because the French were difficult, and to the end he could never understand why even the most pro-German Vichy officials insisted on regarding French Jews as Frenchmen first and Jews afterwards. But, although he was a comparative failure, Dannecker had all the power of the Nazi State behind him. He did not have to work through his nominal chief, Colonel Knochen, though he frequently did so. When he required the assistance of the Army he simply went to General von Stuelpnagel and told him what he wanted.[6] So that we have the remarkable spectacle of this fussy and terrible captain of the S.S. at one moment laying down the law to the elderly Field-Marshal, the next strolling down to the Velodrôme d'Hiver to supervise personally the round-up of unfortunates.

It was the same with Eichmann's emissaries everywhere. S.S. Captain Fuenten in Amsterdam, S.S. Captain Guenther in Prague, S.S. Captain Hunsche in Hungary, S.S. Major Krumey in Vienna, S.S. Captain Zoepff at The Hague, S.S. Captain Wisliceny in Slovakia, Greece, and Hungary again —all these, and many more besides, conducted their appalling operations nominally as sub-section heads of the Gestapo, actually as the executive officers of a large-scale special operation directed from Berlin. Nor were Eichmann, him-

Picture Post

Himmler and Heydrich in Vienna, 1938

Central Press

In the Gestapo Headquarters, Berlin. (*Left to right*) Nebe, Huber, Himmler, Heydrich and Mueller

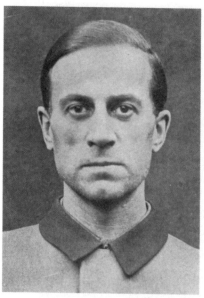

Rudolf Brandt, Himmler's adjutant

Ernst Roehm, S.A. Chief of St

Otto Ohlendorf, *Einsatzgruppe D*

Kurt Daluege, head of Orpo

Ernst Kaltenbrunner, Heydrich's successor, on trial

Joseph Kramer (No. 1), Fritz Klein (No. 2) and Peter Weingartner
(No. 3), on trial before a British Court at Luneberg

Keystone Press

Rudolf Hoess, Commandant,
Auschwitz

Keystone

Martin Sandberger, Security Po
Chief, Estonia and North Ital

Keystone Press

Eduard Strauch, Security Police
Chief, White Russia

Keystone

Herbert Kappler, Security Po
Chief, Rome

self, and his deputy, S.S. Major Brunner, content to sit at their desk. All these staff officers of the Gestapo seem to have been ridden by the demon of conscientiousness; and we find Eichmann careering about all over Europe to make sure that his instructions are understood, that no Jew shall escape the net, to keep his subordinates up to the mark, and to browbeat and argue with reluctant governments.[7] This unremarkable Lieutenant-Colonel was ready to bully, to flatter, or to lie. The Hungarians, for example, he bullied into sending 250,000 Jews to his gas-chambers. But to the Slovaks, who showed concern, he lied, explaining that the Jews were simply to be resettled in special ghettos and would live in comfort and ease in their new homes.[8]

In saying that the Eichmann organisation was largely independent of the nominal chiefs of the Gestapo, the last thing intended is to suggest that these did not know what was going on. Most of them were almost certainly unaware of the scale and range of the extermination camps; but all knew they existed; and all, at one time and another, were called to co-operate with the IVA 4b specialists in arranging for the round-up and deportation of the Jews.

We find Dannecker, for example, elaborately reporting the progress of his actions to his Sipo chief, Knochen;[9] and when Dannecker had been taken away from Paris for corrupt practices (nothing to do with Jews: this inconspicuous little man took it into his head to start a chain of night-clubs on the side)[10] we find his successor, S.S. Captain Roethke, conferring with Knochen about one of the most unspeakable actions of the war.

This was the case of the 4,051 Jewish children who were seized with their parents during the great Paris round-up of July 1942. Nearly 7,000 children and adults were herded into the bleak spaces of the Velodrôme d'Hiver. For five days they had no food, and the only water available came from a single street hydrant. There were ten latrines for the seven thousand. There were many pregnant women, a number of whom gave birth. Many individuals went noisily off their heads, and thirty people died. There they waited while Knochen and Roethke discussed in a leisurely manner with the Vichy officials what was to be done with the children. On the fifth day the mothers were taken away, leaving their children behind, to start the long journey to the gas-chambers on the other side of Europe. D'Arquier, the Vichy official, held that the children should be spared and sent to French orphanages. But Knochen and Roethke took their duties more seriously. Plainly the children should be exterminated too. The only snag was transport. But Eichmann, active as ever, had been busying himself in Berlin, and wired to say that he had been able to arrange for enough transport to take the 4,051 children to Auschwitz too. So, torn from their parents, inadequately looked after by other internees—mainly the very old and the sick—the children were taken to the transit camp at Drancy, the French rail-head for Auschwitz, and, three or four hundred at a time, put on the trains, and trundled off to death.[11]

This action took place not in Eastern Europe, but in Paris, and not under pressure of any Allied advance, but in the summer of 1942, at leisure, and with Germany seemingly victorious. Many people have said that Knochen was a good fellow. No doubt by some standards he was, but the standards are not high enough.

It is clearly impossible, however hard one may try, to limit the responsibility for the worst activities of the Sipo to certain kinds of grades of officials. The responsibility is indivisible. Routine administrative officials were required to co-operate with Captain Nowak, Eichmann's transport officer, in arranging for the transports which took the Jews to Poland. An apparently innocuous official in the administrative branch, Rauff, was responsible for supplying and servicing the gassing-vans. And so on. Nor, it may be believed, were the Germans concerned with who was and who was not responsible. They were simply obeying orders, and indeed they were; and there was nothing else to be done.

S.S. Major-General Ohlendorf of the S.D. put the matter very clearly at Nuremberg. Confessing to the murder of 90,000 Jews when, at the age of thirty-five, he commanded *Einsatzgruppe* D on the Russian Southern Front, he was asked by the Defence Counsel for the Gestapo whether he had ever felt scruples at the tasks he was required to carry out. He answered, "Yes, of course." "And how was it," Defence continued, "that they were carried out regardless of these scruples?" Ohlendorf replied: "Because to me it is inconceivable that a subordinate leader should not carry out orders given by the leaders of the State." And when he was questioned further about the legality of such orders, Ohlendorf replied, perplexed: "I do not understand your question; since the order was issued by the superior authorities, the question of legality could not arise in the minds of these individuals, for they had sworn obedience to the people who had issued the orders." [12]

They were thus absolved in advance from blame for anything they might he called upon to do.

And yet it was not so simple as that. Nobody has any right to demand that another man shall risk his life by standing on his own ideas of right and wrong (it should be remembered, nevertheless, that many of the Gestapo's victims did precisely this, and died as a result). It may reasonably be asked, however, that if a man decides to massacre innocent women and children as ordered from above he should be clear in his own mind whether he is acting in accordance with a philosophy of obedience, for which he would be ready to

go to the stake, or to save his own skin. And it is a fair criticism of the Ohlendorfs that they never seem to have begun to
consider this question: obedience and self-preservation were
hopelessly mixed up in their minds. It may also be reasonably objected that even if an individual decides that he must
carry out the commandments of authority and massacre
women and children, it is not incumbent on him to act with
excessive zeal: the Gestapo almost invariably acted with excessive zeal and obeyed their instructions not only in the
letter but also in the maniacal spirit of their originator.

They had plenty of opportunities for saving the lives of
their victims and some shreds of their own self-respect by
going easy. Instead, they competed with one another in
frightfulness. Ohlendorf, when asked by the Prosecution
why his *Einsatzgruppe* had accounted for fewer Jews than
the other three, replied that he thought that his fellow-
leaders exaggerated the number of their killings.[13] Eichmann, we know, exaggerated considerably the number of
Jews he had sent to the gas-chambers. And, indeed, throughout the early stages of the Russian campaign, there was a
strongly competitive mood: just as the various armies were
inclined to exaggerate the amount of ground and the number
of prisoners they had taken, so the back-area scavengers
exaggerated the number of civilians they had massacred.
There was, as far as is known, no order from Hitler about
this: the Gestapo and the S.D. thought it up for themselves.

Again, while the Gestapo was above the law, so that there
could be no appeal from its decisions, this very fact enabled
it, had it so desired, to go easy. But it did not; nor did it
welcome determined opposition to its actions by a few brave
men, an opposition which, had its reluctance to carry out
Hitler's orders been genuine, it could have magnified on
occasion into an insurmountable barrier (for there were limits

to what the Gestapo could get away with when confronted with opposition) and an excuse for doing nothing.

For example, at a conference between the Army and the Gestapo held shortly after the opening of the Russian campaign the question of screening Soviet prisoners-of-war with a view to executing the undesirables was under discussion; there was a good deal of military objection to this programme, but Mueller was adamant. He insisted that the order must be carried out to the letter, and the only concession he made to the soldiers was that the executions, to be carried out by recruits under command of the Gestapo, should not take place in the presence of troops, in deference to their sensibilities. Mueller, had he wished to soften this order, or even to postpone it, could at least have used the opposition of the soldiers as a means of gaining time; instead, he rode them down, not, it seems, because Hitler so instructed him, but because he would have the support of Hitler if it came to a show-down.[14]

Again, the head of the Gestapo for Silesia, Dr. Mildner, came into head-on collision with the Chief Public Prosecutor at Katowice, early in the Russian campaign, when the Germans were still apparently winning. The Public Prosecutor went so far as to protest to the Reichs Minister of Justice at the summary hanging of alleged Resistance leaders "without notification to the competent court". Mildner fought back. He not only said that the past executions were imperative but went on to declare that "with the authority of the RfSS [Himmler]" (not, it will be noted, "under instructions from Himmler") "these executions by public hanging at the place of the crime" would have to be continued in the future until all the opposition had been destroyed.[15]

As a final example, it has been pleaded that the head of the Paris Gestapo, S.S. Colonel Knochen, strongly disapproved of some of the more spectacularly cruel methods he was called upon to practise.[16]   But in Paris it was easier than anywhere else in Europe for a reluctant Gestapo official to practise obstruction and ca'canny.   It was known and understood in Berlin that the French required very delicate handling, involving concessions on the German side unthinkable in Eastern Europe.   It was known in particular that they showed an incomprehensible reluctance to connive at the deportation and murder of their Jews, and sometimes showed both boldness and ingenuity in frustrating Eichmann's plans.[17]

Against this background S.S. Colonel Knochen, had he really been as kind and gentle as his apologists declare, could have exercised a very strong influence for good.   But he did not.   For example, in the matter of the Jewish children, torn from their parents by Roethke, with the help of Colonel Knochen's men, and condemned to those four ghastly days and nights in the cycle-racing stadium, we find the Vichy Commissioner for Jewish Affairs, d'Arquier de Pellepoix, pleading for the children to be sent to orphanages and Knochen supporting Roethke in his insistence on deporting them to Auschwitz.[18]   D'Arquier himself was a poor and craven creature, who must have been driven to desperation to argue with Knochen: he had recently been given the job because his predecessor, Xavier Vallat, had proved too obstructive and had defeated Dannecker's efforts at every turn, and because the Vichy Chief of Police, Bossuet, refused to have anything to do with deporting French Jews.[19]   Nothing could have been easier than for Knochen to report that it was against German interests to murder the children of French Jews.   Nothing could have been more true.   But Knochen, the mild and reluctant Gestapo chief, insisted on their being murdered according to the book.

CHAPTER 13

Terror and Extermination

THE activities of the Gestapo and the S.D. in occupied Europe fell broadly into two categories: terror and extermination. For the fulfilment of both they depended materially on the assistance of other organisations; on the Concentration Camp Administration (W.V.H.A.) run for Himmler by S.S. Lt.-General Pohl and staffed by the S.S.; on the Waffen S.S.; on Daluege's Orpo; and, to a lesser but highly variable extent, on the Wehrmacht.

Heydrich would have preferred it otherwise. If he had been able to get his own way he would have centralised the whole apparatus of tyranny and massacre on his R.S.H.A. For example, quite early in his career he made a determined effort to get personal control of the concentration-camps,[1] and it was even written into the Law of 10th February 1936, formally setting up the Gestapo, that it should be responsible for their administration. But this was never put into effect.[2] Himmler reserved the concentration-camps for himself, and there is no doubt at all that in withholding them from the Gestapo he was deliberately working to prevent Heydrich from becoming too powerful. He was content to use Heydrich's gifts, his drive, his ruthlessness, his boldness, and his imagination; but he had no intention whatever of allowing Heydrich—or, for that matter, anybody else—to become his deputy and rival.

Heydrich, for his part, habitually looked a very long way ahead, sometimes too far. We have had an example of this in his scheme for corrupting the German Church from within. Another plan of his, which was too ambitious to begin with, was the establishment of special Action Groups or *Einsatzgruppen* for policing the back areas of occupied territory—a plan which was drawn up in the summer of 1938, before Munich, to be put into effect when the Nazis invaded Czechoslovakia.[3]

It was no fault of Heydrich's that the Gestapo had to rely on outside help; but the fact that it did so rely complicates our picture greatly and makes it extremely hard to apportion the responsibility for this or that particular atrocity. It is impossible, furthermore, to consider the performance of the Gestapo in isolation; we are compelled to introduce into our narrative figures who did not belong to the Gestapo and who were not under the orders of the Gestapo, but whose activity, nevertheless, was an integral part of the Gestapo terror.

Thus, while the Gestapo was in no way responsible for the administration of the concentration-camps, it possessed under Article 2 of the decree of the Reich President of 28th February 1933, the exclusive right to send individuals into "protective custody" (e.g. a concentration-camp).[4] It was, moreover, charged with the task of grading the various concentration-camps into three categories, from the mildest— e.g. Dachau—to the bloodiest—e.g. Mauthausen, which was an extermination camp. It had, moreover, permanent representatives in the camps, acting as "political advisers". In a word, when the Gestapo committed a prisoner to "protective custody" it knew precisely what would happen to that prisoner, and desired it.

In the case of the camps designed primarily for immediate extermination—e.g. Auschwitz II (Auschwitz I was a labour camp), Belzek, Treblinka—the connection was even closer.

For these camps were designed as part of the apparatus of the "final solution", the extermination of the Jews in Europe. Heydrich was formally in charge of the "final solution,"[5] and Eichmann and his subordinates who rounded up the Jews and arranged for their delivery to the gas-chambers, which were built and maintained on their behalf, belonged, as we have seen, to Section 4b of the Gestapo. Thus the actual killings, carried out in the main by S.S. subordinates of the Concentration Camp Administration, were in fact ordered by the Gestapo.

The institution from which both the Gestapo and the S.D. tried hardest to disassociate themselves was the notorious *Einsatzgruppe* or Action Group. At Nuremberg the Defence went to extreme lengths of hair splitting to prove that the Action Groups were nothing to do with either the Gestapo or the S.D. as such, but were special-purpose units under Army command which happened to be led in most cases by men who happened to have belonged to the S.D. and also to include in all cases members of the Gestapo. When we come to consider the record of the Action Groups the reason for the anxiety of the Defence will be plain. But at the bottom of all the camouflage, there is documentary proof that the Action Group was in fact the brain-child of Heydrich and the special treasure of the S.D. And it is interesting that although the Action Groups did not get fully into their stride until the early days of the invasion of Russia, when they developed into an instrument of mass murder, the simple and logical end of the whole process of police rule, the idea had been thought up and committed to paper as early as 1938.

In an unsigned draft instruction to the S.D. we read:

"The S.D. should prepare to start its activity in case of complications between the German Reich and Czechoslovakia. . . .

"The S.D. follows, wherever possible, directly behind the advancing troops and fulfils duties similar to those in the Reich, which are the security of political life and at the same time the security as far as possible of all enterprises necessary to the national economy and so, also, of the war economy. . . ." [6]

The document goes on to outline the manner in which the occupied territory is to be divided up—

"so that members of the S.D. intended for employment in Czechoslovakia can be immediately assigned to their tasks."

It then introduces for the first time on record the concept of the Action Group, in general terms:

"The groups detailed for *Einsatz* from the Reich will be collected in a sub-sector corresponding to their intended sphere of activity."

Later on in the document the Gestapo appears:

"Measures in Germany are carried out under the guidance of the Gestapo and with the assistance of the S.D. Measures in the occupied regions are carried out under the leadership of the senior officer of the S.D. Gestapo officials are assigned to certain operations staffs. It is important that, as far as possible, similar preparations, training, and the use of materials should be conducted in the Gestapo as in the S.D."

Finally, the Waffen S.S.:

"It is necessary that an S.S. unit or *Totenkopf* unit be ready for disposal for special purposes."

Here we have the ingredients, or most of them, of the unimaginable teams of murderers who, three years later, led by some of the most able members of Heydrich's entourage, were to ravage the towns and villages of Russia in Europe, from Pskov to the Caucasus: the S.D., the Gestapo, the Waffen S.S.—to which were to be added elements of the Kripo and the Orpo.[7] In 1938, however, the Action Group appeared to be still-born. It was found no longer necessary to invade Czechoslovakia, and we have a countermanding instruction, issued to Dr. Best of the Gestapo, who was later to win fame as the most philosophically minded apologist for the Police State:

> "The suggestion to introduce the Gestapo and the S.D., of which twelve detachments were provided for the Czechoslovakian frontier, will be subject to some modification as a result of the new situation arising from the fact that the Czechs may secede the Sudeten territory. Since some of the detachments will not be employed in the districts which will be ceded, we offer the following changes." [8]

If these documents appear somewhat vague, the reason is clearly that they form a scarcely measurable fraction of the mass of relevant papers which must have been in circulation and have since been destroyed. For suddenly, in a document dated 13th September 1938, we find the Action Group no longer a concept but a concrete establishment:

> "According to the new regulations . . . I enclose herewith a photostatic copy of the *Einsatzkommandos* organisational chart. The chart in its present form has been prepared by Department C." [9]

This communication is addressed to S.S. Lt.-Colonel Jost, as Chief of the S.D. (domestic), and it is signed by S.S. Major Schellenberg, who was to be Chief of the S.D. (foreign). It means that the conception of the Action Group, as a special formation for policing occupied territory, was born in 1938 and in the office of Heydrich's S.D.—which was later, at Nuremberg and elsewhere, to disclaim any organisational connection whatsoever, in a series of gigantic and impudent lies, with the Action Groups, or, indeed, with the Gestapo itself. It was, its members universally declared, purely an intelligence centre with no operational functions of any kind. Schellenberg himself, who rose to be an S.S. Major-General and Himmler's familiar, denied all knowledge of the *Einsatzgruppen* and all connection with the activities of the Gestapo.[10] The fact that certain important members of the S.D. commanded certain *Einsatzgruppen* and supervised their massacres was declared to mean that they had been seconded from the S.D. and ceased to belong to it.[11]

These documents, therefore, are of unusual importance. They penetrate the miasma of confusion and lies which surrounded the whole organisation of the R.S.H.A. And they render in themselves all discussion as to the driving power behind the *Einsatzgruppen*, and the responsibility for the massacres, irrelevant and frivolous. The first document speaks of the Action Group; the second of "detachments" (twelve in number for Czechoslovakia); the third of Action Commandos. In the Russian campaign there came into being four Action Groups—A, B, C, D, each of which consisted of four Action Commandos, or detachments, operating far from Group headquarters. Each of the Groups was theoretically attached to, and under command of, the relevant Army Group; and in fact their commanders had to negotiate with the Army Group Commanders, who knew very well the sort of work they were engaged in, and thus connived at it.[12] But their operational instructions came from Heydrich's office in Berlin, and their operational reports were not submitted to the Army, but only to the R.S.H.A., to which the Gestapo, Kripo, and S.D. all belonged.[13]

Thus the Gestapo and the S.D. were collectively involved in, either directly or indirectly, the totality of the crimes against civilians and prisoners-of-war committed by the Nazis, with the exception of atrocities committed by individuals and units of the Wehrmacht, principally in Poland, Russia, and Yugoslavia, and by the Waffen S.S. on a far larger and more brutal scale (e.g. the massacre of American prisoners in the Ardennes and the reprisal raids in France, such as the massacre at Oradour-sur-Glâne).[14]

It should not be thought that the Gestapo, or even Himmler, originated the régime of mass murder and terror. They were merely the willing executants of a policy conceived by Hitler and accepted with enthusiasm by his court. Once the Generals had bound themselves in their own eyes by taking their oath of allegiance to Hitler, there was no power in the Reich capable of resisting the Fuehrer's most fantastic demands; but still Hitler was conscious of an imponderable weight of public opinion which caused him to go slow: for example, although at any time between 1933 and 1939 he would have been only too pleased to massacre all the Jews in Germany, he knew that this would arouse popular feeling against him to an extent which even he would find it impossible to ignore.[15] It was not until the outbreak of war, with the imposition of war-time controls, and with the public mind diverted, that he felt safe enough to start his deadly action. Similarly, it was not until the invasion of Belgium and Holland in 1940, and the consequent pre-occupation of the Western Allies, that he felt able to ignore foreign opinion completely and launch an out-and-out offensive against the defeated Poles.[16] Only then was he in a position to realise to the full his dreams of destruction; and only then did the Gestapo and the S.D. begin to apply themselves to the technique of mass murder.

We have traced the conception of the Action Group back

to 1938. But it would be wrong to assume that at that time Heydrich was thinking in terms of simple massacre. As far as the Jews were concerned, the idea of the "final solution", if it existed at all, existed only in Hitler's mind. Heydrich was deeply committed to the policy of blackmail and forced emigration, whereby immense sums passed from Jewry into the hands of the Gestapo.[17] As far as the Czechs were concerned, Heydrich had no intention of using his Action Groups to murder them wholesale, but, rather, to establish the sort of terror existing already in Germany, involving the individual killing of leaders and intellectuals likely to prove troublesome.[18]

It was not until Hitler revealed his intention of breaking Poland as a nation by killing off all natural leaders and intelligentsia [19] that the Gestapo and the S.D. began to organise themselves for what was later to become known as genocide (until then it had been called mass-murder). And it was not until after the opening of the Russian campaign that the special machinery required for killing in terms of millions rather than tens of thousands had to be set up. Heydrich and the Gestapo and S.D. invariably strove, if not always with complete success, to prove themselves equal to any demand; but the demand came first, from Hitler and the men of his immediate entourage.

Those who were loudest and most thorough-going in reinforcing Hitler's fantasies should be remembered. They included Goering, whose nature we have examined (but Goering was sometimes the cause of confusion, cross-purposes, and administrative muddle because he demanded for his armament factories more and more workers, even including Jews, who were scheduled for the gas-chambers); [20] Ribbentrop, who developed into an enthusiast for destruction (he liked to think up complicated ideas, which had no appeal to the Gestapo, such as the fomenting of an uprising in the Ukraine which would end in total devastation and the extinction of both the Jews and the Poles); [21] Bormann, Hitler's familiar; and Field-Marshal Keitel, Chief of the O.K.W., Hitler's spokesman to the Army, who somehow managed to add to the most atrocious Fuehrer order the taint of his own peculiar, craven heartlessness. [22]

All the major policy decisions, many of them articulated in minute detail, came from Hitler himself and this inner circle. But they depended for their execution on others. Hitler, once he had given an order, was liable to forget about it and assume that it was being carried out to the letter. Shortly before his death, for instance, he was deeply shocked to find that Heydrich and Kaltenbrunner had failed in their task and that there were still a number of Jews alive in Europe: he had said they were to be exterminated "like bacilli"; [23] therefore they had been exterminated. Similarly, in spite of Keitel's insane obedience in translating his Fuehrer's wildest fantasies into standing orders to the Higher Command, there were Generals who, although they lacked the courage or the will to co-operate with their colleagues in open resistance to their master, nevertheless at times proved capable of ignoring orders and refraining from handing them on. [24]

Himmler, however, *treuer Heinrich*, was the ever-obedient subordinate. And although he was never a member of the Fuehrer's court, and was thus required only to execute the policy laid down by others, he occupied a place of his own. So deep were his own convictions (themselves based on Hitler's pre-war teachings) that his own orders, and his own adaptations of Hitler's orders, added up to a power in their own right—certainly in all those cases where they had to do with the exaltation of Germanism and with the advancement of what Himmler took to be science. When it was a matter of destruction for destruction's sake, or for the imposition of terror, Himmler was content to obey, sometimes apparently reluctantly. When it was a matter of destruction to prepare the world for the new German, or S.S., culture, there entered into his commands and exhortations a note of exaltation, mingled with rueful pride at the arduousness of the task. He sympathised with his men, who had to steel themselves for the sternest action in hard circumstances.

Thus we find him addressing the officers of three S.S. Divisions at Kharkov in 1943. He is talking about the projected extermination of the Jews in occupied Russia, and the "decimation" of the Soviet population:

"Very often the members of the Waffen S.S. think about the deportation of this people here. These thoughts come to me today when watching the very difficult work out there performed by the Security Police, supported by your men, who help them a great deal. Exactly the same thing happened in Poland, in weather 40 degrees below zero, where we had to haul away thousands, tens of thousands, hundreds of thousands; where we had to have the toughness—you should hear this but also forget it again immediately—to shoot thousands of leading Poles."[25]

And again, to his S.S. Generals, at Posen, in the same year:

"I want to talk to you, quite frankly, on a very grave matter. . . . I mean the clearing out of the Jews, the extermination of the Jewish race. It is one of those things it is easy to talk about—'The Jewish race is being exterminated,' says every Party member, 'that is quite clear, it is our programme, elimination of the Jews, and we are doing it, exterminating them.' And then they come, 80 million worthy Germans, and each has his decent Jew. Of course the others are vermin, but this one is an 'A1' Jew."[26]

And then he goes on to a passage already quoted:

> "Not one of all those who talk this way has witnessed it, not one of them has been through it. Most of you must know what it means when 100 corpses are lying side by side, or 500, or 1,000. To have stuck it out and at the same time—apart from exceptions caused by human weakness—to have remained decent fellows, that is what has made us hard." [27]

Himmler was not talking to members of the Security Police and S.D. on that occasion. He was talking to his own officers, the leaders of a force which was later, collectively, to deny all knowledge of such things.

It was when Himmler was carried away by visions that he appeared to be possessed by the mood of stoic exaltation reflected in those passages. But he could switch with the utmost ease to a crisper and more business-like approach.

> "Anti-Semitism is exactly the same as delousing. Getting rid of lice is not a question of ideology, it is a matter of cleanliness. In just this same way anti-Semitism for us has not been a question of ideology but a matter of cleanliness." [28]

He could, indeed, be very matter of fact. The Nazis always found it hard to make up their minds whether to kill prisoners (other than British and American) out of hand, or let them die of starvation and exhaustion, or preserve them as workers for Germany. At first, in the East, they invariably took the line of least resistance and killed; but later they were to regret this. And so we find Himmler again, at Posen, in October 1943, mourning the masses of Russian prisoners captured in the early days of the war and now gone beyond recall:

"At that time we did not value the mass of humanity as we value it today, as raw material, as labour. What, after all, thinking in terms of generations, is not to be regretted, but is now deplorable by reason of the loss of labour, is that the prisoners died in tens and hundreds of thousands of exhaustion and hunger." [29]

But, though matter of fact, he was perpetually dominated by his vision of Germanism, and the S.S. as the elite of Germanism:

"It must be a matter of course that the most copious breeding should be from this racial super-stratum of the Germanic people. In twenty to thirty years we must really be able to present the whole of Europe with its leading class. If the S.S., together with the farmers . . . then run the colony in the East on a grand scale without any restraint, without any question about any kind of tradition, but with nerve and revolutionary impetus, we shall in twenty years push the national boundary five hundred kilometres eastwards." [30]

This was the vision behind his statement that it would be highly desirable if some 30 million Russians should die,[31] by whatever means; it was the logical expression of Hitler's craving for *Lebensraum*.

And yet this complicated figure, full of dreams, full of regrets at the necessity for hardness, could also lapse into destructive hysteria. When things were going badly for Germany, in September 1943, Himmler sent a secret instruction to the S.S. and the S.D. to ensure its collaboration with the soldiers in the total destruction and depopulation of parts of the Ukraine which would have to be evacuated:

"The aim to be achieved is that when areas in the Ukraine are evacuated, not a human being, not a single head of cattle, not a hundredweight of cereals, and not a railway line remains behind; that not a house remains standing, not a mine exists which is not ruined for years to come, that there is no well left unpoisoned. The enemy must really find a land completely burnt and destroyed." [32]

This was the general background against which the Security Police and the S.D. set about their tasks in the East. They were supported by men like Keitel, who declared for the most ruthless measures and explained to the Army that human life in the Eastern territories counted for nothing. [33] They were supported by men like Ribbentrop, who spoke of the whole countryside going up in flames. [34] They were supported by men like Frank, Governor of Poland, who recorded with satisfaction in 1943 that there had been three and a half million Jews in Poland when he had taken over, and now there were not more than 100,000, all at forced labour. [35] They were supported all down the line by Nazi officialdom, and often by the soldiers too. They existed and had their being in a climate of terror and murder which enabled them to carry out their work unreflectingly, as though it were the most natural thing in the world. They were exalted by Himmler and driven by Heydrich and Mueller and the strange intellectuals and semi-intellectuals of Heydrich's S.D. In the East, as already observed, their main task was extermination; in the West, the spreading of terror.

Who were they to resist? In the early days of the Polish war, before Heydrich had achieved his monopoly of murder, and when the troops of the Wehrmacht and the S.S. were indulging in indiscriminate slaughter instead of leaving it to the Security Police and the S.D. following close behind, there was an incident in which the Wehrmacht itself, in the person of the Quartermaster-General's Office, gave its blessing to the sort of procedure for which the Army was later to criticise the Gestapo and S.D. A Field Court Martial of the Kempf Armoured Division had innocently sentenced an S.S artilleryman to three years imprisonment and a sergeant-major of the Military Police to nine years penal servitude for killing fifty Jews.

"After about fifty Jews, who had been used during the day to repair a bridge, had finished their work in the evening, these two men drove them all into a synagogue and shot them without any reason. The sentence is submitted to the Commander of the 3rd Army for confirmation."

The matter went up to Berlin. The nine-years sentence was changed to three, and in fact both sentences were rendered void by an amnesty. But what indicates the atmosphere is the paragraph on extenuating circumstances giving reasons for the revision of the sentence:

"S.S. Sturmmann Ernst is granted extenuating circumstances because he was asked to participate in the shooting by a corporal handing him a rifle. He was in a state of exasperation owing to numerous atrocities committed by Poles against persons of German race. As an S.S. man, particularly sensitive to the sight of Jews and to the hostile attitude of Jewry to the Germans, he therefore acted quite thoughtlessly, in youthful rashness." [36]

This was signed by *Oberkriegsgerichtrath* (Military Judge of the 3rd rank) Lipski. And, of course, the whole matter was soon put on a regular footing by Keitel, who forbade commanders to punish their men for killing Russians and Jews.

CHAPTER 14

The Final Solution

Wᴇ have seen that the first tasks of the *Einsatzgruppen* was the murder of Jews. As originally conceived by Heydrich, in 1938, they were not equipped or trained for mass-murder, but simply for the spreading of terror and the liquidation of recalcitrant individuals. They were used for this, too, and, in Russia, a great deal of stress was laid on the shooting of Commissars—or, more accurately, active Communist officials; but in fact this was almost a side-line. We have the detailed figures of the murders carried out by *Einsatzgruppe* A, working in the Baltic Provinces and North-west Russia, for the first four months of the war with the Soviet Union (June to October 1941). And this record, signed by the Group Commander, S.S. Major-General Stahlecker, claims 135,567 murdered Jews, 4,000 Communists, and 748 lunatics. Before going into the question of how the Jews were murdered we must go back a little.

It was desirable in earlier chapters to dwell on the general history of Nazidom and to recapitulate familiar facts in order to show the parallel development of the Gestapo and S.D. But it is not in the least necessary to work through the processes whereby Jewry under German rule was outlawed, because this had nothing to do with the Gestapo, which enters the picture effectively only when things had reached such a stage that direct physical action against the Jews as a body was called for. This moment was reached after the passing of that long series of decrees, called collectively the Nuremberg laws, at about the time of Munich in 1938. But there was a conflict about what to do.

Heydrich, in his single-minded manner, was for deportation—and he began in October by dumping some thousands of Polish Jews, whom Poland refused to take, in the fields near the Polish border. Schacht, however, was for controlled emigration: he wanted to make the most of Jewish capital and assets, whereas Heydrich was interested only in what ransom money he could get. For a few weeks in the winter of 1938 the Schacht plan was tried. But in January 1939 Heydrich won. Goering, who had favoured Schacht, was compelled by Hitler to hand over full powers in the Jewish question to the Gestapo. Through Frick, still Reichs Minister of the Interior and thus theoretically Himmler's superior, he instructed Heydrich to set up a Central Emigration Office for Jews "to solve the Jewish question by emigration and evacuation in a way that is most favourable under the conditions prevailing". Heydrich was happy with this. He had not at all liked the decorum of the Schacht plan and desired only to force the issue.

His own views on the Jewish question had been made plain on the night of 9th November, when, in order to exploit the wrath of the Germans against the pointless assassination of Ernst von Rath in Paris by the son of one of Heydrich's deportees, the notorious pogrom was organised. It was a police action disguised as a popular riot. Heydrich provided himself with an alibi and expressed surprise and ignorance when a nearby synagogue went up in flames while he was dining; but he had already personally warned the Gestapo of what was to happen and instructed the police throughout the Reich on what they were to do: damage to

German property had to be avoided; shops and flats might be burnt but not looted; synagogues were not to be burnt if there was danger to adjoining property. And Mueller carried these instructions a stage farther by instructing the Gestapo throughout Germany that he wanted 20,000 to 30,000 arrests of Jews, preferably well-to-do ones. In fact, according to Heydrich's report to Goering on 11th November, 20,000 Jews were arrested, 191 synagogues and 171 apartment houses burnt down, and 815 shops smashed and looted —a figure altered next day to 7,500. Thirty-six Jews had been killed.

Heydrich had already had some experience of deporting Jews from Austria after the *Anschluss*; but his first properly organised action was against the Jews of Czechoslovakia, after Hitler's bloodless invasion in March 1939. It is in Vienna that we first meet S.S. Captain Eichmann, as he then was; but it was in Prague that, at the head of a branch establishment of the Central Emigration Office, he created the prototype of what was to become R.S.H.A. IVA 4b, working in close collaboration with the Jewish Community Council, which was made to detail the Jews who were to be deported just as, ever afterwards, local Jewish Councils all over Europe were to be made to register and deliver their fellow Jews marked first for deportation, then for execution—and, in the end, to follow them to the death-pits or the gaschamber. But it was not until the invasion of Poland that IVA 4b, in its own building at 46 Kurfuerstenstrasse, got really under way, and the "final solution" was first mentioned.

Three weeks after the invasion had begun Heydrich held a secret conference. The minutes have not been preserved. But in a covering letter to the Chiefs of the *Einsatzgruppen* (the embryo *Einsatzgruppen*, not the final model that appeared in Russia), Heydrich wrote as follows:

L

"With reference to the conference which took place to-day in Berlin I should like to point out once more that the total measures planned (i.e. the final solution) are to be kept strictly secret. A distinction is to be made between: (1) the final solution (which will take some time), and (2) stages in the carrying out of that solution (which can be achieved within a short space of time). The measures planned require the most thorough preparation from both the technical and the economic point of view. It goes without saying that the tasks in this connection cannot be laid down in detail."

He then went on to say that the first necessity for the attainment of the final solution was the concentration of Jews living in rural areas in large towns.

"As few 'concentration points' as possible are to be established, in order to facilitate later measures. Care must be taken that only such towns be chosen as concentration-camps as are either railway junctions or at least lie on a railway. . . ."

In the light of later knowledge it is possible to read too much into those words. Nobody can say for certain what Heydrich had in mind. But it is highly unlikely that he was then concerned with gathering Jews at strategic points to facilitate their mass execution. It is far more likely that he was concerned with establishing large concentrations in ghettos so that the Jews might be more easily supervised and moved when required from one place to another. Be that as it may, the first concern of Eichmann's office for some time to come was not murder but the deportation of Reich Jews into Poland, the deportation of Polish Jews inside the annexed territories into the General Government, and a wholesale reshuffle of Jews inside the General Government—a process which brought Heydrich into sharp conflict with no less a person than the Governor, Hans Frank, who was interested only in exploiting the resources of the General Government in the interests of the German economy by starving the masses, killing the natural leaders, and collecting slave labour. Frank, not unnaturally, objected to having hordes of the poorest Jews in Europe dumped by Eichmann on his territory. But he had to put up with it. And it was not until March 1941, when Hitler was giving preliminary orders for the invasion of Russia, that the formal decision was taken to embark upon a policy of extermination.

This decision was not taken lightly. As we have seen, Hitler could be impressed by the weight of outside opinion. Once he was at grips with Russia he could afford to throw off all pretences, for what went on in Russia, he was sure, the outside world would never hear. But there was still America to be considered. Mr. Reitlinger has suggested that had there been no Pearl Harbour Hitler would have cared too much for American opinion to launch his policy of total extermination outside Russia. And he has pointed out that it was not until nine days after Pearl Harbour that Hans Frank made his celebrated remark to his Cabinet about what to do with the Jews in Poland: "Do you think they will be settled in villages in the Ostland? . . . Liquidate them yourselves." And it was not until six weeks later that Heydrich gave to a larger audience at a conference at Gross-Wannsee an outline of what it was proposed to do.

CHAPTER 15

Massacre in the East

OTTO OHLENDORF, who at thirty-three became an S.S. Major-General, and at forty was condemned to death at Nuremberg, was to many the image of what a good German should be. This is not the view of a prejudiced non-German: it was the view of those women spectators at his trial who sent flowers to his cell, so moved were they by his appearance and bearing.[1] They did this in the knowledge that two years earlier, also at Nuremberg, where he was a witness for the prosecution of the S.D., he had confessed to the murder of over 90,000 men, women, and children.[2]

We have mentioned Ohlendorf's killings before; but it should not be thought that he was a unique figure. He was simply for a period the commander of Action Group D, one of Heydrich's four Action Groups operating in Russia, which, in the words of the Nuremberg prosecutor, "totalling not more than 3,000 men, killed at least 1,000,000 human beings in approximately two years' time".[3] To understand the operations of the Gestapo and the S.D. it is necessary to explore the activities of their Action Groups, and Ohlendorf was the only commander of one of these organisations who was brought to trial at Nuremberg. Group A, which operated in the Baltic Provinces and the Leningrad Front, was commanded by Franz Stahlecker, who had been head of Section VIA of the R.S.H.A. (S.D. foreign intelligence) before Schellenberg, and who was killed by Esthonian partisans. Group B, which operated in White Russia and behind the Moscow front, was commanded by Artur Nebe, the friend of Gisevius, the intriguer against Diels in the early days of the Prinz Albrecht Strasse, the idealist, who vanished, supposedly shot by Kaltenbrunner's men after the attempt on Hitler on 20th July 1944. Group C, which operated in the Ukraine, was commanded by Otto Rasch, formerly Inspector of Security Police (IdS) for Königsberg, who, suffering from Parkinson's disease, was declared unfit to plead at Nuremberg.

Among the subordinates of these men and their successors a number were brought to trial at Nuremberg; but Ohlendorf is our only specimen of a Group Commander. Like the others, he went straight from an office desk in Berlin to take command of an almost unbelievable collection of scallywags, ranging from failed intellectuals to simple brutes, who roamed the torn and ravaged Russian landscape looking for people to kill—Jews, gypsies, Communists (they had the list of the S.D. to work on).[4] Exactly what went on in their minds we can never know. Why did Stahlecker, the head of the whole foreign-intelligence section of the R.S.H.A., which was soon, under Schellenberg, to swallow the whole of military intelligence too—why did this inoffensive intellectual put on jack-boots and proceed to the Baltic lands to take charge of the massacre of civilians, putting his name to the most appalling reports of organised slaughter it is possible to conceive?[5] The answer appears to be that he wished to ingratiate himself with Heydrich, with whom he was in disfavour.[6] It was also an order. Why did Nebe, the veteran C.I.D. man, who is supposed to have been plotting actively against Hitler, leave his familiar Berlin office and proceed to the Moscow front in charge of a mere 900 men? Perhaps because, feeling vulnerable, he wished to prove his zeal?

Certainly because the leader of Action Group B was designated the future Police Chief of Moscow.[7] Again, it was an order. Why did Ohlendorf, the young lawyer and economist, who had risen high in the S.D. and come to command, at thirty-three, Section III of the R.S.H.A., which had a monopoly of internal intelligence, follow suit and break off his brilliant career (he resumed it later as an official in the Ministry of Economics)? He gave no reason—other than that it was inconceivable that any subordinate should disobey an order.[8]

We always come back to obedience: *Befehl ist Befehl.* And it counted for a very great deal. How much, will have to be considered later. But not for everything. Because the pattern of total obedience is spoilt by the example of Otto Rasch of Action Group C, the man who could not plead at Nuremberg. In an affidavit he declared that it was not until the end of August 1941, two months after starting operations, that he fully understood what he was required by Hitler to do. And then he jibbed.[9] After some false starts he did at last succeed in getting free of the whole apparatus of the Security Police and in the end, in spite of tempting offers, settled down as Mayor of Wittenburg and a company director.[10] He proved—and he was not alone in this—that it was possible not to obey Heydrich—and to survive. The general idea of the Nuremberg defence was that if one disobeyed one was shot.[11] Ohlendorf obeyed. Stahlecker in one of his massacre reports added the following remark: "It should be mentioned that the leaders of the Waffen S.S. and of the uniformed police, who were now on the reserve, have declared their wish to stay with the Security Police and the S.D."[12]

The testimony of Ohlendorf was valuable because it went a long way to establish the relationship of the Action Group with the Reichswehr. It established that the Army knew what the Action Groups were doing and provided facilities for them—rations, transport, etc. The instructions were that all Jews as well as the Soviet Political Commissars were to be liquidated. "Since this liquidation took place in the operational area of the Army Group ... they had to be ordered to provide support. Moreover, without such instructions to the Army, the activities of the Action Groups would not have been possible".[13] As far as Ohlendorf's Group was concerned, the Army was in two minds. It was attached to the 11th Army, operating in the extreme South, and on one occasion it received instructions from Army H.Q. that "liquidations were to take place only at a distance of not less than 200 kilometres from the H.Q. of the commanding general" (125 miles sounds a long way, but it is not far in Russia).[14] On another occasion, however, at Simferopol, "the army command requested the *Einsatzkommandos* in its area to hasten the liquidations, because famine was threatening and there was a great housing shortage".[15]

It was also valuable because it confirmed in minute detail and in straightforward and soldierly language the reports of survivors, or less disciplined witnesses, of the manner in which the killings were carried out.

> "Do you know," the Prosecution asked, "how many persons were liquidated by *Einsatzgruppe* D under your direction?"
>
> "In the year between June 1941 and June 1942 the *Einsatzkommandos* reported 90,000 people liquidated."
>
> "Did that include men, women and children?"
>
> "Yes."

And later, again as question and answer:

> "Did you personally supervise mass executions of these individuals?"

"I was present at two mass executions for purposes of inspection."

"Will you explain to the tribunal in detail how an individual mass execution was carried out?"

"A local *Einsatzkommando* attempted to collect all the Jews in its area by registering them. This registration was performed by the Jews themselves."

"On what pretext, if any, were they to be rounded up?"

"On the pretext that they were to be resettled."

"Will you continue?"

"After the registration the Jews were collected at one place; and from there they were later transported to the place of execution, which was, as a rule, an anti-tank ditch or a natural excavation. The executions were carried out in a military manner, by firing squads under command."

"In what way were they transported to the place of execution?"

"They were transported to the place of execution in trucks, always only as many as could be executed immediately. In this way it was attempted to keep the span of time from the moment in which the victims knew what was going to happen to them until the time of their actual execution as short as possible."

"Was that your idea?"

"Yes."

"And after they were shot what was done with the bodies?"

"The bodies were buried in the anti-tank ditch or excavation."

"What determination, if any, was made as to whether the persons were actually dead?"

"The unit leaders or the firing-squad commanders had orders to see to this and, if need be, finish them off themselves." [16]

This young economist from Hohen-Egelson was proud of the orderly, ship-shape, and humane manner in which his Commandos carried out their duties. He objected, for example, to what went on in the areas of some of the other Action Groups:

"Some of the unit leaders did not carry out the liquidation in the military manner, but killed the victims singly by shooting them in the back of the neck."

"And you objected to that procedure?"

"I was against that procedure, yes."

"For what reason?"

"Because both for the victims and for those who carried out the executions it was, psychologically, an immense burden to bear." [17]

The burden to bear, the psychological strain, was one of Ohlendorf's obsessions. This was testified to also by his adjutant, Heinz Schubert. Schubert, twenty-five when he went to Russia straight from the Hitler *Jugend*, was a descendant of the great composer's family, and a serious and earnest young man. Speaking particularly of the massacres at Simferopol, he said: "I knew that it was of the greatest importance to Ohlendorf to have the persons who were to be shot killed in the most humane and military manner possible, because otherwise the spiritual strain (*seelische Belastung*) would have been too great for the execution squad." [18] And, of course, the strain was there. Himmler, we have seen, was affected by it when he watched the sample massacres at Minsk, and cried aloud when two Jewish women were not killed outright. He told Nebe, who carried out the execution, that more humane means had better be devised, and the answer was the gas-van,[19] manufactured by the firm of Saurer in Berlin, and supplied and maintained by Rauff, the transport officer of the R.S.H.A.[20]

But the gas-vans, when they arrived in 1942, were to cause Ohlendorf further spiritual burdens. He preferred shooting, and so did his men. The general concept was a plain van so constructed that when the motor was started up "gases were conducted into the van causing death in ten to fifteen minutes. . . . The vans were loaded with the victims" (Ohlendorf is speaking) "and driven to the place of burial, which was usually the same as that used for the mass executions. The time needed for transportation was sufficient to ensure the death of the victims." [21] The vans varied in size and could take fifteen to twenty-five people. The reason why Ohlendorf and his subordinates did not like the gas-vans was not because they were inhumane—he was sure the victims did not know what was happening to them—but because "the unloading of the corpses was an unnecessary mental strain".[22] It was less tiresome to stand people on the edge of a ditch and shoot them down and shovel earth over their bodies. But when Ohlendorf was asked what he meant by "an unnecessary mental strain" he replied in terms which indicated quite clearly that the victims were aware of what was happening to them: "As far as I can remember the conditions at that time—the picture presented by the corpses and probably because certain functions of the body had taken place leaving the corpses lying in filth." [23]

The victims, of course, were aware. We know that from other witnesses. The "death vans" became notorious, and more often than not they failed to work either quickly or humanely. When they were used in a purposeful manner in the neighbourhood of Taganrog in the Ukraine, before Auschwitz got into its stride, there were many complaints from their designer, Lieutenant Becker, of their improper use.[24] Although they added their own flourish to the fantastic world inhabited not only by the Gestapo and the S.D. but by every German soldier and official behind the lines in Russia and

Poland, their contribution to the number killed in Russia was really very small.[25]

Ohlendorf was questioned at length about his preference for what he called shooting in the military manner, and in the course of his explanation he threw some official light on the habitual form:

"On the one hand, the aim was that the individual leaders and men should be able to carry out the executions in a military manner acting on orders and should not have to make a decision of their own; it was, to all intents and purposes, an order which they were to carry out. On the other hand, it was known to me that through the emotional excitement of the executions ill-treatment could not be avoided, since the victims discovered too soon that they were to be executed and could not therefore endure prolonged nervous strain. And it seemed intolerable to me that individual leaders and men should in consequence be forced to kill a large number of people on their own decision." [26]

When questioned as to what he meant by "ill-treatment", Ohlendorf replied:

"If, for instance, the manner in which the executions were carried out caused excitement and disobedience among the victims, so that the Commandos were forced to restore order by means of violence . . . if, as I have already said, in order to carry out the liquidation in an orderly fashion it was necessary, for example, to resort to beating." [27]

It is as well that we have this testimony of the gifted and highly educated commander of *Einsatzgruppe* D. It prepares us for the impression created by these orderly and humane operations on others.

On 30th October 1941 the Commissioner of the territory of Slutzk in White Russia wrote to the Commissioner General of Minsk, criticising the actions of the *Einsatzkommandos* belonging to *Einsatzgruppe* B (commanded by our old friend Artur Nebe). Here are excerpts from his letter:

"On 27th October, in the morning at about eight o'clock, a first lieutenant of the Police Battalion Number 11, from Kovno (i.e. an officer of Daluege's Orpo), Lithuania, appeared and introduced himself as the adjutant of the battalion commander of the Security Police. The first lieutenant explained that the police battalion had received the assignment to effect the liquidation of all Jews here in the town of Slutzk within two days. The battalion commander with his battalion in the strength of four companies, two of which were made up of Lithuanian partisans, was on the march here, and action would have to begin immediately. I replied to the first lieutenant that I had to discuss the action in any case first with the commander. About half an hour later the police battalion arrived in Slutzk. Immediately after the arrival a conference with the battalion commander took place according to my request. I first explained to the commander that it would not very well be possible to effect the action without previous preparation, because everybody had been sent to work and it would lead to terrible confusion. At least it would have been his duty to inform me a day ahead of time. Then I requested him to postpone the action one day. However, he refused this with the remark that he had to carry out this action everywhere in all towns and that only two days were allotted for Slutzk. Within two days the town of Slutzk had by all means to be cleared of Jews."

That was how it began. It was not one of Ohlendorf's

tidy actions. It took place in the streets of Slutzk. After further preamble the letter continues:

"For the rest, as regards the execution of the action, I must point out, to my deepest regret, that the latter almost bordered on sadism. The town itself during the action offered a picture of horror. With indescribable brutality on the part both of the German police officers and particularly of the Lithuanian partisans, the Jewish people, and also with them White Ruthenians, were taken out of their dwellings and herded together. Everywhere in the town shots were to be heard, and in different streets the corpses of Jews who had been shot accumulated. The White Ruthenians were in the greatest anguish to free themselves from the encirclement. In addition to the fact that the Jewish people, among whom were also artisans, were barbarously maltreated in sight of the White Ruthenian people, the White Ruthenians themselves were also beaten with clubs and rifle butts. It was no longer a question of an action against the Jews. It looked much more like a revolution. . . ."

It goes on to describe the looting:

"In conclusion I find myself obliged to point out that the police battalion looted in an unheard-of manner during the action and that not only in Jewish houses but equally those of the White Ruthenians. Anything of use, such as boots, leather, cloth, gold, and other valuables was taken away. According to statements of the troops, watches were torn off the arms of Jews openly on the street and rings pulled off their fingers in the most brutal manner. A disbursing officer reported that a Jewish girl was asked by the police to obtain immediately 5,000 roubles to have her father released. The girl is actually said to have run about everywhere to obtain the money."

The outraged official could not bring himself to stop there. He finished up on a burst of indignation:

"I am submitting this report in duplicate so that one copy may be submitted to the Reich Minister. Peace and order cannot be maintained in White Ruthenia with methods of that sort. To have buried alive seriously wounded people, who then worked their way out of their graves again, is such extreme beastliness that this incident as such must be reported to the Fuehrer and the Reich Marshal." [28]

This was the impression made on a German official, who had already in the nature of his job seen many dreadful things, who was prepared to see the Jews of Slutzk completely liquidated provided he had a day's warning to organise the affair in an orderly manner, but who, nevertheless, was so shocked and affronted by the reality that, after brooding about it for three days, he still could not overcome his indignation and, taking his courage in both hands, laid bare his heart to his Fuehrer, via Goering. He was an innocent, of course. The Fuehrer had ordered that these people should be killed, and did not care how.

The Commissioner at Slutzk seems to have sat in his office and listened to the shots and heard the reports brought in by his men and the troops. We now turn to the report of another German, a civilian, an engineer belonging to the building firm of Joseph Jung, who managed the branch office at Sdolbunov in the Ukraine. He was responsible, amongst other things, for a building site in Rovno, where, during the night of 13th July 1942, all the Jews, about 5,000 of them, were liquidated. Engineer Hermann Graebe was an interested party because a number of the Jews living in the Rovno ghetto were his employees. He had heard rumours of a forthcoming action against them, and had marched his Jews

out of harm's way. Then the rumours had been officially
denied by S.S. Major Puetz, commanding the Rovno Security Police and S.D. But later it was admitted, and, after a
great deal of bargaining, Engineer Graebe managed to obtain a written paper, officially stamped by the Rovno Area
Commissioner, that his hundred worker Jews should be
spared. This is what Engineer Graebe saw, as described in his
Nuremberg affidavit:

"On the evening of this day I drove to Rovno and posted
myself with Fritz Einsporn [his foreman] in front of the
house in the Bahnhofstrasse in which the Jewish workers
of my firm slept. Shortly after 10 p.m. the ghetto was en-
circled by a large S.S. detachment and about three times as
many members of the Ukrainian militia. Then the electric
arc-lights which had been erected in and around the ghetto
were switched on. S.S. and militia squads of four to six
men entered or at least tried to enter the houses. Where the
doors and windows were closed and the inhabitants did not
open at the knocking, the S.S. men and militia broke the
windows, forced the doors with beams and crowbars, and
entered the houses. The people living there were driven
on to the street just as they were, regardless of whether
they were dressed or in bed. Since the Jews in most cases
refused to leave their houses and resisted, the S.S. and
militia applied force. They finally succeeded, with strokes
of the whip, kicks, and blows from rifle butts, in clearing
the houses. The people were driven out of their houses in
such haste that small children in bed had been left behind
in several instances. In the streets women cried out for
their children and children for their parents. That did not
prevent the S.S. from driving the people along the road
at running pace, and hitting them, until they reached a
waiting freight train. Car after car was filled, and the

screaming of women and children and the cracking of whips and rifle shots resounded unceasingly. Since several families or groups had barricaded themselves in especially strong buildings and the doors could not be forced with crowbars or beams, the doors were blown open with hand-grenades. Since the ghetto was near the railroad tracks in Rovno, the younger people tried to get across the tracks and over a small river to get away from the ghetto area. As this stretch of country was beyond the range of the electric lights, it was illuminated by small rockets. All through the night these beaten, hounded, and wounded people moved along the lighted streets. Women carried their dead children in their arms, children pulled and dragged their dead parents by their arms and legs down the road toward the train. . . .

"About six o'clock in the morning I went away for a moment leaving behind Einsporn and several other German workers who had returned in the meantime. I thought the greatest danger was past and that I could risk it. Shortly after I left, Ukrainian militia men forced their way into 5 Bahnhofstrasse and brought seven Jews out and took them to a collection point inside the ghetto. On my return I was able to prevent further Jews from being taken out. I went to the collecting point to save these seven men. I saw dozens of corpses of all ages and both sexes in the streets I had to walk along. The doors of the houses stood open, windows were smashed. Pieces of clothing, shoes, stockings, jackets, caps, hats, coats were lying in the street. At the corner of a house lay a baby, less than a year old, with his skull crushed. Blood and brains were spattered over the house wall and covered the area immediately around the child. The child was dressed only in a little shirt. The commander, S.S. Major Puetz, was walking up and down a row of about 80 to 100 male Jews who were crouching on the ground. He had a heavy dog-whip in his hand. I walked up to him, showed him the written permit of *Stabsleiter* Beck and demanded the seven men whom I recognised among those who were crouching on the ground. Puetz was very furious about Beck's concession and nothing could persuade him to release the seven men. He made a motion with his hand encircling the square and said that anyone who was here once would not get away. Although he was very angry with Beck, he ordered me to take the people from 5 Bahnhofstrasse out of Rovno by eight o'clock at the latest. When I left Puetz, I noticed a Ukrainian farm-cart with two horses. Dead people with stiff limbs were lying on the cart. Legs and arms projected over the side boards. The cart was making for the freight train. . . ." [29]

Engineer Graebe did not follow that freight train to its destination, which was the death pit at Kostopol, so we cannot through his observant eyes follow the 5,000 Jews of Rovno (it was, incidentally, Rovno's second massacre: most of the 5,000 did not belong to the place, but had been moved from other parts of Poland to the ghetto for easier handling). But a few months later, on 5th October 1942, he was able to do the next best thing. He attended a mass execution of very similar people at Dubno in Volhynia, on a disused aerodrome where his firm had a building site. He saw the vans arriving with prisoners, and went to look; and his account, read by Sir Hartley Shawcross in his final speech at Nuremberg, filled even those who for week after week had accustomed themselves to tales of unimaginable horror with an emotion deeper than any they had yet experienced.

". . . an old woman with snow-white hair was holding this one-year-old child in her arms and singing and tickling it. The child was cooing with delight. The parents

M

were looking on with tears in their eyes. The father was holding the hand of a boy about ten years old and speaking to him softly; the boy was fighting his tears. The father pointed towards the sky, stroked the boy's head, and seemed to explain something to him. At that moment the S.S. man at the pit shouted something to his comrade. The latter counted off about twenty persons and instructed them to go behind the earth mound. The family I have described was among them. I well remember the girl, slim and with black hair, who, as she passed me, pointed to herself and said: 'Twenty-three years old.'

"I then walked round the mound and found myself confronted by a tremendous grave. People were closely wedged together and lying on top of each other so that only their heads were visible. Nearly all had blood running over their shoulders from their heads. Some of the people shot were still moving. Some lifted their arms and turned their heads to show that they were alive. The pit was already two-thirds full. I estimated that it held a thousand people. I looked for the man who did the shooting. He was an S.S. man who sat at the edge of the narrow end of the pit, his feet dangling into it. He had a tommy gun on his knees and was smoking a cigarette. The people—they were completely naked—went down some steps which were cut in the clay wall of the pit and clambered over the heads of those who were lying there to the place to which the S.S. man directed them. They lay down in front of the dead and wounded. Some caressed the living and spoke to them in a low voice. Then I heard a series of shots. I looked into the pit and saw that their bodies still twitched or that their heads lay motionless on top of the other bodies before them. Blood ran from their necks.

"I was surprised that I was not ordered off, but I saw

that there were two or three postmen in uniform near by. Already the next batch was approaching. They went down in the pit, lined themselves up against the previous victims and were shot. When I walked back round the mound I noticed that another truck-load of people had arrived. This time it included sick and feeble people. An old, terribly thin woman was undressed by others, who were already naked, while two people held her up. The woman appeared to be paralysed. The naked people carried her round the mound. I left with my foreman and drove in my car back to Dubno.

"On the morning of the next day, when I visited the site, I saw about thirty naked people lying near the pit— about thirty to fifty metres away from it. Some of them were still alive; they looked straight in front of them with a fixed stare and seemed to notice neither the chilliness of the morning nor the workers of my firm who stood around. A girl of about twenty spoke to me and asked me to give her clothes and help her to escape. At that moment we heard a fast car approach and I noticed that it was an S.S. detail. I moved away to my site. Ten minutes later we heard shots from the vicinity of the pit. Those Jews who were still alive had been ordered to throw the corpses into the pit, then they themselves had to lie down in the pit to be shot in the neck." [30]

Ohlendorf's shootings in the "military" manner were tidier, but in other respects identical. The people, men, women, and children, were rounded up in their houses, torn forcibly from them, transported to the death-pits, and shot. But Ohlendorf did not make them undress completely.

The Rovno massacre accounted for only 5,000 Jews. Between June and October 1941 some 350,000 were killed directly in this manner,[31] perhaps the greatest slaughter of ll having taken place at Kiev, where S.S. Major-General Franz Jaeckeln, Higher S.S. and Police Leader with the Southern Army Group, forced the pace in a manner usually associated with Heydrich's young men of the S.D. It was the greatest single massacre, and *Einsatzgruppe* C reported to Heydrich that 33,771 Jews had been killed in two days, on 29th and 30th September, on the very outskirts of Kiev in the Babi Yar ravine.[32] The hero of this operation was the commander of *Einsatzkommando* 4a, another of Heydrich's intellectuals, an architect turned into a Colonel of the S.S., Paul Blobel— who, later, when the Germans were retreating, was made Director of Exhumation Activities by Heydrich, whom he had displeased. His job then was to dig up the death-pits and supervise the burning of the corpses, a laborious and unsalubrious task, before the advancing Russians found them. One of the pits he had to exhume was in the Babi Yar ravine, where, at Nuremberg, he admitted to digging up the contents of one pit sixty yards long and more than eight feet deep.[33]

But this is not a history of the massacres in Poland and Western Russia. The reader who wishes to grasp the magnitude of these killings and to acquaint himself with the careers and characters of the individuals who carried them out is referred to Mr. Reitlinger's sombre and elaborate study of *The Final Solution*. We are concerned with these terrible events only in so far as they throw light on the nature of the Gestapo and the S.D., and the relationship of the Gestapo and the S.D. with other organisations. It is necessary to show the kind of work they did together.

It may seem that we have come a long way from the Prinz Albrecht Strasse and allowed ourselves to get mixed up with a strange and questionable mob far removed from the pure Gestapo. What were the Lithuanian partisans doing at the massacre at Slutzk? How was it that a civilian Area Commissioner was asked by the Security Police for his help, and afterwards protested to Goering? Why was Engineer Graebe allowed to watch the round-up at Rovno and the massacre at Dubno, when these things were supposed to take place in total secrecy, so that only a handful of Germans knew of them? There are many questions of this kind. How was it, for example, that Higher S.S. and Police Leader Jaeckeln led the massacres at Riga, Kovno, Kiev, and elsewhere—when, according to the defence, Higher S.S. and Police Leaders had no jurisdiction over the Gestapo and the S.D.? And then we have the curious order from Field-Marshal von Rundstedt, the dear old, straight-backed, honourable old General who knew nothing about the massacres, like all the other dear old Generals:

> "Action against Communists and Jews is only to be undertaken by the special commandos of the Security Police and S.D., who carry out such orders on their own responsibility. Participation of members of the Armed Forces in Ukrainian excesses against the Jewish population is forbidden, also the witnessing and photographing of the measures taken by the special commandos. This order must be made known to the personnel of every unit. All officers and N.C.Os are responsible for carrying it out." [34]

It all seems very muddled, and indeed it was. We have been at some pains to discover that these massacres were carried out under the leadership of the R.S.H.A.—of the Security Police, that is, and the S.D.—which was strongly denied at Nuremberg. But it is already clear that a great many others were involved as well in actions which the Germans as a nation have firmly maintained were known only to the handful of men who carried them out: the 3,000 men of the four *Einsatzgruppen*.

And those involved were not only Germans. In *Einsatz-gruppe* A Lithuanian mercenaries took to the work with great fervour, and in a short time formed the main elements in Stahlecker's firing squads. Although they were said to lose their enthusiasm after a time and failed to emulate their German colleagues in plodding, conscientious devotion to duty, this fact about the Lithuanians has to be recorded.[35] Considerable use, also, was made of the indigenous Ukrainian anti-Semitism. At one time certain Germans, Ribbentrop among them, had dreams that the Ukrainians would do all their work for them; but as time went on the Group Commanders found, as the Russians had found before them, that the Ukrainians were unbiddable and that their animal high spirits got in the way of orderly extermination and the compilation of accurate records.[36] There were also the Roumanians, who carried out important massacres of their own, above all in Odessa. They offended the Germans on the spot by not troubling to bury their victims; and they offended the R.S.H.A. by their failure to keep proper records and by their uncontrolled looting.[37] It was above all, however, the volunteers from Lithuania and the Ukraine who provided the mainstay of local help for the hard-pressed Group commanders.

And, indeed, they were hard-pressed. They had immense areas to cover. Stahlecker's Group was responsible for the extermination of the Jews in a territory half the size of Western Europe.[38] His was the largest Group, certainly; but to set against that, he had the biggest concentrations of Jews, so that he was able to forge ahead of the rival Groups (although Ohlendorf with his 90,000 in a year protested that he exaggerated). Stahlecker's elaborately detailed figures for the first four months totalled 135,567, though this figure included nearly 4,000 Communists and 748 lunatics. To cover all this ground he had barely more than a thousand men divided into four commandos, and it took him a very long time to get round the area, until he was given his private aeroplane.

It is perfectly obvious that his commandos could not operate over these vast distances without assistance from the civil and military authorities. As a rule they received it as their right; only occasionally were the people on the spot obstructive—and then, as a rule, not because they wished to resist the "final solution", but because they objected to being rushed. Or because they thought such actions were detrimental to the German cause, as indeed they were.

CHAPTER 16

Auschwitz

THERE were more Jews, however, than the *Einsatz-gruppen* could kill by shooting. The Germans recognised this, and their problem was expressed by Governor Frank in the very early days of the Russian campaign:

"We cannot shoot or poison 3,500,000 Jews," he told his Cabinet, "but we shall nevertheless be able to take measures which will lead somehow to their annihilation, and this will be done in connection with the gigantic measures to be determined in discussions in the Reich. The General Government must become free of Jews, just as the Reich is. Where and how this is to be achieved is a matter for certain offices which we must set up and create here. These activities will be brought to your notice in due course." [1]

Frank, of course, was speaking from a parochial point of view. He was interested in killing only the Jews in the General Government of Poland, and he was anxious to direct this operation himself. He was already in conflict with Himmler—not as to methods and aims, but as to who was to be the scourge of Poland: he objected strongly to being side-tracked by Himmler, the Gestapo, and the Higher S.S. and Police Leaders in the matter of creating terror. And he had quarrelled with S.S. Lt.-General Odilo Globocnik, an

Austrian Nazi, who had taken an extremely active part in the
conspiracies which resulted in the *Anschluss*.[2] Globocnik was
appointed by Heydrich to liquidate the Polish Jews in
November 1939, when he was made Higher S.S. and Police
Leader for Lublin province. He was a handsome brute in a
coarse and heavy way, who, having been disgraced for corrupt practices as the first Nazi Gauleiter of Vienna, found, at
thirty-five, his spiritual home as a conspiratorial dictator of
the heart of Polish Jewry.[3] He had to be a conspirator because he was required to double-cross Frank. But he was one
of those born conspirators and racketeers who can function as
well when they are drunk as when they are sober. Globocnik was almost always drunk. It would be a pleasure to be
able to believe that he was sober when, five years later, he met
his death at the hands of Yugoslav partisans in Istria. But
he was probably drunk then too. His activities have been
conveniently summarised by Goebbels:

> "Beginning with Lublin," he wrote in his diary on
> March 27 1942, "the Jews in the General Government are
> now being evacuated eastward. The procedure is pretty
> barbaric and is not to be described here more definitely.
> Not much will remain of the Jews. About 60 per cent of
> them will have to be liquidated. Only about 40 per cent
> can be used for forced labour. The former Gauleiter of
> Vienna (Globocnik), who is to carry out this measure, is
> doing it with considerable circumspection and in a way
> that does not attract much attention . . . the ghettos that
> will be emptied in the cities of the General Government
> will now be refilled with Jews thrown out of the Reich.
> The process is to be repeated from time to time." [4]

This was the process known as "resettlement", the moving
of the Jews by stages farther and farther into the East, until
they ended in the gas-chambers or in the mass graves of the

Einsatzgruppen. In the beginning they were either shot in or around the ghettos, or taken to one of the early death-camps (e.g. Treblinka, Belsec-Sodibor). The action, as it developed into wholesale extermination, was known as *Aktion Reinhard,* in honour of Heydrich, who, in June 1942, was assassinated at Lidice. The scenes described by Engineer Graebe were typical of the "action", though separate from it.[5]

It was not the easiest thing in the world to manage, and we can sympathise with Globocnik, at the end, asking for a distribution of medals among his officers and men.[6] One of the most remarkable achievements of Globocnik and Himmler working together was the way in which they bullied the Army into giving up much needed railway space for train-loads of starving Jews to be shuttled about between ghetto and ghetto, and ghetto and death-camp, at a time of extreme military exigency. We find a letter from the Ministry of Transportation to Himmler's Adjutant, S.S. Lt.-General Karl Wolff, dated 28th July 1942:

> "Since July 22nd one train a day with 5,000 Jews goes from Warsaw to Treblinka via Malkinia, as well as two trains a week with 5,000 Jews each from Przemysl to Belsec. Bedob is in constant touch with the S.D. in Cracow. . . ."

S.S. Lt.-General Karl Wolff, who has been a free man ever since 1949, sent a congratulatory reply:

> "I was especially pleased to learn from you that already for a fortnight a daily train, taking 5,000 of the Chosen People every time, had gone to Treblinka. . . ." [7]

Mr. Reitlinger remarks as follows:

> "As a witness at the trial of Oswald Pohl on June 5th 1947, Karl Wolff had 'not the slightest recollection' why

he had taken such a close interest in these trains. He was not unduly pressed on the subject. Karl Wolff was a 'good German'. He had gone as Kesselring's peace envoy to Berne in March 1945, and in May he had signed the capitulation of the army in Italy, as a consequence of which he was allowed to wear his general's insignia in court at Nuremberg. The sight was apparently so impressive that no one thought of asking him what he thought happened to 70,000 people, who were moved in the course of a fortnight to a single improvised camp, from which there was no transport to take them any further. Nor was Karl Wolff asked under what conditions of hygiene he supposed that 5,000 old people and children could travel in a single goods-train." [8]

The gas-chambers at Treblinka, to which the trains of Karl Wolff's special interest were directed, were the direct successors of the euthanasia establishments in Germany, originally used for the destruction of lunatics and useless mouths.[9] It became customary to detail individuals from the concentration-camps to these euthanasia establishments (those from Dachau went to Schloss Hartheim for gassing); but the facilities were so inadequate and the waiting list became so long that it was soon found expedient to build gas-chambers inside the individual concentration-camps. They were inefficiently designed and inefficiently run.

Dr. Figl, the gallant Chancellor of the Austrian Republic from 1945 to 1952, an engineer by profession, was a prisoner in Dachau; and, told to design a gas-chamber and a crematorium, succeeded in saving many lives by quiet sabotage: he would specify materials he knew could not be obtained and produce designs which would not work. But sooner or later every camp had its death-chamber. The original idea was to exterminate the sick, as well as unwanted Jews, but the idea spread. And under Globocnik the Gestapo and the S.D. in Poland established three camps to assist them in their task of eliminating the Jews in Poland: Belzek, Treblinka, and Sodibor. The Camp Commander at Treblinka, which had the best record of gassings, was S.S. Major Christian Wirth, with the rank of *Kriminal Kommissar*, a favourite of Globocnik's. He had a curious job, because not only was he Chief of the Death-camps organisation in Poland, but he also actually ran Treblinka. He developed a technique of his own for using Jews to handle their own co-religionists, and gave them a vested interest in this activity by allowing them to plunder the corpses, particularly of gold from their teeth. These men, living in the shadow of death, could accumulate great riches in no time at all, which they would squander in festivity, knowing that soon they themselves would be gassed in their turn. One of the witnesses for the S.S. at Nuremberg told a fantastic story of a Jewish wedding near Lublin, a fabulous banquet with over a thousand guests, which was given by the members of Wirth's special Jewish commandos on the proceeds of their loot.[10]

To trace Wirth's career is impossible: he seems to have held rank in the Kripo. But he occupied one of those strange positions so familiar in Nazi Germany which makes it impossible to pin him down; but it is clear that he had the most intimate connections with Hitler's Chancellery, through Phillip Bouhler, a young Major-General of the S.S. who was Hitler's expert on euthanasia. Wirth had worked with him in the more peaceful days, and had so developed the feeling that he alone understood the business of mass killing.[11] In fact, Wirth was not very clever, and his death-apparatus was inefficient in the extreme.

His original method, once the gas-vans had been discarded as not good enough, was to pump the exhaust gases of the engines into permanent chambers, each holding several hun-

dred people.[12] But the installation at Belzek kept on breaking down, and the victims of the Lublin "resettlement" were
left either in the box-cars to die of suffocation and exhaustion
in the sidings, or else turned out into the open (this was
March 1942) and left naked and without food and water.
The same thing happened at Sodibor. On top of this, the
engines were perpetually breaking down for short periods.
The gas expert, Kurt Gerstein, has told how it once took two
and three-quarter hours to start the engines, and while the
mechanics fiddled and cursed, 3,000 people were left packed
in the four gas-chambers, waiting, moaning.[13] Treblinka,
however, had more efficient engines, self-contained Diesels,
not simply the engines of the discarded death-vans. In the
end it had thirteen gas-chambers and a very smart "Potem-
kin" railway station—a complete model of an ordinary working station, put up in the middle of the camp siding, with
bogus time-tables, posters, and advertisements,[14] to make the
victims feel at home, and to conceal from them that Treblinka
station was the terminus and, for them, the terminal of their
lives.

But the camp which has stamped its imprint on the mind
of the Western world is Auschwitz. This is partly because
more Jews were gassed there than anywhere else—though
not as many as its commander laid claim to; partly because
this commander, S.S. Lt.-Colonel Franz Hoess, was found at
Nuremberg to be a most communicative witness; but more
than anything else because it was above all to Auschwitz that
the Jews from all over Europe were sent, so that there are far
more people in France, or Holland, or Belgium to say nothing of Hungary, who have had friends and relations murdered at Auschwitz than in any other camp.

Rudolf Hoess was described by Wirth as his "untalented
disciple". But Hoess, who was quiet and efficient, with the
quietness and efficiency of a born confidential clerk, regarded

Wirth as an untidy amateur. Although he was only an S.S. Camp Commander (promoted step by step from the day when he became a Block overseer, while serving a sentence for political murder in Buchenwald), he had the closest ties with the Gestapo and the R.S.H.A., since he was their chief agent for the disposal of the Jews they rounded up. Few men have been more difficult to rattle. He could handle small groups of victims or the largest consignments with perfect imperturbability. Even when Eichmann landed 250,000 Hungarian Jews on his doorstep with very little warning, he simply set to and passed them through his gas-chambers as part of the day's work. The only thing that ever worried him, even slightly, was the fact that although he could kill 10,000 prisoners a day in his gas-chambers without disorganisation, it was not so easy to dispose of the bodies. It took much longer to incinerate 10,000 bodies than to put them to death, and the burning was harder to conceal.[15]

We have no verbal evidence from Wirth, who disappeared with Globocnik, allegedly killed by Istrian partisans. But from Hoess we have a good deal; and it is best to hear in his own words what an extermination camp of the most up-to-date kind was like, and how it functioned.[16]

Hoess described how after a year at Auschwitz, originally an ordinary concentration-camp, he was called to Berlin in the summer of 1941 by Himmler.

"He told me something to the effect—I do not remember the exact words—that the Fuehrer had given the order for a final solution of the Jewish question. We, the S.S., must carry out that order. If it is not carried out now, then the Jews will later destroy the German people. He had chosen Auschwitz on account of its easy access by rail and also because the extensive site offered space for measures ensuring isolation."

It should be recorded in this connection that no written order for the extermination of European Jewry is known to exist. The Fuehrer's order of March 1941 for the killing of Russian Commissars was put on paper. But when it comes to the Jews the order seems to have been transmitted verbally to the relevant executives from Hitler all down the line. It was during the course of transmission that the term "final solution" came to be accepted by an increasing number of authorities as the proper term for the elimination of European Jewry as a whole, and the terms "special treatment" and "resettlement" as the code names for murder.

Hoess went back to Auschwitz full of his new mission:

"The Auschwitz camp as such was about three kilometres away from the town. About 20,000 acres of the surrounding country had been cleared of all former inhabitants, and the entire area could be entered only by S.S. men or civilian employees who had special passes. The actual compound, called 'Birkenau', where later on the extermination camp was constructed, was situated two kilometres from the Auschwitz camp. The camp installations themselves, that is to say, the provisional installations used at first were deep in the woods, and could from nowhere be detected by the eye."

It was to a siding specially built at Birkenau that the trains would come from all over Europe:

"During the whole period up until 1944 certain operations were carried out at regular intervals in the different countries, so that one cannot speak of a continuous flow of incoming transports. It was always a matter of four to six weeks. During those four to six weeks two to three trains containing about 2,000 persons each, arrived daily. These trains were first of all shunted to a siding in the Birkenau region and the locomotive then went back. The guards who had accompanied the transport had to leave the area at once, and the persons who had been brought in were taken over by guards belonging to the camp.

"They were there examined by two S.S. medical officers as to their fitness for work. The internees capable of work at once marched to Auschwitz or to the camp at Birkenau, and those incapable of work were first taken to the provisional installations, then later to the newly constructed crematoria."

The "certain operations . . . carried out at regular intervals in the different countries" referred to by Hoess were the systematic round-ups of Jews carried out by Eichmann and his subordinates and agents of Section IV A 4 b of the R.S.H.A. They were rounded up for deportation and resettlement. They were dragged slowly in their box-cars, packed to suffocation, starved, filthy, frozen in winter, baked in summer, dying by the score, across the breadth of Europe. Those who were plainly incapable of work, and all children, were disembarked at Birkenau and sent straight to the gas-chambers, undressed completely, naked, stripped of all their valuables, having been told that they were going to undergo a delousing operation, and assisted by other internees, members of the Jewish *Sonderkommandos*, whose turn was yet to come. Those who went to work were driven until they were too ill or exhausted to be of any use, and then packed off to the gas-chambers themselves.

In his outline of what happened at Auschwitz as a defence witness for Kaltenbrunner at Nuremberg, Hoess was matter of fact enough in manner but unreliable as to figures. In an affidavit he had dictated before the trial he was more eloquent and detailed, but still inaccurate: [17]

"I commanded Auschwitz until 1st December 1943, and estimate that at least 2,500,000 victims were executed and exterminated there by gassing and burning, and at least another half million succumbed to starvation and disease, making a total dead of about 3,000,000. This figure represents about 70 to 80 per cent. of all persons sent to Auschwitz as prisoners, the remainder having been selected and used for slave labour in the concentration-camp industries; included among the executed and burned were approximately 20,000 Russian prisoners-of-war (previously screened out of prisoner-of-war cages by the Gestapo), who were delivered at Auschwitz in Wehrmacht transports operated by regular Wehrmacht officers and men. The remainder of the total victims included about 100,000 German Jews, and great numbers of citizens, mostly Jewish, from Holland, France, Belgium, Poland, Hungary, Czechoslovakia, Greece, or other countries. We executed about 400,000 Hungarian Jews alone at Auschwitz in the summer of 1944. . . ."

These figures, as Mr. Reitlinger has proved, were, like Eichmann's, exaggerated, in spite of the fact that Hoess had the mind of a book-keeper and maintained the most meticulous records. (The proper figure seems to be in the neighbourhood of one million.)[18] But when Hoess gets on to ways and methods he is more reliable, and his testimony is confirmed by others. First his actions on returning to Poland after receiving Himmler's instructions:

"At that time there were already in the General Government three other extermination camps: Belzek, Treblinka, and Wolzek. These camps were under the *Einsatzkommandos* of the Security Police and S.D. I visited Treblinka to find out how they carried out their exterminations. The Camp Commandant at Treblinka told me that he had liquidated 80,000 in the course of one half-year. He was principally concerned with liquidating all the Jews from

N

the Warsaw Ghetto. He used monoxide gas, and I did not think that his methods were very efficient. So when I set up the extermination building at Auschwitz, I used Cyklon B, which was a crystallised prussic acid which we dropped into the death-chamber from a small opening. It took from three to fifteen minutes to kill the people in the death-chamber, depending upon climatic conditions. We knew when the people were dead because their screaming stopped. We usually waited about a half-hour before we opened the doors and removed the bodies. After the bodies were removed our special Commandos took off the rings and extracted the gold from the teeth of the corpses.

"Another improvement we made over Treblinka was that we built our gas-chamber to accommodate 3,000 people at one time, whereas at Treblinka their ten gas-chambers only accommodated 200 people each. The way we selected our victims was as follows: We had two S.S. doctors on duty at Auschwitz to examine the incoming transports of prisoners. The prisoners would be marched by one of the doctors, who would make spot decisions as they walked by. Those who were fit for work would be sent into the camp. Others were sent immediately to the extermination plants. Children of tender years were invariably exterminated, since by reason of their youth they were unable to work. Still another improvement we made over Treblinka was that at Treblinka the victims almost always knew that they were going to be exterminated and at Auschwitz we endeavoured to fool the victims into thinking that they were to go through a delousing process. Of course, frequently they realised our true intentions, and we sometimes had riots and difficulties due to this fact. Very frequently women would hide their children under their clothes, but of course when we found them we would send the children in to be exterminated. We were required to carry out these exterminations in secrecy, but of course the foul and nauseating stench from the continuous burning of bodies permeated the entire area, and all of the people living in the surrounding communities knew that exterminations were going on at Auschwitz."

During Hoess's examination at Nuremberg he was asked:

"Did you yourself ever feel pity with the victims, thinking of your own family and children?"
"Yes."
"How was it possible for you to carry out these actions in spite of this?"
"In view of these doubts which I had, the only one and decisive argument was the strict order and the reason given for it by the Reichsfuehrer Himmler." [19]

Dr. Gilbert, who, as a psychiatrist, spent a great deal of time behind the coulisses at Nuremberg trying to find out what made the prisoners tick, has this to say about Hoess:

"There was nothing about this apathetic little man to suggest that he was the greatest murderer who ever lived. The only clue to the nature of the personality that had lent itself so readily to such a thing was that apathy, the hallmark of the schizoid personality. . . . There was no indication of emotional reaction of any sort as he calmly related how he had received and executed Himmler's orders to exterminate Jewish families by the train-load. Only a certain air of remoteness in his expression, the cold eyes gazing out into space when he looked at you, gave outward evidence of a personality that was not entirely of this world." [20]

Since to say that a man has a schizoid personality is to tell one as much, or as little, as to say that he has red hair, this is not as illuminating as it might be: the tendency of psychiatrists to attach a life of their own to technical terms which are simply labels, like black and white, can be misleading. Mr. Reitlinger's description of the man as revealed in his photographs, on the other hand, seems to mean something:

"In the photographs, taken in his prime, the political enthusiast, who had found his way to murder even in 1923, looks like an adequate lance-corporal but with the pale, rather dilated eyes of those who find life hard to understand." [21]

That is enough of S.S. Lt.-Colonel Hoess. And here it must be emphasised strongly that Hoess's narrative is not introduced as evidence of the number of Jews and others destroyed at Auschwitz (which we are not concerned with here) but as an example of the sort of thing that went on within the purview of the Gestapo and was made possible by the Gestapo. Those who are concerned to find out whether the Germans killed six million Jews or four, and where, and how, must refer to Mr. Reitlinger and others. Hoess is a highly unreliable witness. He had to destroy all his records, and Mr. Reitlinger thinks he was simply repeating Eichmann's boasts, uttered to impress Himmler with his, Eichmann's, efficiency and indispensability. Hoess may be caught out in many particulars. For example, although he told the Tribunal that he had accounted for two and a half million men, women, and children, he reduced this figure, speaking to Dr. Gilbert, to one million three hundred thousand.[22] Even his chronology is wrong. Treblinka was dealing with the deportees of the Warsaw Ghetto in 1942, not 1941, and, in fact, most of the victims of this particular action were shot, or clubbed to death, as they arrived at Treblinka, because the gas-chambers were not ready.[23]

In fact, the mass gassing of Jews did not begin until the summer of 1942, after Heydrich's death; and it took place under the ægis of his successor, Kaltenbrunner, the Austrian lawyer who, at Nuremberg, did not know anything about anything. But, when it came to practical detail, Hoess's mind functioned more accurately. It is desirable to be clear about this because the evidence of Hoess, and of others equally unreliable, has been treated as factual by too many investigators. For example, in his book *Human Behaviour in the Concentration Camps*, Dr. Elie Cohen accepts the Hoess figure of two and a half million gassed or burned and another half million dead of exhaustion and disease. So long as there are Germans (and there are still many) who believe that all they have to do to prove that the Nazis were not as black as they were painted is to show that they did not kill quite as many as was originally believed, it is important to be conservative about the numbers.

The evidence here presented in this affair of mass-murder has come entirely from Germans. It is better that this should be so, because it might be considered that the stories of the survivors who escaped the gas-chambers are likely to be biased. It may even be thought that the evidence of Germans at Nuremberg is questionable. And so, as a final contribution to the record, let us take an item from the great mass of evidence contained in diaries and reports written by those who participated in these murders while they were in progress, and long before it had occurred to them that they might one day fall into enemy hands.

Here are excerpts from the diary of Professor Dr. Hans Kremer of the University of Westphalia. He was one of the doctors, referred to by Hoess, who stood on the platform as the new arrivals were unloaded from the trains and, as they

filed past, made the sign which was to send the majority to
the gas-chambers, the minority to forced labour. He was
suddenly plunged into the middle of it all, having, as a
member of the S.S., been sent off to deputise for another
doctor who had fallen ill: [24]

"September 2nd, 1942—Present for the first time at a
special action at three in the morning. Compared with
this Dante's Inferno seems a comedy. It is not for nothing
that Auschwitz is called the extermination camp.

"September 5—Present this afternoon at a special
action from the women's camp (Musselmen).* The most
horrible of horrors. Thilo, the Troops' M.O., was right
when he told me this morning that we were at *anus mundi*.
In the evening at approximately seven o'clock again present at a special action from the Netherlands. Men all
want to take part in these actions because of the special
rations they get, consisting of a fifth of a litre of schnapps,
five cigarettes, 100 grammes of sausage, and bread. Today and tomorrow on duty.

"September 6—Today, Sunday, excellent lunch: to-
mato soup, half a hen with potatoes and red cabbage,
sweets and marvellous vanilla ice. . . . In the evening at
eight o'clock outside for special action.

"September 9—This morning the most pleasant news
from my lawyer, Professor Dr. Hallermann in Muenster:
I was divorced from my wife on the first of this month.
(*Note*: I see colours again: a black curtain has been drawn
back from my life.) Later on, present as M.O. at a corporal
punishment of eight prisoners and an execution by shooting with small calibre rifles. . . . In the evening present at
my fourth special action.

* Musselmen was the term used in the German concentration-camps for
prisoners who had been reduced to walking skeletons.

"September 10—Present in the morning at my fifth special action.

"September 20—Listened to a concert of the prisoners' band this afternoon in bright sunshine. Bandmaster: conductor of the Warsaw State Opera. Eighty musicians. For lunch we had pork, for dinner baked tench.

"September 23—Present last night at sixth and seventh special actions. In the morning Lt.-General Pohl [Chief of the Concentration Camp Administration under Himmler] arrived with his staff at the house of the Waffen S.S. ... At eight o'clock in the evening dinner with Lt.-General Pohl in the *Fuehrerhaus*, a real banquet. We had baked pike, as much as we wanted, good coffee, excellent ale and rolls."

Professor Dr. Hans Hermann Kremer stayed at Auschwitz until 18th November, returning then to normal duty. He took part in fourteen special actions all told, and cared less and less about them, although the eleventh was tiresome —a special action against Dutch women on a cold, wet, Sunday morning, some of whom so far forgot themselves as to beg for mercy: "Shocking scenes with three women, who beseech us for bare life." But he was settling down to his new existence, enjoying the food, and conducting interesting experiments with liver, spleen, and pancreas taken from living prisoners. On 1st November he had to fly off to Prague, but he got back six days later and felt happy to be home at Auschwitz, "where I had a really good meal again and ate myself good and properly full". His last special action was on 8th November. "In the evening we had a good time in the Leaders' Club, invited by Colonel Wirth. We had Bulgarian red wine and Croatian plum-schnapps."

It is of interest to note that Professor Dr. Kremer of the University of Westphalia was sentenced to death by a Polish

Court at Cracow and was duly executed. It is not certain that this would have happened had he been tried farther West.

There are no extant descriptions by Germans of the horrors of the special actions, so to picture the scenes which Professor Kremer had to witness before getting back to his comfortable meals we must put together the evidence of survivors. When pressure was not too great the proceedings were orderly. Naked and shorn, the prisoners were marched to the gas-chambers, some of which were sunk in the ground, others on the same level as the crematoria which disposed of the corpses. It was all very clean and tidy, with a neat lawn all around, broken only by what might have been ventilation shafts, but which, in fact, were the orifices through which the blue crystals of Cyklon B were dropped into hollow columns of perforated sheet metal, which ran down to the floor of the chamber. There were douches in the ceiling to maintain the impression of a bath-house, but these were dummies, and there were no drainage channels in the floor, which was level and not sloped.

It was through these perforated columns that the gas made its way into the chamber, and, whatever the people may have felt while they waited, they knew in their last minutes what was happening, and then they would stampede away from the columns and pile up against the great metal door, shrieking, and fighting in mass panic, even in the moment of death. The shrieks would die down to nothing, and then, as Hoess said in his affidavit, those outside would wait perhaps half an hour; the great metal door would slide back, and the Jewish *Sonderkommandos* would go into action with hoses to wash out the blood and excrement and with hooks and ropes to drag the intertwined mass of naked corpses apart. But sometimes it was not as orderly as this. When Auschwitz was working at its highest pitch, in the summer of 1944, when, in a last maniacal effort, Eichmann was trying to sweep all the Jews left in Europe into his gas-chambers before it was too late, the pressure was too great.

Then the victims would be driven into the chambers with their hands held high so that more could be squeezed in, and the children were piled up on top of them. The *Sonderkommandos* would have to work like fiends to deal with the packed mass, and, as they worked, the S.S. overseers would be flogging them with sticks and rubber truncheons to make them work faster, while, outside, because they could not be packed in, others would be moving among the waiting victims, gathering them into little groups and shooting them down then and there to save space.[25] It was this kind of pressure which proved the inadequacy of the crematoria, and it was found quicker by far, though also more conspicuous, to flood the bodies with petrol and burn them in the open. At the Lueneberg trial it was stated by Dr. Bendel that all five furnaces of Crematorium No. 4, so ingeniously constructed by the firm of Toepf of Erfurt, could consume only 1,000 corpses a day, whereas in open pits, with petrol, they could burn the same number in an hour.[26]

None of the people we have lately encountered belonged to the Gestapo, which here, as in other matters, cannot serve as an alibi. On the other hand, every man, woman, and child in that fantastic death-factory was consigned there by the Gestapo.

CHAPTER 17

Night and Fog in the West

IT is said sometimes of the Gestapo, and not only of the Gestapo, but also of the S.S. in general, and of those members of the Armed Forces and of the civilian bureaucracy (they may fairly regard themselves as an ill-used minority) who have been unable to escape being implicated in the slaughter of the Jews and the Slavs, that they had become so conditioned to regarding these people as not people at all, as sub-human types, that they felt not merely no compunction in removing them from the earth but also a positive pride. This contention has a basis of truth. We remember Himmler's description of the extermination of the Jews as a delousing operation, and we may cite the words of S.S. Lt.-General Erich von dem Bach-Zelewski at Nuremberg, when asked to comment on the massacres of the *Einsatzgruppen*: "I am of the opinion that when, for years, for decades, the doctrine is preached that the Slav race is an inferior race and Jews not even human, then an explosion of this sort is inevitable." [1] Bach-Zelewski was an educated man, an old soldier, a Higher S.S. and Police Leader in charge of operations on the Russian Front, and a member of the Reichstag from 1932 until the end.

We shall return to this view later. The point to be made immediately is that the Gestapo, the S.S., and others did not confine their extraordinary activities to people whom they considered inferior or sub-human. They operated with equal cruelty against the nations of the West. It is true that there was no campaign of extermination directed against, for example, the French; but this was due to a political decision made by Hitler. We have no reason to doubt that had the Fuehrer decided to eliminate ten million Frenchmen in order to make room for Germans, the relevant organisations, including the Gestapo and the S.D., would have carried out his orders, even though they had not been taught for years that the French were sub-human. Indeed, although extermination of whole sections of the population was never practised in Western Europe—always excepting the Jews, whom the the people of several nationalities, and especially the French, perversely insisted on regarding as their own compatriots—there were some by no means inconsiderable massacres, not only of civilian populations but also of prisoners-of-war; and on those occasions when the Gestapo were required to act with severity against groups and individuals, there was nothing to choose between their behaviour in Bourges and their behaviour in Borisov. Only those who think that, in these days, individual murder must be multiplied a thousand-fold before it may be considered reprehensible will find any fundamental variation in the general attitude and behaviour of the Gestapo wherever it happened to be stationed. If there is some confusion about this, it may be found to be due very largely to the invention of a new word to describe what was, at Nuremberg, considered to be a new crime: the word genocide, which may be seen as one of those camouflage terms. It is meant to sound formidable; but in fact it serves all too well to conceal the simple fact of murder.

There was plenty of murder in Western Europe, but no genocide. Most of it took place—always excepting the mass-murder of the Jews—when Germany was hard put to it to hold her own against the Allies; and most of it came into the category of killing for punishment, or as a deterrent, rather than into the category of killing to exterminate. There was the shooting of hostages on a large scale, to cow the spirit of resistance; there was the torturing and killing of individuals suspected of sabotage; there was the killing of prisoners-of-war, mainly British, who made a nuisance of themselves; there was the killing of captured parachutists and Commandos, mainly British, to discourage the others. There were special expedients, such as the decree which instructed the police not to interfere with angry crowds when they started lynching Allied bomber-crews who had been shot down, or such as the notorious *Nacht und Nebel* (Night and Fog) Decree, which provided that all suspected resisters who could not be shot out of hand were to be sent in conditions of the utmost secrecy to Germany, where their fate would be concealed, even after death, from their families—the object of this being to create an atmosphere of secret and mysterious terror inimical to the spirit of resistance. In all these operations the Gestapo and the S.D. operated in the foreground, as in the rounding-up and deportation of the Jews—not, as they were compelled to do at Auschwitz and elsewhere, in the background at comparatively long range.

At Nuremberg on 4th February 1946, the court-room was suddenly invaded by a sense of humanity. Until then the onlookers had become so attuned to tales of wickedness and horror that their feelings had been numbed; and even when, as very often, they were required to listen to the pitiful evidence of individuals, ordinary men and women who had been assailed by the Nazi machine, but had miraculously escaped, the scale of inhumanity was so immense that the personal disaster seemed to count not as a human tragedy but simply as one more squalid item in the tremendous case being so laboriously assembled. But now, for once, there was a real human being speaking and in language all could understand:

the Belgian scholar, the historian, van der Essen, General Secretary of the University of Louvain.

Nothing much had happened to Professor van der Essen. He had had a lucky war. His beloved university library had been wrecked by the Germans, but he had not been hurt, and he had moved about, a free man, during the whole period of the occupation. He was detached from the suffering all around him (if he had allowed himself to participate he would have gone mad) and, his body unbroken, his mind unclouded, and in no immediate personal fear, he was in a position to observe the afflictions of the less fortunate. Thus his evidence, though unspectacular and almost dull, in which he gave an account of life as lived in the shadow of the Gestapo, has a point and actuality which helps to make sense of the catalogue of horrors to which we must soon return.

"I think I understand," said M. Faure, a member of the French Prosecution, who was later to become Prime Minister of France, "that you yourself were never arrested or seriously worried by the Germans. I would like to know whether you consider that a free man, against whom the German administration or police have nothing in particular, could during the Nazi occupation lead his life in accordance with the concept a free man has of his dignity?"

So this rare, this almost unique, apparition at Nuremberg, a man who had neither suffered physical violence nor inflicted it, set himself earnestly to trying to give a sober impression of the German occupation as experienced by a man with nothing to fear. He held the court. His story on the face of it was an anti-climax; but in fact it underlined more than anything else the reality behind the fantasy of murder and cruelty which, until then, had dominated the whole proceedings. He started off by saying that he weighed 82 kilos "before the 10th May 1940, before the aeroplanes of the

Luftwaffe suddenly came without any declaration of war and spread death and desolation in Belgium." He now weighed 67 kilos. There was that small fact to begin with. One of the German defence counsel, who failed to sense the mood of the court, Herr Dr. Babel, tried a remark that was half a joke and half a sneer: "During the war, I also, without having been ill, lost 35 kilos. What conclusion would you draw from that, in your opinion ?" There was laughter in court, but the President cut in: "Go on, Dr. Babel we are not interested in your experiences." [2]

Professor van der Essen said:

"I don't want to dwell on personal considerations or enter into details of a personal nature or of a theoretical or philosophical nature. I should like simply to give an account—it will not take more than two minutes—of the ordinary day of an average Belgian during the occupation.

"I take a day in the winter of 1943: at six o'clock in the morning there is a ring at the door. One's first thought—indeed we all had this thought—was that it was the Gestapo. It wasn't the Gestapo. It was a city policeman who had come to tell me that there was a light in my office and that in view of the necessities of the occupation I must be careful about this in future. But there was the nervous shock.

"At seven-thirty the postman arrives bringing me my letters; he tells me that he wishes to see me personally. I go downstairs and the man says to me: 'You know, Professor, I am a member of the secret army and I know what is going on. The Germans intend to arrest today at ten o'clock all the former soldiers of the Belgian Army who are in this region. Your son must disappear immediately.' I hurry upstairs and wake my son. I make him prepare his kit and send him to the right place. At ten o'clock I take

the tram for Brussels. A few kilometres out of Louvain
the tram stops. A military police patrol makes us get
down and lines us up—irrespective of our social position—
in front of a wall, with our arms raised and facing the wall.
We are thoroughly searched, and having found neither
arms nor compromising papers of any kind, we are allowed
to go back into the tram. A few kilometres farther on the
tram is stopped by a crowd which prevents the tram from
going on. I see several women weeping, there are cries
and wailings, I make enquiries and am told that their men
folk living in the village had refused to do compulsory
labour and were to have been arrested that night by the
Security Police. Now they are taking away the old father
of eighty-two and a young girl of sixteen and holding them
for the disappearance of the young men.

"I arrive in Brussels to attend a meeting of the academy.
The first thing the President says to me is:

" 'Have you heard what has happened? Two of our
colleagues were arrested yesterday in the street. Their
families are in a terrible state. Nobody knows where they
are.'

"I go home in the evening and we are stopped on the
way three times, once to search for terrorists, who are said
to have fled, the other times to see if our papers are in
order. At last I get home without anything serious having
happened to me.

"I might say here that only at nine o'clock in the evening
can we give a sigh of relief, when we turn the knob of our
radio set and listen to that reassuring voice which we hear
every evening, the voice of Fighting France. 'Today is the
189th day of the struggle of the French people for their
liberation', or the voice of Victor Delabley, that noble
figure of the Belgian Radio in London, who always finished
up by saying, 'Courage, we will get them yet, the Boches!'

That was the only thing that enabled us to breathe and
go to sleep at night." [3]

It is all very quiet and unsensational, and Professor van
der Essen was not hurt. And yet so many aspects of Gestapo
rule are there, just below the placid surface. The knock at
the door, which is not the milkman; the son being packed off
into hiding at a moment's notice; the round-up of ex-soldiers
to be sent to concentration-camps or forced labour; the seiz-
ing of hostages—the old man and the young girl, for shooting in case of need; the arrest of university dons in broad
daylight in the streets of Brussels and their disappearance
into Night and Fog; the listening to the nine-o'clock news
from London—but in French, not English—because the
English intonation would be noticeable in itself, and listening to the English wireless meant arrest.

Professor van der Essen was not an innocent. He knew
what was going on. He was not an active resister, but it was
only luck that saved him; the luck of not being a Jew that
saved him from almost certain death; the luck of not being
picked up as a hostage that saved him from probable shooting, certain imprisonment. "When hostages were taken it
was nearly always university professors, doctors, lawyers,
men of letters." This was a settled policy. It was laid down
for the whole of occupied Europe that hostages, to be shot if
a German was killed, often in the proportion of 100 to one,
were to be people who were well known in their districts,
well liked, and certain to be widely missed.[4]

And behind these actions were the men who, on the other
side of Europe, were slaughtering millions in conditions of
inconceivable barbarism and calling their slaughter a delousing action.

It was in France, after the total occupation, and at a time
when the Resistance had become serious, that the local com-

manders of the Gestapo and the S.D. showed that they were made of the same stuff as the Globocniks, the Kruegers, the Mildners, and the rest. And, as in the East, they found they could always call on the Waffen S.S. and nearly always on the Wehrmacht. In the closing stages of the war, when the Germans were on the run, the Gestapo could not begin to cope with the militant Resistance, and then the Waffen S.S. as at Oradour-sur-Glâne, carried out by themselves the sort of actions which they had so often practised in the East.[5]

But earlier the Security Police and the S.D. were able to manage fairly well on their own. They maintained a constant pressure of terror, which might strike at any time. Professor van der Essen was extremely lucky:

"Professors from Louvain were sent to Buchenwald, to Dora, to Neuengamme, to Gross-Rosen, and perhaps to other places too. I must add that it was not only professors from Louvain who were deported, but also intellectuals who played an important rôle in the life of the country. I can give you immediate proof. At Louvain, on the occasion of the reopening ceremony of the university this year, as Secretary General of the University, I read out the list of those who had died during the war. The list included 348 names, if I remember rightly. Perhaps some thirty of these names were those of soldiers who died during the Battles of the Scheldt and the Lys in 1940, all the others were victims of the Gestapo, or had died in camps in Germany, especially in the camps of Gross-Rosen and Neuengamme."[6]

At Nuremberg the French Prosecution gave a list of figures, which was an anonymous roll of honour. The figures referred to the number of hostages taken from the civilian population and shot by the Germans in revenge for attacks on the occupation forces. And yet the list is not quite

o

anonymous, because the figures break down into regions.
And some of the many memorials scattered along the tourist
roads of France commemorate the names behind these figures
Here they are, region by region: [7]

Lille —	1,143
Laon —	222
Rouen —	658
Angers —	863
Orleans —	501
Rheims —	353
Dijon —	1,691
Poitiers —	82
Strasbourg —	211
Rennes —	974
Limoges —	2,863
Clermont-Ferrand —	441
Lyons —	3,674
Marseilles —	1,513
Montpellier —	785
Toulouse —	765
Bordeaux —	806
Nancy —	571
Metz —	220
Paris —	11,000
Nice —	324

The total is 29,660. Notices of the executions would be
put up on posters, or published in the Press. Here is one
such notice taken from *Le Phare* of 21st October 1941: [8]

NOTICE

"Cowardly criminals in the pay of England and of
Moscow killed, with shots in the back, the *Feldkomman-
dant* of Nantes on the morning of 20th October 1941. So
far the assassins have not been apprehended.

"As expiation for this crime I have ordered that fifty hostages be shot initially. Because of the gravity of the crime, fifty more hostages will be shot if the guilty have not been arrested between now and 23rd October midnight."

Most of the executed hostages in this case, as in many others, were known Communists, and they were chosen from a list furnished by the Vichy Minister of the Interior, Peucheu, who was to be tried and hanged by his countrymen at Algiers in 1943. What went on at these shootings is described by the Abbé Moyon, who was a witness of a part of the consequences of the Nantes affair:

"It was a beautiful autumn day. The temperature was particularly mild. There had been lovely sunshine since morning. Everyone in town was going about his usual business. There was great animation in the town, for it was Wednesday, which was market day. The population knew from the newspapers and from the information it had received from Nantes that a senior officer had been killed in a street in Nantes, but refused to believe that such savage and extensive reprisals would be applied [it was still only 1941]. At Choisel Camp the German authorities had, for some days, put into special quarters a certain number of young men who were to serve as hostages in case of special difficulties. It was from among these men that those who were to be shot on this evening of 22nd October were chosen.

"The Curé of Béré was finishing his lunch when M. Moreau, Chief of Choisel Camp, presented himself. In a few words the latter explained to him the object of his visit. Having been delegated by M. Lecornu, the sub-prefect of Châteaubriant, he had come to inform him that twenty-seven men selected from among the political prisoners at

Choisel were going to be executed that afternoon; and he asked Monsieur le Curé to go immediately to attend them. The priest said he was ready to undertake this mission, and he went to the prisoners without delay.

"When the priest appeared to carry out his mission, the sub-prefect was already with the condemned. He had come to announce the horrible fate which was awaiting them, and he asked them to write letters of farewell to their families without delay. It was under these circumstances that the priest presented himself at the entrance to the quarters." [9]

That was at Châteaubriant. The same thing was going on in the prison of La Fayette at Nantes itself, where sixteen were to be shot:

"The condemned were all very brave. It was two of the youngest, Gloux and Grolleau, who were students, who constantly encouraged the others, saying that it was better to die in this way than to perish uselessly in an accident.

"At the moment of leaving, the priest, for reasons which were not explained to him, was not authorised to accompany the hostages to the place of execution. He went down the stairs of the prison with them as far as the car. They were chained together in twos. The thirteenth had on handcuffs. Once they were in the truck, Gloux and Grolleau made another gesture of farewell to him, smiling and waving their hands, which were chained together." [10]

The priest had not been able to go to the place of execution at Châteaubriant, either. But a French police-officer, Roussel, saw the condemned men being driven off, and later, brought back:

"The 22nd October, 1941, at about three-thirty in the afternoon, I happened to be in the rue du 11 Novembre at Châteaubriant, and I saw coming from Choisel Camp four or five German trucks, I cannot say exactly how many, preceded by an automobile in which was a German officer. Several civilians with handcuffs were in the trucks and were singing patriotic songs, the 'Marseillaise', the 'Chant du Depart', and so forth. One of the trucks was filled with armed German soldiers.

"I learnt subsequently that these were hostages who had just been fetched from Choisel Camp to be taken to the quarry of Sablière on the Soudan Road to be shot in reprisal for the murder at Nantes of the German Colonel Hotz.

"About two hours later these same trucks came back from the quarry and drove into the court of the Châteaubriant, where the bodies of the men who had been shot were deposited in a cellar until coffins could be made.

"Coming back from the quarry the trucks were covered and no noise could be heard, but a trickle of blood escaped from them and left a trail on the road from the quarry to the castle.

"The following day, on 23rd October, the bodies of the men who had been shot were put into coffins without any French persons being present, the entrances to the château having been guarded by German sentinels. The dead were then taken to nine different cemeteries in the surrounding communes, that is, three coffins to each commune. The Germans were careful to choose communes where there was no regular transport service, presumably to avoid the population going *en masse* to the graves of these martyrs." [11]

Police-officer Roussel could not know it, but there was a standing order about this, and for the reasons which he guessed.[12] For the shooting of hostages, as nothing else bound the population together; and it is without surprise that we read the protest of General Falkenhausen, Military Governor of Belgium, to Keitel, dated 16th September 1942:

"Enclosed is a list of the shootings of hostages which have taken place until now in my area and the incidents on account of which the shootings took place.

"In a great number of cases, particularly in the most serious, the perpetrators were later apprehended and sentenced.

"The result is undoubtedly very unsatisfactory. The effect is not so much deterrent as destructive of the feeling of the population for right and security; the gulf between the people influenced by Communism and the remainder of the population is being bridged; all circles are becoming filled with a feeling of hatred towards the occupying forces, and effective inciting material is given to enemy propaganda. Thereby military danger and general political reaction of an entirely unwanted nature . . ." [13]

A similar protest was sent in also to Keitel, by the Commander of the Wehrmacht in Holland.[14] But the shootings went on, sometimes carried out by the Security Police, sometimes by the Wehrmacht, who in the West as in the East were relied on to make up for the numerical weakness of the Gestapo.

From early in 1942, however, the dominating horror of the occupation was the notorious *Nacht und Nebel* Decree. It was thought up by Hitler, promulgated by Keitel, and issued to the Security Police by Himmler in the following form:

"I. The following regulations published by the Chief of the High Command of the Armed Forces, dated 12th December 1941, are being made known herewith.

"(1) The Chief of the High Command of the Armed Forces. After lengthy consideration, it is the will of the Fuehrer that the measures taken against those who are guilty of offences against the Reich or against the occupation forces in occupied areas should be altered. The Fuehrer is of the opinion that in such cases penal servitude or even a hard labour sentence for life will be regarded as a sign of weakness. An effective and lasting deterrent can be achieved only by the death penalty or by taking measures which will leave the family and the population uncertain as to the fate of the offender. Deportation to Germany serves this purpose.

"The attached directives for the prosecution of offences correspond with the Fuehrer's conception. They have been examined and approved by him."

Himmler elaborated on this:

"The decree introduces a fundamental innovation. The Fuehrer and Supreme Commander of the Armed Forces orders that offences committed by civilians in occupied territories . . . are to be dealt with by the competent military courts in the occupied territories only if: (a) the death penalty is pronounced, and (b) sentence is pronounced within eight days of the prisoner's arrest.

"Unless both these conditions are fulfilled, the Fuehrer and supreme Commander of the Armed Forces does not anticipate that criminal proceedings within the occupied territories will have the necessary deterrent effect.

"In all other cases the prisoners are, in future, to be transported to Germany secretly, and further treatment of the offenders will take place here; these measures will have a deterrent effect because: (a) the prisoners will vanish without leaving a trace; (b) no information may be given as to their whereabouts or their fate." [15]

There followed instructions as to the reporting of cases for deportation to Germany directly to the Director of the Kripo at the R.S.H.A. in Berlin.

Six months later we have a letter from the Chief of Security Police and S.D. which goes over the old ground and emphasises that the mystery surrounding *Nacht und Nebel* prisoners is to persist after their death:

"I therefore propose that the following rules be observed in the handling of cases of death:

"(*a*) Notification of relatives is not to take place.

"(*b*) The body will be buried at the place of decease in the Reich.

"(*c*) The place of burial will, for the time being, not be made known".[16]

The Security Police in the Reich and all over Europe had absolute jurisdiction over the whole population. They could arrest. They could interrogate and torture. They could arrange with summary military courts whether a death sentence was desirable or not. And, if it was not, the victims were deported to Germany and passed by the home-based Security Police to the concentration-camps, where most of them died.

But it was not only over the civilian populations that the Security Police held this absolute sway. There were also categories of the Allied Armed Forces which had to be surrendered to them by the Wehrmacht. In every camp for Russian prisoners-of-war there was a small Gestapo screening-team whose job it was to comb out undesirables—i.e. "political, criminal, or in some other way intolerable elements among them."[17] Russian prisoners-of-war, like all others, were the responsibility of the Army. But it was laid down that the Security Police screening-squads could in no way be interfered with and were the absolute arbiters of which prisoners should be taken away and executed. In a Gestapo directive of 17th July 1941 the squads were told how to set about their task:

> "The Commandos must make efforts from the beginning to seek out among the prisoners elements which would appear reliable, regardless of whether they are Communists or not, in order to use them for intelligence purposes inside the camp and, if advisable, later in the occupied territories also.
>
> "By use of such informers and by use of all other existing possibilities, the discovery of all elements to be eliminated among the prisoners must proceed, step by step, at once. The Commandos must find out definitely in every case, by a short questioning of those reported and possibly by questioning other prisoners, what measures should be taken. The information of one informer is not sufficient to designate a camp inmate to be a suspect without further proof. It must be confirmed in some way, if possible. . . ."[18]

These instructions give in a very convenient form a clear idea of the methods of the Gestapo everywhere. What they came to in practice was indicated by General Lahousen, not of the S.S., in his evidence for the Prosecution at Nuremberg. Lahousen belonged to the Military Intelligence organisation, or *Abwehr*, of Admiral Canaris, who was later executed for plotting against Hitler. Canaris and his *Abwehr* were at daggers drawn first with Heydrich, then with Kaltenbrunner and the Security Police in general; and this was not only because the Security Police and the S.D. in particular was constantly poaching on the preserves of Military Intelligence (in the end, after Canaris's execution, the S.D. took the whole outfit over, so that the German Army was unique in the world in having no Intelligence of its own) but also because

Canaris and his friends were wholly revolted by the methods of the Security Police and the S.D. General Lahousen said:

"The prisoners were sorted out by commandos of the S.D. and according to peculiar and utterly arbitrary ways of procedure. Some of the leaders of these *Einsatzkommandos* were guided by racial considerations, particularly of course, if someone were a Jew or of Jewish type or could otherwise be classified as racially inferior, he was picked for execution. Other leaders of the *Einsatzkommandos* selected people according to their intelligence. Some had views all of their own and most peculiar, so that I felt compelled to ask Mueller: 'Tell me, according to what principles does this selection take place? Do you determine it by the height of a person or the size of his shoes?' " [19]

(We are reminded of the notorious Gestapo round-ups in France, ostensibly to send Frenchmen to work in Germany, actually, as a rule, to consign them to concentration-camps. "Certain German policemen were especially entrusted to pick out Jewish persons, according to their physiognomy. They called this group 'The Physiognomists Brigade'.") [20]

Sometimes the Russian victims of the Gestapo screening-operations were shot then and there—but some way from the camp. More frequently they were sent off to concentration-camps, where they were executed or worked to death. It is worth recalling that the man in Berlin who directly supervised these activities was S.S. Colonel Kurt Lindow, the gentlemanly Gestapo man who gave evidence at the trial of Heinrich Baab, and was afterwards taken away. [21]

Soviet prisoners-of-war were not the only ones to come into the hands of the Gestapo. On 4th March 1944 Mueller issued an instruction to the Security Police and the S.D.

which became known as the *Kugel Erlass*, or Bullet Decree,
which provided that certain categories of prisoners-of-war
were "to be discharged from prisoner-of-war status" and
handed over to the Secret State Police by the Army. These
categories included all Soviet prisoners-of-war recaptured
after escaping; all Soviet prisoners-of-war who refused to
work, or were considered a bad influence on other prisoners;
all Soviet prisoners-of-war screened by the Security Police
as described above); all Polish prisoners-of-war involved in
sabotage. All prisoners-of-war of all nations except Britain
and America, for whom a special order was made by the
O.K.W.[22]

This was called the Bullet Decree, because prisoners
handed over to the Security Police and S.D. under its provisions for "special treatment" were sent to Mauthausen concentration-camp and shot.[23] As a rule the prisoners were
taken directly to the "bathroom", where they had to undress.
The "bathroom" was used for gassing unwanted inmates of
the concentration-camp, and when there were many prisoners "for special treatment" they were gassed like so many
civilians. But, as a rule, they were disposed of in what Major-
General Ohlendorf would doubtless have considered a more
military manner. They were shot in the neck by a sort of
humane killer; "the shooting took place by means of a meas-
uring apparatus—the prisoner being backed towards a metri-
cal measure with an automatic contraption releasing a bullet
into his neck as soon as the moving plank determining his
height touched the top of his head."[24]

British and American prisoners alone were unaffected by
the Bullet Decree. But they too on occasion were liable to be
"discharged from prisoner-of-war status" and handed over to
the Gestapo. These included captured Commando Officers
and men, who came under the provisions of the Commando
Decree of October 1942, and the fifty escapees from Stalag

Luft III at Sagan, who were shot by the Gestapo on special orders from Hitler.

The notorious Commando Order was a no less blatant infringement of international law in general, and the Geneva Convention in particular, than the Bullet Decreė. It was Hitler's personal response to the inconvenience caused by British Commando raids on the Atlantic Coast, and it offers one more example of his obsession with terror as a deterrent. The gist of the matter was contained in paragraphs three and four of the original order.

"III. I therefore order that from now on all opponents engaged in so-called Commando operations in Europe or Africa, even when it is outwardly a matter of soldiers in uniform or demolition parties with or without weapons, are to be exterminated to the last man in battle or while in flight. In these cases it is immaterial whether they are landed for their operations by ship or aeroplane or descend by parachute. Even should these individuals, on their being discovered, make as if to surrender, all quarter is to be denied on principle. . . .

"IV. If individual members of such Commandos working as agents, saboteurs, etc., fall into the hands of the Wehrmacht by other means, such as through the police in any of the countries occupied by us, they are to be handed over to the S.D. immediately. It is strictly forbidden to hold them in military custody or in prisoner-of-war camps, even as a temporary measure."

Paragraph 6 showed that Hitler and Keitel were well aware of the opposition this order would arouse within the Wehrmacht.

"VI. In the case of non-compliance with this order, I shall bring to trial before a court-martial any commander or other officer who has either failed to carry out his duty in instructing the troops about this order or who has acted contrary to it." [25]

The only modification permitted was set out in a covering letter from the Fuehrer which stated: ". . . . should it prove advisable to spare one or two men in the first instance for interrogation reasons, they are to be shot immediately afterwards."

Thus from October 1942 the Allied Commandos were up against not only the combined forces of the German Army, which was instructed to kill them to a man, but also, in the last resort, found themselves face to face with the Security Police and the S.D., whose methods we have been exploring. Sometimes they were shot on the spot; sometimes they were interrogated and then shot. Official instructions were that the cause of death should be recorded as "killed in action".[26] On the other hand, there is evidence that some commanders did in fact disobey the order, in spite of Hitler's threat.

The fifty R.A.F. officers who escaped from Stalag Luft III were all said to have been shot while trying to escape. In fact, they were as a rule picked up by the Gestapo and then shot. The Security Police and the S.D. all had their orders direct from the R.S.H.A. in Berlin. One officer got as far as Alsace, across the whole width of Germany, before he was recaptured and taken to Strasbourg Gestapo H.Q. Berlin told Strasbourg what to do:

"The British prisoner-of-war who has been handed over to the Gestapo by the Strasbourg Criminal Police, by superior orders, is to be taken immediately in the direction of Breslau and to be shot *en route* while escaping. An undertaker is to be directed to remove the body to a crematorium and have it cremated there. The urn is to be sent to the head of the Criminal Police Headquarters

R.S.H.A. The contents of this teleprint and the affair itself are to be made known only to the officials directly concerned with the carrying out of this matter, and they are to be pledged to secrecy by special handshake. . . ."

The procedure followed was that on the way to Natzweiler concentration-camp, where the cremation was to take place, the prisoner should be allowed to get out of the car to relieve himself, one member of his Gestapo escort was to hold him in conversation, while the other shot him from behind.[27] This procedure was followed in other cases as well.

CHAPTER 18

Full Circle

We seem to have come a long way from Berlin; but we have not. To this immense city in the heart of Europe, with its music, its theatres, its unquench-able pride, came the stream of teleprints and mimeographed reports of all that we have recorded, and a hundred times as much besides. From it went out the orders, meticulously de-tailed, condemning millions to unspeakable suffering and death.

Hitler is no longer there, in the spring of 1944: he lives with Keitel and his other friends underground at his field-headquarters behind the Russian Front, cut off from all real-ity, a sick and exhausted shadow of himself, to all intents and purposes off his head. But his Generals, all but a handful of them, still obey him. Goering, the savage and the bold, the buccaneering figure, the only recognisable human type among all that gang, is in eclipse and will remain in eclipse until his impressive come-back in the dock at Nuremberg. The city is ruled in practice by Himmler, with Goebbels as a sort of cheer-leader.

Berlin is no longer the city it was. It has been badly knocked about already by the Allied bombing; but it is still a functioning city. The luxurious building in the Prinz Al-brecht Strasse has been damaged, and some officials have had to find quarters elsewhere. Others work in rooms with the windows boarded up, and in basements. But it is still Gestapo H.Q.

Heydrich is dead. He had a remarkable career for a cashiered naval lieutenant, finishing up not only as head of the R.S.H.A. but also as an exalted Government functionary, Protector of Bohemia. He had the massacre at Lidice for a funeral pyre and Globocnik's *Aktion Reinhard* as a memorial; and he was recommended to posterity by Himmler in his funeral oration as "that good and radiant man".[1] Kaltenbrunner, his morose successor, who seems incapable of getting any real enjoyment from the exercise of unlimited power and the practice of unlimited murder, carries on. And since Kaltenbrunner's installation the old familiar atmosphere of intrigue has returned with a vengeance. There was no room for effective intrigue under Himmler and Heydrich: the only intrigue allowed was the plotting of the S.S. against the German Army and the world. But Himmler, now alone, rules over a divided house. Schellenberg, the brightest of Heydrich's bright young men, and chief of Amt VI of the R.S.H.A., the foreign branch of the S.D., had hoped to succeed his master, Heydrich, and so became Kaltenbrunner's bitter and ingenious enemy.[2] This egregious young blond, who, at the end of the war, managed to dissociate himself from nearly everything, and, after a short time in prison, died in his bed in Rome, was to have his triumph in the moment of his country's final disintegration.

When the Stauffenberg attempt failed and the whole apparatus of the elaborate plot against the Fuehrer was broken, and the only soldiers who had the courage and the decency to understand their duty were shot or slowly strangled, young Schellenberg had already achieved his ambition and won for the S.S. a total monopoly of all German Intelligence.[3] It did not help. As Intelligence Chief of the Reich, the man who had started the war by kidnapping Messrs. Best and

Stevens finished it by conspiring with Himmler to persuade Count Folke Bernadotte to recommend the *Reichsfuehrer* S.S. to the Allies as a suitable person to do business with.[4] At the same time Kaltenbrunner, his immediate superior, was using S.S. Lt.-Colonel Willy Hoettl to talk to Mr. Alan Dulles with the same end in view.[5] It seems never to have occurred to any of these remarkable characters that the Allies might not care for them.

But in this chaos of renewed vendetta and intrigue we find many of the old familiar faces. Mueller is still there, with his flickering eyes, still more or less efficiently directing the terror machine of the New Order, which has already lost a great deal of land. Eichmann is still there, dauntless to the end, purposefully touring Europe in the intervals of issuing his appalling imperatives from Berlin, and scooping up into Auschwitz, preparing for its last high summer, the Jews that were left. 1944 was to be an important year for him. His great achievement was the delivery of Hungarian Jewry, who moved into the gas-chambers of S.S. Lt.-Colonel Hoess while the Reich began to crumble at the edges. At the same time, in Budapest, instead of slinking about anonymously with his artificially low rank, "like a pest in a street full of men", he felt bold enough to throw off his camouflage and display himself publicly as the man with the power of life and death over millions.[6]

Hoess is still at Auschwitz, but will soon come to Berlin to work in the head office of the W.V.H.A. under Pohl. Ohlendorf is already back in Berlin, doubling his work for the S.D. with a job in the Ministry of Economics. Daluege is a sick man, superseded by Wuennenburg, but later to be executed; if we have scarcely heard anything of him at all, it is partly because he was careful of what papers he kept (he left two behind with his signature on, mass deportation orders for Jews),[7] and partly because eye-witnesses so

P

often mixed up the Orpo with the Sipo. For we have seen the work of his men many times in the course of this narrative, without always quite knowing what we saw: officers and men of the special battalions of the Orpo who worked with the Security Police and the S.D. in their special actions, as at Slutzk.

Even our old friend Artur Nebe is still there, still head of the Kripo, and now a full General of the S.S. We pick him up again, curiously enough, in the matter of the Sagan shootings, in which the Kripo were deeply involved. One of his subordinates, Major Wielen, who gave evidence at Nuremberg before he was himself tried and sentenced, was in charge of the search, which extended over the whole of Germany and beyond. It was he who issued the order for the *Grossfahndung*, the emergency hue and cry, which completely shattered the quiet, everyday routine of the whole of the German Police. And when all the escaped prisoners had been recaptured, he was called to Berlin by Nebe himself:

"I gave him a short, concise report on the whole matter as it stood at that time. He then showed me a teleprint order signed by Dr. Kaltenbrunner, in which it was stated that on the express personal orders of the Fuehrer more than half the officers escaped from Sagan were to be shot after their recapture. The officer in charge of Department IV, Lt.-General Mueller, had received corresponding orders and would give instructions to the State Police. Military headquarters had been informed."

Wielen then went on to say:

"General Nebe himself appeared shocked at this order. He was very distressed. I was afterwards told that for nights on end he had not gone to bed but had passed the night on his office settee." [8]

That seems to bring us back to our beginning. One would have thought that after all he had seen Artur Nebe's capacity for being shocked would have been exhausted. In 1933, in the early days of the Prinz Albrecht Strasse, we first met Artur Nebe, the secret Nazi, the disguised idealist, being shocked into speechlessness by the temporary triumph of Rudolf Diels, in those halcyon days of the Gestapo when they were not overworked and had only to kill in tens instead of in millions. And he goes on being shocked for the next eleven years: by the massacre of 30th June; by the news that Jews were being gassed in Poland.[9] And here, nearly at the end, he is still as emotional as ever. He is shocked by the order to kill fifty R.A.F. prisoners-of-war even as he passes it on. And in the meantime he has commanded *Einsatzgruppe* B in Russia; and in his room there reposed the only existing copy of a film of a gas van in action ever to be found.[10] Yet all the time, according to Gisevius and others, he was taking part in the conspiracy against Hitler, which ended on 20th July 1944, with the savage killing of the more active-minded conspirators and the disappearance of Nebe—to his death at the hands of Kaltenbrunner's hangman, according to Gisevius, a martyr to the liberal cause.[11]

In actual fact Nebe seems to have been an unscrupulous careerist with a twisted mind and no clear views on anything but his own advancement. It is true that he kept in close touch with the conspiratorial circles. He certainly had one motive—to reinsure himself, as he had reinsured himself when he became a secret Nazi before Hitler came to power. Probably he had another—while reinsuring himself, to keep an eye on the conspiracy so that he could choose his moment to expose it, if this seemed desirable and useful to his career. He was never at the heart of the plot; and the information he passed on to the devoted band of soldiers and civilians who were ready to risk their lives, and finally did risk them and lose them, was never of real importance.[12] So it is fair to conclude that the failure of the attempt gave Nebe his last shock, from which he never recovered.

What are we to make of all this? We have not followed the activities of the Gestapo in detail. Its crimes fill volumes. We have not so much as touched on the conspiratorial activities of Heydrich and Kaltenbrunner and Mueller after the accession to power (for example, the fantastic story of the bogus attempt on Hitler's life in 1939 on the anniversary of the Munich *Bierkeller Putsch*).[13] The whole immense field of the foreign activities of the S.D., under Walter Schellenberg, has had to be ignored. But we have traced the founding and the growth of the Gestapo; and we have seen enough of the things it did, and of the individuals inside it, or closely connected with it, to have a fair idea of its performance.

And in the course of this examination it has become clear that the Gestapo did not function as a dark and sinister tyranny, compact and aloof, ruling first Germany, then most of Europe, alone, in secrecy, and unobserved; but, once absolute power had been achieved, merged itself inextricably with the general mood of Germany as a whole, so that in occupied Europe, especially in the East, it is hard to separate the cruelties of the Gestapo and the S.D. from the cruelties of the Wehrmacht, and quite impossible to separate them from the cruelties of Daluege's uniformed police and from the General S.S. and the Waffen S.S.

And we have seen how deeply all sorts of Germans were involved in activities which, according to the Nuremberg defence, were known only to a selected few. The Army had to supply and house the *Einsatzgruppen* and assist the Security Police and S.D. in sorting out prisoners-of-war for execution. The civil administration of the occupied countries, as well as

of Germany, had to assist in many ways, and only sometimes
protested, and then weakly: Area Commissioners in the East
had to provide facilities for mass executions; Gauleiters and
their subordinates in Germany itself had to assist in the fulfilment of the Bullet Decree. Transport officials in Germany
and all over Europe had to provide Eichmann with his trains.

When Globocnik in Lublin sent in his report to Himmler
announcing the winding up of *Aktion Reinhard* he had a great
deal to say about the proceeds in cash and kind: rings,
ladies' gold wrist-watches, gentlemen's gold pocket-watches,
ladies' watches with brilliants, ladies' watches of platinum,
spectacles, shaving equipment, pocket knives, alarm clocks,
silver cigarette-cases, clinical thermometers—all detailed to
the last mark, and adding up to 43,662,000 Reichsmark.
There were 1,900 waggon loads of clothing, underclothes,
rags, and bed-feathers, adding up to 26 million Reichsmark.
There were millions of marks of currency of all kinds, so that
by the end of December 1943 the total loot amounted to
178,745,000 Reichsmark—from *Aktion Reinhard* alone.[14]

"I want you to look at Page 16 of this report," said the
American Prosecution: "Other valuables: 5 gold revolv-
ing pencils; 576 gentlemen's wrist-watches; 13,455
gentlemen's pocket watches and miscellaneous ladies'
jewellery; then the item 22,324 spectacles; and then, next
but one to that, 11,675 rings; then all the precious little
possessions of these people, necklaces, a pair of mother-
of-pearl opera glasses, each one itemized down to the last
sordid Reichsmark." [15]

Some of these things were doled out directly to the troops
and the civilian population. The great bulk—and not only
from *Aktion Reinhard*, but from Auschwitz and elsewhere—found their way, via the Concentration Camp Administration, into the vaults of the Reichs Bank in Berlin,

under the personal direction of Herr Funk.[16] This remarkable transaction was not effected without many people knowing, wondering, and guessing. And there were the tens of thousands of German civilians who saw the prisoners from the concentration-camps being taken to and from their work in the factories and quarries outside; and the deportees packed almost to death in their trains.

Sometimes, of course, there were protests. We have encountered one or two. We have Major Roesler, Commander of the 528th Infantry Regiment, putting in a report to the Commander of the 9th Military District in which he gives his own account of a mass execution which is almost identical with the account of the German engineer, Graebe, which we have quoted in full. He was deeply shocked by what he saw, and his report was forwarded to the chief of the army armament and equipment department in Berlin with a covering note:

"Subject: Atrocities perpetrated on the civilian population of the East.

"With regard to the news of mass executions in Russia which we are receiving, I was at first convinced that they had been unduly exaggerated. I am forwarding herewith a report from Major Roesler which fully confirms these rumours. . . .

"If these things are done openly they will become known in the fatherland and give rise to criticism.

"Signed: Schirwindt." [17]

And we have the protest to Rosenberg of the Reichs Commissioner for Eastern Territories:

"It should be possible to avoid atrocities and bury those who have been liquidated. To lock men, women, and children into barns and set fire to them does not appear to be a suitable method of disposing of partisans, even if it is desired to exterminate the population. This method is not worthy of the German cause, and damages our reputation severely." [18]

But even these protests were strictly limited in scope. Liquidation as such is not in question: it is simply a problem of method.

In considering how these things came to be, whether they reveal a particular wickedness of the German people, and whether circumstances could arise elsewhere in which other nations might find themselves behaving in this way, several lines of enquiry may be seen to open themselves.

In the first place it is inaccurate to say that only Germans were engaged in the horrors we have seen. Austrians, many of them with Slavonic blood, were deeply implicated. Hitler himself was an Austrian; so, to name only two, were Kaltenbrunner and Globocnik. Eichmann had been brought up as an Austrian. There were many others.

Furthermore, it is inaccurate to think purely in terms of Teutonism. The *Einsatzgruppen* recruited and trained elements from the occupied countries, above all the Lithuanians and the Ukrainians. At Slutzk the Lithuanian mercenaries outdid the German Police in their zeal, and were accounted extremely useful up to a point—the point being reached when they lost their first enthusiasm for killing and were then found to lack the steady training and tradition which enabled the Germans to go on killing even when they were bored. [19]

When it came to the high-spirited slaughter of Jews the native Ukrainians, employed at first with great hopes, became altogether too much for the Germans and had to be discouraged because they got out of hand. [20] The Roumanians, too, showed a great aptitude for mass-murder and conducted their own massacres at Odessa and elsewhere. [21] In Western Europe certain officials, police and civil, of the

Vichy Government showed the greatest ardour in assisting Oberg, Knochen, and Eichmann. Quisling could be harsher and more ruthless than the German Police Chiefs themselves.

We also know that in Spain in the thirties atrocities of extreme savagery were committed by both sides. We know about the Soviet deportations and the horrors of forced labour in the Soviet arctic camps and elsewhere, involving human degradation on a truly massive scale. We know that both Americans and British are still capable, as individuals, of atrocious behaviour to those whom they consider to be their racial inferiors.

Thus we are clearly going about things the wrong way if we allow ourselves to start with the assumption that only Germans could behave in the manner recorded in these pages.

Otto Ohlendorf, the scholarly commander of *Einsatzgruppe* D, had thought long about this, and, according to his lights, deeply. In the last days of the Reich he emerged from the seclusion of the Ministry of Economics and went to Himmler, his old chief, and tried to persuade him to surrender to the Allies so that he might justify the ways of the S.S.[22] He failed in this; but, at his own trial, he tried to remedy the error, ranging through the whole history of mankind to show that, on occasion, mass-murder has been indulged in by most peoples for ends generally considered desirable, and bringing the matter up to date by insisting that posterity would be unable to perceive the difference between his mass-executions on the Russian Front and the dropping of the atomic bomb on Hiroshima and Nagasaki.[23]

But in that case posterity will be wrong. The dropping of atom bombs without specific warning may have been inexcusable; but the decision to do so was taken by harrassed men in the extremity of a life and death conflict. It aroused immediate feelings of revulsion. The mass murder of Jews and Russians was a deliberate policy made possible by the war but had nothing to do with the winning of it. It was carried out systematically and in cold blood by men who knew what they were doing and watched their victims die.

We all have citizens who, given the necessary power and a total absence of restraint, would behave like S.S. Captain Kramer, "the Beast of Belsen". But do we all have citizens who, in given circumstances, would behave, precisely, like Otto Ohlendorf? And do the rest of us have as many citizens liable, at the drop of the hat, to turn into Kramers? And would so many of us, again in the requisite circumstances, condone such behaviour?

The elementary approach to the German problem fixes on the tradition of absolute obedience to authority which is drummed into every German from childhood on. This is the approach of simple men like Captain Best, who managed to hold his own for the duration of the war in various concentration-camps, and it is shared by trained psychiatrists like Elie Cohen, the Dutch author of *Human Behaviour in the Concentration Camp*, who managed to survive Auschwitz, although his wife and children were murdered there. This system, in which mother and children are brought up to fear the father; in which school-children are brought up to fear the teacher; in which "every German is there to be kicked by another German, and has, below him, another German to kick", has, without any doubt, a strong bearing on the mentality which expresses itself over and over again in the shrugging phrase, *Befehl ist Befehl*—"Orders are orders". But it seems to raise as many questions as it answers.

Professor Cohen has committed himself to the belief that:

"If Netherlanders and Germans were reared from their birth in the same social atmosphere (family, school, youth clubs included), then I believe the differences which are now noticeable between the two peoples would cease to be so. In my view it is not the German as such, but the German individual *malformed* through his German education, that is the determining factor in the behaviour of the German people." [24]

This raises the question: what is it in the Germans that conditions their educational system so disastrously?

Dr. Karl Jaspers, one of the few Germans who has speculated freely on the question of Germany's guilt, takes the matter a stage further:

"Orders are orders!—this meant and still means emotionally for many people the expression of their supreme duty. But this phrase implied at the same time a shedding of responsibility, when it allowed a man to accept with a shrug everything that was evil and foolish. This behaviour under the inner compulsion of obedience became altogether sinful in the moral sense, this instinctive behaviour which pretended to itself to be listening to the voice of conscience, whereas in fact it had entirely done with listening to this voice." [25]

This would seem to take us quite a long way if the Germans had shown themselves content to leave it at that. But they did not.

When General Beck was trying to gather round him a powerful opposition to Hitler he was met on every side by his colleagues, who respected him, with the unassailable response that they had taken their military oath to Hitler and must abide by it or lose their honour. But at Nuremberg General after General exhibited the greatest anxiety to prove that he, personally, had disapproved of such and such an order and had in fact ignored it, or omitted to pass it on. This applied particularly to the notorious Commissar Order in the

East and the Commando Order in the West. There were, indeed, many examples of disobedience in the field.

The Germans, however, cannot have it both ways. Either the idea of disobeying an order was inconceivable to them, as asserted by characters as disparate as Keitel, Ohlendorf, and Hoess, or it was not. If it in fact was inconceivable, then it follows that all the actions described in this narrative may be ascribed to that one inhibition. But indeed it was by no means inconceivable, at least as far as the high-ranking officers of the Army, as well as of the S.S., were concerned. It has been demonstrated beyond all possible doubt that they were prepared to disobey the Fuehrer on a truly remarkable scale when it seemed to them, individually, desirable, convenient, and expedient to do so. When it did not, they took refuge in the mystique of total obedience.[26]

Nowhere is this brought out in a more striking way than in the long, tortuous, and broken-backed history of the plots against Hitler's person. From 1938 until the end there was not a moment when some Generals were not actively considering the removal of Hitler, by arrest or assassination, first in order to prevent him from declaring war, then in order to substitute another régime for the purpose of negotiating peace with the Allies. This long-drawn-out procession of unhappy conjunctures has received elaborate and illuminating treatment by Wheeler-Bennett in *The Nemesis of Power*. It is a history not of honour but of dishonour. Time and time again when the Generals felt that Hitler was leading them to disaster, a quite astonishing proportion of them were ready to discuss with the few steadfast and single-minded conspirators ways and means of getting rid of their Fuehrer. Time and time again, when Hitler seemed to be winning, these same individuals remembered their oath of allegiance. Towards the end, when it was clear to all but the lunatic fringe that defeat was certain, and when more and more members of the Officer Corps felt nothing but bitterness against the Leadership, their waverings became squalid in the extreme. Now they invoked their honour as soldiers not for the sake of Germany but for the sake of their own individual skins. Each was afraid that if something went wrong he, General X, might have to sacrifice himself. This was too much to ask. The upstart Keitel had started the rot with his betrayal of his father-in-law in 1938—the poor, wretched Field-Marshal von Blomberg, who had married a whore. The rest of the Marshals and Generals, with a handful of splendid exceptions, thankfully took their tone from Keitel, whom they all so heartily despised.

In the late summer of 1943 there was a remarkable episode involving General von Bock, who had once been disgraced by the Fuehrer as a scapegoat for his, the Fuehrer's, own errors in Russia, but was now back in command on the Southern Russian Front. Then, nearly a year before the maturing of the Beck–Goerderler–Stauffenberg plot, the deeply wronged Marshal was approached by the conspirators, who needed his help. Von Bock knew that the game was up. He knew that Hitler was driving Germany to ruin. He knew that only the removal of Hitler could save his country from total destruction. Things were so bad that he did not even bother to remember his oath of allegiance. Instead he declared categorically that he would have no part in any *Putsch* which was not supported by Himmler and the S.S.[27] It was 30th June 1934 all over again. Yet, so desperate were some of the conspirators (but not Beck and Goerderler) that they made an approach to Himmler, who let it be understood that he was not averse from a change in the Leadership.

Again, there was the episode of Field-Marshal von Kluge, who also weighed his chances. Von Kluge was one of those who were supposed to loathe the Gestapo and all its works.

He was also one of those who for many months fluctuated in agonised indecision when invited to take part in the rescue of Germany from Hitler. His oath did not come into it either. He agreed that he would join in a *Putsch* with all his forces once Hitler was dead. He was then Commander-in-Chief West, trying to cope with the Normandy invasion. And, on 20th July 1944, there was a moment when it was believed by the conspirators, grouped round Field-Marshal Beck, that the Fuehrer really was dead—killed at his field headquarters by Stauffenberg's bomb.

Von Stuelpnagel, the Military Governor of France, was one of the stalwarts of the conspiracy. Before he could take action in Paris he heard the disastrous news that the bomb attempt had failed and that Hitler was still alive; but he realised that even though the plans for the Berlin *Putsch* might be ruined, a revolt of the Army in France could save the day. So he acted, relying on von Kluge, faced with a *fait accompli*, to back him up. He acted so successfully that in no time at all he had the whole nest of the Security Police under lock and key; our old friends Higher S.S. and Police Leader Oberg, S.S. Colonel Knochen, Captain Roethke and all, found themselves, a little dazed, under arrest in Frêsnes prison. And there they should have stayed, and would have stayed, but for the gallant and high and mighty Commander-in-Chief West, who, when he heard that Hitler was not after all dead, rang up Keitel and allowed himself to be persuaded.[28] Not because of his oath of allegiance. Not because of his soldierly honour, but in spite of it. Simply because he was afraid of what might happen to him if, by some miracle, the Fuehrer should survive a revolt of the Western armies. So von Kluge let the Gestapo out of prison and allowed it to arrest his old comrade von Stuelpnagel and hang him in Berlin.

It is against this sort of background that we have to

consider the parrot-cry that for a German officer the idea of disobeying an order was inconceivable.

And it is against the background of highly involuted intrigue within the orbit of Himmler himself that we have to consider the obedience fetish of the R.S.H.A.

When Himmler was approached by one section of the standing conspiracy on the insistence of von Bock, he encouraged his old friend and confidential adviser, Dr. Karl Langbehn, to go to Switzerland to see how the land lay. Langbehn had already been there for the same reasons under the protection of the S.D. in 1942—probably at the instance of Schellenberg. But this time things went wrong. It looked for a moment as though Himmler himself was fatally compromised, and Schellenberg and Mueller, both bearing the motto "My Honour is Loyalty" on their S.S. belts, got together to exploit the seeming peril of their *Reichsfuehrer* in the interests of their personal ambitions. Himmler, however, was far too clever for them all. For an ex-agriculturalist he had a remarkable capacity for playing both ends against the middle without appearing to take the initiative or, indeed, to exert himself at all. He explained everything to the satisfaction of Hitler, had his old friend Langbehn put in a concentration-camp, and later tortured and hanged, continued to employ Schellenberg and Mueller, and went on being *treuer Heinrich*.[29] It was a virtuoso performance, the details of which are still obscure; and this performance in itself was enough to make nonsense of the theory that Himmler was a mediocrity upheld by his brilliant subordinates.

Later on, of course, at the end, Himmler came out into the open and, egged on again by Schellenberg (or, perhaps, allowing it to appear that Schellenberg was the active agent), amiably discussed with Count Folke Bernadotte the question of throwing Hitler over—while Kaltenbrunner, with his own plot on hand in Switzerland, did his gloomy best to upset the negotiations.[30] Even Ohlendorf, the paragon, the most rigid of all the upholders of the claim that disobedience was unthinkable, was found trying to persuade Himmler to negotiate a peace behind the Fuehrer's back—in order to prove to the Allies that the S.S. had been an admirable body of men. . . .[31]

So much for honour, loyalty, and obedience. There remains the problem of sub-humanity.

We remember the old *Junker* officer, turned S.S. man and Higher S.S. and Police Leader, Erich von dem Bach-Zelewski, whose task it was, in the course of partisan warfare, to wipe out as many Russians, men, women, and children, as he could—and by whatever means. We remember his observation at Nuremberg: "If for years, for decades, a doctrine is preached to the effect that the Slav race is an inferior race, that the Jews are not even human beings, then an explosion of this sort is inevitable."

Von dem Bach-Zelewski was speaking then not only of the extermination of the Jews by the *Einsatzgruppen* of the Security Police and S.D., and in the gas-chambers of Wirth and Hoess and Eichmann; he was speaking also of the wholesale massacre of the population of the Soviet Union by units and formations of all kinds, and particularly those employed by him as Chief of Anti-partisan Operations—the massacre, that is to say, which Himmler had in mind when, in his speech at Wewelsburg, he dwelt on the necessity of reducing by some 30,000,000 souls the population of the Soviet Union.[32]

It is true that the doctrine of the inferiority and subhumanness of the Slavs and the Jews was actively preached, by Hitler himself and by the schoolmasters of the Reich. We remember Himmler's own comparison of the action against the Jews with a delousing operation carried out in the interests of national hygiene. We remember Dr. Hirt's memorandum about the skulls of his "Jewish-Bolshevik

Commissars—the prototype of the repulsive sub-human".
But this doctrine had not been preached by anybody in
authority "for decades". Only twelve years had gone by
since Hitler's accession to power. He had begun to preach
the doctrine as a dubious character in the wilderness, and the
German people had lifted him to power, doctrine and all.

Furthermore, it is clear that, apart from a few psychopaths, the Germans, even the Germans of the S.S., were never
able to sink themselves into such a state of mind that they
were totally oblivious of the human qualities of Jews and
Russians. Those most concerned with their organised
slaughter were always most acutely aware, and showed it by
their actions, that what they were doing was morally wrong.
Even Eichmann, who gloried in his killings and exaggerated
them to his colleagues, took the greatest care never to commit himself on paper. We have the evidence of his colleague
in murder, Dieter Wisliceny:

"Eichmann was in every respect a painstaking bureaucrat. He at once recorded in the files every discussion he
ever had with any of his superiors. He always told me that
the most important thing was to be covered at all times by
one's superiors. He shunned all personal responsibility
and took care to shelter behind his superiors—in this case
Mueller and Kaltenbrunner—and to inveigle them into
accepting liability for his actions." [33]

This description of Eichmann's methods is evidently true;
but the diagnosis was not true; Eichmann was not a born
bureaucrat. We find a clear picture of his mind in the record
of a telephone conversation between him and Roethke, his
Paris representative, dated 14th July 1942. Roethke had
been having very serious trouble with the French authorities,
who were refusing to give up Jews with French citizenship,

and agreeing only to hand over stateless Jews. This led to
the unheard of cancellation of one of Eichmann's trains:

"The train due to leave on 15th July 1942 had to be
cancelled because, according to information received by
the S.D. *Kommando* at Bordeaux, there were only 150
stateless Jews in Bordeaux. There was no time to find
other Jews to fill this train. S.S. Colonel Eichmann replied
that it was a question of prestige. They had to conduct
lengthy negotiations about these trains with the Reichs-
minister of Transportation, which turned out successfully;
and now Paris cancels a train. Such a thing had never happened to him before. The matter was highly shameful.
He did not wish to report it to S.S. Lt.-General Mueller
straight away, for the blame would fall on his own shoulders. He was considering whether he would not do without France as an evacuation country altogether." [34]

Wisliceny also told how when Eichmann had explained
to him the real meaning of the "final solution", he was
horrified:

"It was perfectly clear to me that this order spelled the
death of millions of people. I said to Eichmann, 'God
grant that our enemies never have the opportunity of doing the same to the German people', in reply to which
Eichmann told me not to be sentimental; it was an order
of the Fuehrer's and would have to be carried out." [35]

These incidents do not give a picture of men unthinkingly
carrying out atrocious orders simply because it has not occurred to them that Jews might be regarded so human. They
knew very well that they were, or at least were so regarded
by almost everybody but themselves. We find countless
examples of this. We find Eichmann himself cajoling the
Slovakian government and lying to them to make them hand

Q

over their Jews.[36] We find, perhaps most revealingly of all, the R.S.H.A. in Berlin telling Dannecker in Paris that in order to give an impression (to whom?) that the French Jews were being deported in family units, the children, who had been torn away from their parents during the terrible round-ups, were to be mingled discreetly with the convoys of adults—which might or might not include their own parents: "The Jews arriving from the unoccupied zone will be mingled at Drancy with Jewish children now at Pithviers and Beaune-la-Rolande. . . . According to instructions from the R.S.H.A. no trains containing Jewish children only are to leave." [37]

It is possible to believe that a certain category of human beings is sub-human. But it is not possible for such a belief to find free and unthinking expression if, at every turn, one is forced to disguise and conceal one's conduct from others who do not share this belief. Throughout the period of the German domination of Europe the working of a guilty conscience in the killers and torturers is clearly to be seen. It was never clearer than in the shocking operation which called for the exhumation and burning of hundreds of thousands of corpses during the great retreat in the East, or in the conflicting orders issued in the last days of the war in the West about what was to be done with the prisoners in concentration-camps—some leading lights in the R.S.H.A. wishing to kill the prisoners off and pretend that the camps had been bombed by the Allies, others thinking it more expedient to release the prisoners in the path of the Allied advance.[38]

What then?

In all modern societies there are men and women who, released from all restraints, will behave like beasts towards their fellows. But in the twentieth century it has been only in Germany and in Russia that such men have been able to achieve absolute power; and it is only in Germany that they have deliberately delegated their power without reserve to psychopaths and the criminal riff-raff of their country, absolving them from all restraint.

The German system of education, with its exaltation of unquestioning obedience to authority and the consequent encouragement of bullying on the one hand and irresponsibility on the other, must contribute to the sort of behaviour contemplated in these pages. It has taken the Germans themselves to develop this system. Have they abolished it ?

Further, the habit of obeying authority without question, even when that authority is clearly seen to be evil, accounts in some measure for the remarkable readiness with which intelligent, educated, and, in some ways, highly developed men committed unheard-of crimes. But that this compulsion was by no means absolute is shown by the fact that these same men could on occasion bring themselves to disobey their Leader and even consider plotting against his life. (The situation more than once arose in which an otherwise hard-headed soldier would argue that while Hitler was alive the oath of allegiance was binding; but if he was murdered, then the oath would no longer bind.) In the case of von Kluge and Keitel (there are very many others), it was only fear of the consequences of failure which held them to their oath.

The habit of regarding Jews and Russians as inferior or sub-human helped to condition the minds of many to the acceptance of mass-slaughter; but it is important to bear in mind that other peoples than the Germans have regarded other peoples than the Jews and Russians as inferior, or sub-human, without seeking to exterminate them (we are speaking still of the twentieth century, which is the relevant epoch); notably the British in Africa and India, and the American whites *vis-à-vis* the American Negroes. In this

Q 2

connection a comparison between the German and British records in their African colonies is illuminating.

In other words, it is clear that the habit of considering other people as sub-human, the habit of unquestioning obedience to authority, and the tyranny of a dictator of ruthless temper and unbridled cruelty working on the lusts and fears of his subjects, are all in themselves conducive to the sort of behaviour under examination. Other people beside the Germans have accepted the tyranny of a wicked man; others instinctively regard certain categories of their fellowmen as being inferior to the point of being sub-human. We need go no farther than Soviet Russia or Fascist Italy for examples of the one; than the British settlers of Kenya or the Dutch of South Africa for examples of the other. But in no other country has murder and outrage been carried so far as in Nazi Germany, and in no other country have so many individuals from all classes of society been actively involved in murder and outrage.

The callousness and harshness of the Bolsheviks, working through their own Security Police, is a by-word; but in all the Russian actions against humanity, in so far as they can be documented, there has been a marked absence of that sustained and supererogatory zeal which was such a feature of the handiwork of the Ohlendorfs and the Stahleckers, the Wirths and the Lindows. The Russian psychopaths and cynics have carried out the actions, and their subordinates, though tainted with that fatal irresponsibility which goes with the acceptance of authority, however evil, have, in countless recorded cases, shown an individual kindliness to the victim which is almost wholly absent from the German record.

It seems to be clear that in certain circumstances other peoples than the Germans would find themselves well on the way to producing a fair imitation of the Gestapo and the S.D. The Russians have done so: indeed, their Security

Police served as a model for Mueller and Heydrich. The South African Dutch, also possessed by a rigid ideology, seem to be moving towards it. The Italians, however, with a rigid dictatorship, never came anywhere near it, and in fact showed themselves more resistant to modelling themselves on the Germans than any other people in Europe, including the French. Many Jews in Italy and the South of France owe their lives to the flat refusal of the Italian Fascist authorities, civil and military, to co-operate with Eichmann, and to their ingenuity in frustrating his plans.[39]

Dr. Werner Best, who is now at large and prospering in Western Germany, an ex-S.S. General, a constant member of the Gestapo, and a pleader for it at Nuremberg, published in 1941 a text-book called *The German Police*, which was officially circulated as a handbook for senior officials and officially recommended as suitable to be given as a prize for meritorious juniors. This handbook contains the following passage which illuminates the darker recesses of the German mentality. The translation cannot do it justice because, to get it into recognisable English at all, violence has had to be done to the pristine incoherence of the original:

"It is not a question of Law, but of Destiny, whether the rules for police action laid down by the will of the Leader are 'right'—i.e. possible and necessary—and therefore form a body of 'Police' Law which is suitable and advantageous for the people. For the abuse of the right of Law-making on the part of the people's Leader—whether in the direction of harmful severity or of harmful leniency—will receive its punishment with greater certainty from Destiny itself, according to the very Law of Life which has been violated, than from any State Tribunal; and the punishment, before History, will be calamity, downfall, and ruin."

Dr. Werner Best, at Nuremberg, claimed that this was intended as a warning to the leadership. It seems, rather, that it was a reflection of the nihilistic, fate-defying rhetoric which was not spoken, but *lived*, by thousands of Germans who ought to have known better. It expresses with extraordinary aptness the flight from reality into an unpeopled void. It reflects nothing less than the death-wish.

The Germans are a kindly people in their personal relations. Many of the characters in this narrative were good fathers of families, who bought sweets and Christmas-trees for their children, and then went out to do some more killing, killing of children and women and old people especially, because these could or would not work for Germany. But the almost total absence of any recorded kindliness on the part not only of the police but also of countless thousands of S.S. men to those whom they regarded as sub-human is a very striking aspect of this whole story. It would seem to correspond with a rejection of real life. The British, on the other hand, may regard certain Asian and African peoples as inferior, and yet at the same time develop for them a strong and quite deep affection. With their empirical approach they understand instinctively that life as it is must be accepted, and that life is nothing but people—and people are more than one's immediate family circle, which, when it comes to it, may be seen simply as a reflection of oneself.

We have glanced at some, though by no means all, of the attitudes and characteristics which, taken separately, may lead a nation to behave badly and, taken together, may lead it to disaster. But these are not enough to explain the Gestapo and the S.D. They are enough to serve as a warning to us all, since, in some degree, we all share some, if not all, of these characteristics. But in the last resort the German failure, which so far differentiates Germany from all the other nations of the West, including Russia, is "a rejection of that reality which includes one's neighbours", and an attempt to substitute a false abstraction. It is idealism gone rotten ; and until they can learn to accept a reality which includes people, the Germans, in their restless and insane striving for something better, will remain dangerous to those who content themselves with trying to make the best of the world as we know it to be.

APPENDIX I

Text References

Note.—The Proceedings of the International Military Tribunal at Nuremberg, and the Documents in Evidence, are abbreviated thus: IMT IV 242; Doc 2751-PS—referring to the fourth volume, page 242, and Prosecution Document 2751.

The twelve later trials, conducted by American Tribunals, are referred to by their serial numbers: e.g. Case IX (The *Einsatzgruppen* Case). Relevant documents are referred to by the numbers given in Court.

CHAPTER 1 *(pages 15–18)*

1. Gisevius, Hans Bernd, *To the Bitter End* (London, 1948).
2. IMT IV 329 (Ohlendorf's evidence); IMT XI (Kaltenbrunner's evidence).

CHAPTER 2 *(pages 19–32)*

1. Alquen, Gunther d', S.S. *Standartenfuehrer*, *Die S.S.* (Berlin).
2. Bernadotte, Count Folke, *The Curtain Falls* (New York, 1945).
3. IMT XX (Examination of Sievers); Docs 085–091-NO.
4. *The Memoirs of Felix Kersten* (New York, 1947).
5. IMT V (Dr. Blaha's evidence); also Case I (The Doctors' Trial).
6. IMT Doc 1919-PS.
7. Kersten, Felix, *op. cit.* (New York, 1947).
8. Case IX, Doc 2693-NO; and Bach-Zelewski's affidavit published in *Aufbau-Rekonstruktion*, Vol. 12, No. 24 (New York, 1946).
9. Trevor-Roper, H. R., *The Last Days of Hitler* (London, 1947).
10. Bernadotte, Count Folke, *op. cit.*
11. Dornberger, Major-General Walter, *V 2* (London, 1954).

CHAPTER 3 *(pages 33–38)*

1. Hagen, Walter, *Die Geheime Front* (Linz-Wien, 1950). *Note* Walter Hagen is the pseudonym of S.S. Lt.-Colonel Willy Hoettl, one time of the R.S.H.A. Amt VI.
2. *Ibid.*; also Diels, Rudolf, *Lucifer Ante Portas* (Zurich, 1950).
3. Hagen, Walter, *op. cit.*

CHAPTER 4 *(pages 39–50)*

1. Gisevius, Hans Bernd, *op. cit.*; Diels, Rudolf, *op. cit.*
2. *Ciano's Diary* (London, 1947).
3. Diels, *op. cit.*; IMT IX (Goering's evidence).
4. *Ibid.*; also IMT IX (Kesselring's evidence).
5. Diels, *op. cit.*; Gisevius, *op. cit.*
6. Diels, *op. cit.*
7. *Ibid.*
8. Litten, Irmgard, *A Mother Fights Hitler* (London, 1940).
9. Diels, *op. cit.*
10. *Ibid.*

CHAPTER 5 *(pages 51–62)*

1. Diels, *op. cit.*; Gisevius, *op. cit.*; IMT XII (evidence of Gisevius).
2. *Ibid.*; see also Schlabrendorf, Fabian von, *Offiziere Gegen Hitler* (Zurich, 1946).
3. Bach-Zelewski's affidavit. Refer Chapter 2, Note 8.
4. Gisevius, *op. cit.*, 60–61. Compare *Lucifer Ante Portas* for Diels's version of the whole story.
5. Gisevius, *op. cit.*, 62.
6. Diels, *op. cit.*, 244.
7. Gisevius, *op. cit.*, 62.
8. Diels, *op. cit.*, 246.
9. Gisevius, *op. cit.*, 62.
10. *Ibid.*, 63. IMT XII (Gisevius's evidence).
11. Gisevius, *op. cit.*, 60.
12. Diels, *op. cit.*
13. *Ibid.*, 237.

CHAPTER 7 *(pages 68–75)*

1. *The Goebbels Diaries* (London, 1948).
2. IMT Doc 3593-PS for interrogation of Hermann Goering.

3. Diels, *op. cit.*, 143 *et seq.*
4. *Ibid.*
5. Gisevius, *op. cit.*, 64 *et seq.*
6. IMT Doc 1390-PS.
7. For the detailed story of Hitler's rise to power see especially *Hitler: A Study in Tyranny*, by Alan Bullock (London, 1952).

CHAPTER 8 (*pages* 76–87)

1. Wheeler-Bennett, John W., *The Nemesis of Power*, 309 (London, 1953).
2. *Ibid.*, 311.
3. *Ibid.*, 312.
4. *Ibid.*, 317.
5. *Ibid.*, 318.
6. Gisevius, *op. cit.*, 165.
7. *Ibid.*, 173.
8. *Ibid.*, 167.
9. *Ibid.*

CHAPTER 9 (*pages* 88–98)

1. Dornberger, Major-General Walter, *op. cit.*
2. Trevor-Roper, H. R., *op. cit.*
3. Hagen, Walter, *op. cit.*

CHAPTER 10 (*pages* 99–116)

1. IMT XXII 537 (Judgement on Kaltenbrunner); see also *The Venlo Incident*, by Captain S. Payne Best (London, 1950), for a personal account of the evacuation of Dachau.
2. Their testimonies are to be found scattered through the Nuremberg trials.
3. IMT XI (Kaltenbrunner's evidence and examination).
4. See Ch. 11 below.
5. IMT IV (Bach-Zelewski's evidence).
6. IMT IV and Case IX (The *Einzatsgruppen* Case) (Ohlendorf's evidence).
7. IMT IV (Wisliceny's evidence).
8. Reitlinger, Gerald, *The Final Solution*, 27 (London, 1953).
9. IMT XI and Case IV (The Concentration Camps Case—Hoess's evidence).
10. IMT IV 242 (Naujock's affidavit); Doc 2751-PS.

11. IMT IV 282.

12. Frischauer, Willy, *Heinrich Himmler* (London, 1950).

13. But Himmler also said in 1936, speaking of the S.S.: "I know there are people in Germany now who become sick when they see these black coats. We know the reason, and we do not expect to be loved by too many." IMT IV 182 and Doc 1851-PS.

14. See particularly IMT IV (Ohlendorf's evidence and Bach-Zelewski's evidence); also Case IX.

15. Wheeler-Bennett, John, *op. cit.*, 365.

16. *Ibid.*, 366.

17. *Ibid.*, 370.

18. For the detailed story of the failure of the Generals see *The Nemesis of Power*, by John Wheeler-Bennett, cited above.

19. IMT IV (Naujock's affidavit).

20. *The Manchester Guardian*, 17th March 1938.

21. IMT Doc D-897.

22. Hagen, Walter, *op. cit.*

CHAPTER 11 *(pages 117–131)*

1. "The People with Names", by Kay Boyle, *The New Yorker*, 9th September 1950; reprinted in *The Smoking Mountain* (London, 1952).

2. See particularly IMT VI (evidence of Lampe, Vaillant-Couturier, Veith, Dupont, Boix, Cappelen, Balachowsky); also Case IV (The Concentration Camps Case). For a swift general impression of the sort of people who ran the concentration camps, see *The Scourge of the Swastika*, by Lord Russell of Liverpool (London, 1954).

3. Lord Russell of Liverpool, *op. cit.*

4. IMT VI 334 *et seq.*, Doc 218-PS, L-159, etc.

5. Tickell, J., *Odette* (London, 1949).

6. Marshall, Bruce, *The White Rabbit* (London, 1952).

7. See particularly IMT V & VI (case of the French Prosecution); IMT VII (case of the Soviet Prosecution); also Bruce Marshall, *op. cit.*, and Lord Russell of Liverpool, *op. cit.*

8. Best, S. Payne, *The Venlo Incident* (London, 1950).

9. IMT VII (case of the Soviet Prosecution).

10. IMT VI, 172 (Labussière's affidavit).
11. IMT VI, 174 (deposition of Doummergues).
12. See particularly IMT Doc 4069-PS concerning the murder of General Mesny.

CHAPTER 12 *(pages 132–144)*

1. For elaboration of the activities and responsibilities of the HSSuPF in occupied territory see Reitlinger, *op. cit.*
2. Hagen, Walter, *op. cit.*
3. IMT XXII (Rauff's affidavit); IMT IV (Ohlendorf's evidence). Also for a reconstruction in the history of the gas-vans, Reitlinger, *op. cit.*
4. IMT VI (Vaillant-Couturier's evidence).
5. Best, S. Payne, *op. cit.*; Trevor-Roper, H.R., *op. cit.*
6. Reitlinger, *op. cit.*, 307.
7. *Ibid.*
8. IMT IV, 357 (Wisliceny's evidence).
9. The activities of Dannecker and his successor, Roethke, are described in detail in *The Final Solution*, by Gerald Reitlinger.
10. Reitlinger, *op. cit.*, 317.
11. *Ibid.*, 317 and IMT Docs RF 1225 and 1226.
12. IMT IV (Ohlendorf's evidence).
13. *Ibid.*
14. IMT II (Lahousen's evidence).
15. IMT IV 274 and Doc 674-PS.
16. This did not prevent him from taking the initiative and pressing it, even when the resistance of the military commander in Paris, von Stuelpnagel, would have given him every excuse to go slow.
17. Reitlinger, *op. cit.*, Chapter 12.
18. *Ibid.*, 318.
19. *Ibid.*, 315.

CHAPTER 13 *(pages 145–158)*

1. Hagen, Walter, *op. cit.*
2. IMT IV 233; Doc 2108-PS.
3. IMT XX 212; Doc USSR 509.
4. IMT XXI 517.

5. IMT XI (Lammers's evidence; Hoettl's affidavit).

6. IMT XX 212; Doc USSR 509.

7. IMT IV (Ohlendorf's evidence).

8. IMT XX 220.

9. *Ibid.*

10. IMT IV (Schellenberg's evidence).

11. IMT XXII (Defence Counsel for the S.D.).

12. IMT IV (Ohlendorf's evidence); Doc 3716-PS (Rode's affidavit).

13. *Ibid.*

14. These actions, and many others (including the Lidice affair), have been omitted from this narrative because the Gestapo as such had nothing to do with them. Details of atrocities committed by the S.S., the Waffen S.S. and the Army may be found in the IMT volumes and also in *The Scourge of the Swastika*, by Lord Russell of Liverpool, cited above.

15. Reitlinger, *op. cit.*

16. *Ibid.*

17. *Ibid.*

18. IMT XX, 212 *et seq.*; Doc USSR 509.

19. IMT II (Lahousen's evidence); IMT XI (Keitel's evidence).

20. Reitlinger, *op. cit.*

21. IMT II (Lahousen's evidence).

22. All Hitler's orders to the Army were transmitted by Keitel.

23. IMT I 287.

24. There was naturally a good deal of controversy about this; but the Nuremberg trials produced firm evidence that a number of German commanders on various occasions refused to transmit or implement some of the more atrocious orders from Hitler, especially the Commando Order.

25. IMT Doc 1918-PS. (Himmler's Metz speech).

26. IMT Doc 1919-PS. (Himmler's Posen speech).

27. *Ibid.*

28. *Ibid.*

29. *Ibid.*

30. *Ibid.*

31. IMT IX 645.

32. IMT XX 558; Doc 007-NO.

33. IMT VII 109; Doc 389-PS.
34. IMT II (Lahousen's evidence).
35. IMT Doc 2233-PS (Frank's Diary). Also IMT V 78.
36. IMT XX 450; Doc D-421.

CHAPTER 14 (*pages* 159–163)

Special Note.—The detailed story of the genesis of *The Final Solution* will be found, elaborately and meticulously documented, in Reitlinger, *op. cit.*, which also reconstructs the whole history of the attempted extermination of European Jewry. Aspects of this action are described in Chapters 15 and 16 below. The Gestapo comes into the story: (1) because Eichmann's office (sub-section 4b of the Gestapo apparatus) was responsible for rounding up the Jews and delivering them to the death-camps (2) through the *Einsatzgruppen*.

CHAPTER 15 (*pages* 164–183)

1. Reitlinger, Gerald, *op. cit.*
2. IMT IV (Ohlendorf's evidence).
3. IMT IV (U.S. Prosecution).
4. See the proceedings of Case IV for the story of the *Einsatzgruppen*; also Reitlinger, *op. cit.*
5. See particularly IMT II 121; Docs L-180 and 2273-PS.
6. Reitlinger, *op. cit.*, 189.
7. *Ulrich von Hassell's Diaries*, 176 (London, 1947).
8. IMT IV (Ohlendorf's evidence).
9. Case IX, transcript 312, 313.
10. *Ibid.*
11. See particularly IMT XXI (final plea of Gestapo counsel).
12. IMT Doc L-180.
13. IMT IV 317.
14. IMT IV 318.
15. IMT IV 319.
16. IMT IV 319.
17. IMT IV 319.
18. IMT IV 321.
19. Reitlinger, *op. cit.*, 208; IMT IV, 322.
20. IMT IV 351.
21. IMT IV 322.

22. IMT IV 334.
23. *Ibid.*
24. Reitlinger, *op. cit.*, 139.
25. IMT IV (Ohlendorf's evidence).
26. IMT IV 324.
27. IMT IV 331.
28. IMT IV 247; Doc 1104-PS.
29. IMT IV 253 (Graebe's affidavit); Doc 2992-PS.
30. *Ibid.*
31. Reitlinger, *op. cit.*
32. Case IX, Doc. NO 3159. (*Einsatzgruppe* Report, 31st October 1941.)
33. Case IX (Blobel's affidavit).
34. Case XII (The High Command Case); Doc NOKW 541.
35. Case IX.
36. Reitlinger, *op. cit.*, 143.
37. Case IX (Ohlendorf's evidence).
38. Reitlinger, *op. cit.*

CHAPTER 16 *(pages 184–201)*

1. IMT Doc 2233-PS (Frank's Diary).
2. Reitlinger, *op. cit.*, 245.
3. *Ibid.*
4. *The Goebbels Diaries* (London, 1948).
5. For Globocnik's own report on *Aktion Reinhard* see IMT Doc 4024-PS.
6. *Ibid.*
7. Case IV (Interrogation of Wolff).
8. Reitlinger, *op. cit.*, 257.
9. For light on this aspect of the New Order see Case I.
10. IMT XX (Morgen's evidence).
11. *Ibid.*
12. *Black Book of Polish Jewry* (1943).
13. Cases I and IV; Reitlinger, *op. cit.*
14. IMT XX (Morgen's evidence).
15. Hoess's evidence is contained in IMT XI and in Case IV.
16. IMT XI 396 *et seq.*
17. IMT Doc D.749.

18. Reitlinger, *op. cit.*, 460.

19. IMT XI (Hoess's evidence).

20. Gilbert, Dr. G. M., *Nuremberg Diary* (New York, 1947).

21. Reitlinger, *op. cit.*, 108.

22. Gilbert, *op. cit.*

23. Reitlinger, *op. cit.*, 141.

24. Case IV, Doc NO3408.

25. See *The Belsen Trial*, edited by Raymond Phillips (London, 1948). (Evidence of Dr. Bendel and Ada Bimko).

26. *Ibid.*

CHAPTER 17 *(pages 202–222)*

1. IMT IV (Bach-Zelewski's evidence).

2. IMT VI (cross-examination of Professor van der Essen by Counsel for Goering).

3. IMT VI (van der Essen's evidence).

4. IMT VI, 121 *et seq.* Doc 1585-PS, etc.

5. See Note 14, Chapter 13 above. The massacre of Oradour-sur-Glâne was committed by the Waffen S.S., not the Gestapo. It is fully documented in IMT VI, and Lord Russell gives a full account in *The Scourge of the Swastika*, cited above.

6. IMT VI (van der Essen's evidence).

7. IMT VI; Doc RF-266.

8. IMT VI; Doc RF-285.

9. *Ibid.*

10. *Ibid.*

11. *Ibid.*

12. IMT VI. French prosecution offers a long series of German orders on the shooting of hostages.

13. IMT VI; Doc 1594-PS.

14. IMT VI; Doc 1587-PS.

15. IMT Doc 668-PS.

16. *Ibid.*

17. IMT IV; Doc 502-PS.

18. *Ibid.*

19. IMT II (Lahousen's evidence).

20. IMT VI 156.

21. IMT IV (Lindow's affidavit).

22. IMT Doc 1514-PS.

23. IMT Doc 1650-PS.
24. IMT IV (affidavit of Lt. Jean Veith and Lt.-Col. Guivante de Saint Gast).
25. IMT IV Docs 503-PS, 506-PS, 512-PS, 551-PS, etc.
26. *Ibid.*
27. IMT IV (Wielen's evidence).

CHAPTER 18 *(pages 223–247)*

1. Frischauer, Willy, *op. cit.*
2. Hagen, Walter, *op. cit.*
3. IMT XI (Kaltenbrunner's evidence); IMT XV.
4. Bernadotte, Count Folke, *op. cit.*
5. *Ibid.*
6. Reitlinger, *op. cit.*
7. *Ibid.*
8. IMT XI (Wielen's evidence).
9. Gisevius, *op. cit.*; IMT XII (Gisevius's evidence).
10. Reitlinger, *op. cit.*
11. Gisevius, *op. cit.*; Hagen, *op. cit.*
12. Hagen, *op. cit.*
13. *The Venlo Incident*, by S. Payne Best (cited above) contains a detailed first-hand account of the incident by Georg Elser, the man who claims to have planted the bomb on orders from Heydrich.
14. IMT XX (Globocnik's report); Doc 4024-PS.
15. IMT XX (Prosecution summary).
16. IMT XXI (Funk's evidence).
17. IMT VII 534.
18. IMT Doc 1475-PS.
19. IMT IV 247.
20. Case IX. Doc NO3403. (*Einsatzgruppe* Report No. 119.)
21. Case IX. Doc NO2651.
22. Case IX (Ohlendorf's evidence).
23. *Ibid.*
24. Cohen, Elie, *Human Behaviour in the Concentration Camp* (London, 1954).
25. Jaspers, Karl, *Die Schuldfrage* (Zurich, 1946).

26. See Wheeler-Bennett, *op. cit.*, for elaboration of this point. Also evidence concerning guilt of Keitel, especially IMT X and IMT XI.

27. Wheeler-Bennett, *op. cit.*

28. *Ibid.*

29. *Ibid.*

30. Bernadotte, Count Folke, *op. cit.*

31. Case IX (Ohlendorf's evidence).

32. IMT VII 192.

33. IMT IV (Wisliceny's evidence).

34. IMT VII 40; Doc RF 1226.

35. IMT IV (Wisliceny's evidence).

36. *Ibid.*

37. IMT VII 42; Doc RF 1234.

38. Captain S. Payne Best, *op. cit.*, throws useful light on the conflict over the liquidation of prisoners. For the exhumation and burning of corpses see Case IX (Blobel's affidavit); also Reitlinger, *op. cit.*

39. See Reitlinger, *op. cit.*, for detailed account of French and Italian manœuvres to save Jews from deportation at the hands of Eichmann.

Glossary

Amt. Office or Bureau.

BdO (*Befehlshaber der Orpo*). Commander of Order Police in Occupied Territory.

BdS (*Befehlshaber der Sipo*). Commander of Security Police in Occupied Territory.

Einsatzgruppe. Action Group, or Task Force, for special purposes.

Einsatzkommando. Einsatzgruppen were divided into a number of *Kommandos.*

Gestapo (Geheime Staats Polizei). Secret State Police: the Gestapo was *Amt IV* of the R.S.H.A.

HSSuPF (*Hoeherer S.S. und Polizei Fuehrer*). Himmler's direct and senior representatives as chiefs of the S.S. and the Police throughout the New Order.

IdO (*Inspektor der Orpo*). The equivalent of the BdO within the boundaries of Greater Germany.

IdS (*Inspektor der Sipo*). The equivalent of the BdS within the boundaries of Greater Germany.

Kripo (Kriminal Polizei). The German equivalent of the C.I.D. Under the Nazis deeply involved with the Gestapo.

Kommissar. Gestapo officials of a certain rank were known as *Kommissaren.* They wore plain clothes, as a rule, although members of the S.S.

OKW (*Oberkommando der Wehrmacht*). Hitler's combined services General Staff, headed by Keitel.

OKH (*Oberkommando des Herres*). Army General Staff.

Orpo (Ordungspolizei). Order Police: a branch of the uniformed police, formed into armed units and living in barracks.

R.S.H.A. (*Reichssicherheitshauptamt*). Reich Security Main Office. Heydrich's creation, designed to amalgamate all the security services of Nazi Germany, including the Gestapo and the Kripo.

RMdI (*Reichs Ministerium des Inneren*). Home Office (Himmler).

S.D. (*Sicherheitsdienst*). The Security Service of the S.S. Amt VI of the R.S.H.A.

Sipo (*Sicherheitspolizei*) Name for the security police (Gestapo and Kripo) as opposed to uniformed police (Orpo, Schupo, etc.).

S.A. (*Sturm Abteilung*). Storm Troops (Brown shirts).

S.S. (*Schutz Staffel*). Guard Detachment (Himmler's Black Shirts).

The officers ranks of the S.S., with their military equivalents, were as follows. Ranks are sometimes confusing, because a given officer might have one rank in the S.S. and another in the Police.

RfSS (*Reichsfuehrer Schutz Staffel*). Himmler's personal style.

Obergruppenfuehrer. General.

Gruppenfuehrer. Lieut.-General.

Brigadefuehrer. Major-General.

Oberfuehrer. Brigadier.

Standartenfuehrer. Colonel.

Obersturmbannfuehrer. Lieut.-Colonel.

Sturmbannfuehrer. Major.

Hauptsturmfuehrer. Captain.

Obersturmfuehrer. Lieutenant.

Untersturmfuehrer. 2nd Lieutenant.

APPENDIX III

Select Bibliography

Documentation of atrocities committed by the Gestapo, S.D., etc., has been confined in this narrative with some rigidity to the testimony of Germans and of witnesses at the Nuremberg trials. Except in one or two cases it has been found unnecessary to cite from the mass of material in the form of survivor reports and the proceedings of trials and investigating committees conducted in Germany by Germans and in East Europe, including the Soviet Union, where the rules of evidence sometimes left a good deal to be desired.

The two major sources are:

(1) *The Trials of the German War Criminals before the International Military Tribunal.* Vols. I–XXIII, *Proceedings.* Vols. XXIV–XLII, *Documents in Evidence* (Nuremberg, 1947–49).

(2) *Trials of War Criminals before the Nuremberg Military Tribunals.* Vols. I–XV (Washington, Government Printing Office, 1951–52).

The first of these is a complete verbatim record of the proceedings in question, with the relevant documents in evidence in the original German bound up in separate volumes. Some of the documents, referred to in the *Text References* at the end of this narrative by their Court numbers, are in themselves major works—as, for example, No. 2233-PS, which consists of a great part of the diary of Hans Frank, German Governor General of Poland.

The second, which is a record of twelve trials conducted by American Tribunals, is not complete. But Vols. V and VI, dealing with Case IV (The Concentration Camp Case), and Vol. IV, dealing with Case IX (The *Einsatzgruppen* Case), contain a great deal of material relevant to this narrative.

R 261

Summaries of some of the twelve trials referred to above may be found in *Law Reports of Trials of War Criminals Selected and Prepared by the United Nations War Crimes Commission.* Vols. I–XIV (London, H.M. Stationery Office, 1947).

Books Dealing with the Organisation and General Attitude and Activities of the German Police

ALQUEN, Gunther d': *Die S.S.* (Munich, 1939).

BEST, Werner: *Die Deutsche Polizei* (Berlin, 1940).

DIELS, Rudolf: *Lucifer Ante Portas; Zwischen Severing und Heydrich* (Zurich, 1950).

GISEVIUS, Hans Bernd: *To the Bitter End* (London, 1948).

HIMMLER, Heinrich: *Die S.S. als Anti-Bolchewismus Kampforganisation* (Munich, 1936).

Books Dealing with Particular Personalities and Activities of the German Police

ABSHAGEN, Karl Heinz: *Canaris* (Stuttgart, 1949). The story of the chief of German Military Intelligence; the attitude of Himmler and the Gestapo to the conspiracies against Hitler.

BEST, S. Payne: *The Venlo Incident* (London, 1950). Personal reminiscences of Heydrich, Mueller, Schellenberg and others; direct light on the Munich bomb incident; first-hand description of the evacuation of Dachau.

BERNADOTTE, Count Folke: *The Curtain Falls* (New York, 1945). Count Bernadotte's negotiations with Himmler and Schellenberg to end the war and obtain the release of prisoners.

BOYLE, Kay: *The Smoking Mountain* (London, 1952). Description of the Trial of Heinrich Baab.

COLVIN, Ian: *Chief of Intelligence* (London, 1951). The Story of Admiral Canaris.

DORNBERGER, Walter: *V2* (London, 1954). Major-General Dornberger was in charge of the development of Germany's rocket weapons. His personal narrative contains reminiscences of Himmler and Mueller and shows the S.S. trying to capture rocket development for themselves.

FRISCHAUER, Willy: *Himmler* (London, 1950).

HAGEN, Walter: *Die Geheime Front* (Linz-Wien, 1950). An account of the workings of the foreign intelligence organisation of the S.D. Hagen, as S.S. Lt.-Colonel Willy Hoettl, was chief of Amt VI of the R.S.H.A. Light on Himmler, Heydrich, Mueller, Schellenberg, etc.

KERSTEN: *The Memoirs of Felix Kersten* (New York, 1947). Kersten was Himmler's masseur and confidant.

MARSHALL, Bruce: *The White Rabbit; the Story of Wing-Commander F. F. E. Yeo-Thomas* (London, 1952). The Gestapo in action against a British agent in France.

TICKELL, J.: *Odette; the Story of a British Agent* (London, 1949). Further aspects of the Gestapo in action.

LITTEN, Irmgard: *A Mother Fights Hitler* (London, 1940). Heinz Litten was a young lawyer who was arrested for defending anti-Nazi personalities in the Berlin courts. His mother tells of her determined but vain efforts to obtain his release. Encounters with Rudolf Diels, when head of the Gestapo.

SCHLABRENDORFF, Fabian von: *Offiziere gegen Hitler* (Zurich, 1946). The story of the conspiracies leading up to the 20th July 1944. (For this story see also Gisevius and Wheeler-Bennett, *op. cit.*)

TREVOR-ROPER, H. R.: *The Last Days of Hitler* (revised edition, London, 1950). Character of Himmler and activities of Himmler and Mueller in the last days of the Nazi régime.

Books Dealing with Mass Murder and Concentration Camps

BURNEY, Christopher: *The Dungeon Democracy* (London, 1946).

COHEN, Elie: *Human Behaviour in the Concentration Camp* (London, 1954). An impersonal account of the behaviour of prisoners, guards, and executioners at Auschwitz by a Dutch psychologist, whose wife and children were murdered in the gas-chambers but who himself survived.

GILBERT, G. M.: *Nuremberg Diary* (New York, 1947). Studies of some of the Nuremberg figures, including Hoess of Auschwitz, by a Court psychiatrist.

KOGON, Eugen: *The Theory and Practice of Hell* (London, 1951). A detailed and impersonal survey of the concentration-camp system by an ex-prisoner.

LINGENS-REINER, Ella: *Prisoners of Fear* (London, 1948).

LIVERPOOL, Lord Russell of: *The Scourge of the Swastika* (London, 1954). A brief survey of German war crimes, including some committed by the Gestapo and affiliated organisations.

PHILIPS, Raymond: *The Belsen Trial* (London, 1942).

POLIAKOV, Leon: *La Breviaire de la Haine* (Paris, 1951).

REITLINGER, Gerald: *The Final Solution: The Attempt to Exterminate the Jews of Europe, 1939–45* (London, 1953). The definitive work on this subject. Much light on the individual activities of Gestapo and S.D. officials. Contains also a valuable bibliography.

ROUSSET, David: *"L'univers Concentrationnaire"* (Paris, 1946).

Books Dealing with Aspects of the Development of the Third Reich

BULLOCK, Alan: *Hitler: A Study in Tyranny* (London, 1952).

Ciano's Diary, 1937–38 (London, 1952).

Ibid., 1939–43 (London, 1947).

The Goebbels Diaries, edited by Louis Lochner (London, 1948).

GOERING, Hermann: *Reden und Aufsatze* (Munich, 1938).

HITLER, Adolf: *Mein Kampf* (Munich, 1936).

HEIDEN, Konrad: *Der Fuehrer; Hitler's Rise to Power* (London, 1945).

MOWRER, Edgar: *Germany Puts the Clock Back* (London, 1933).

OLDEN, Rudolf: *Hitler* (New York, 1936).

HASSELL, Ulrich von: *The Ulrich von Hassell Diaries* (London, 1948).

SHIRER, William: *Berlin Diary* (New York, 1941).

WHEELER-BENNETT, John W: *The Nemesis of Power: The German Army in Politics, 1918–45* (London, 1953).

The above is a brief selection from an immense literature: Bullock and Wheeler-Bennett, *op. cit.*, contain invaluable bibliographies.

Index